RUSSIAN LITERARY ATTITUDES
FROM PUSHKIN TO SOLZHENITSYN

Russian Literary Attitudes from Pushkin to Solzhenitsyn

by

RICHARD FREEBORN, M.A., D.Phil.
Professor of Russian Literature
University of London

GEORGETTE DONCHIN, B.A., Ph.D.
Reader in Russian Literature
University of London

N. J. ANNING, B.A.
Lecturer in Russian Language and Literature
University of London

Edited by
RICHARD FREEBORN

First published 1976 by
THE MACMILLAN PRESS LTD
London and Basingstoke
Associated companies in New York
Dublin Melbourne Johannesburg and Madras

SBN 333 19314 8

Printed in Great Britain by
THE BOWERING PRESS LTD
Plymouth

Contents

Preface

Much amplified and recast though the short studies in this book may be, they follow the general pattern of a series of lectures delivered under the aegis of the University of London Department of Extra-Mural Studies between January and March 1975. Their purpose is to offer simple, compact evaluations of the literary attitudes of leading Russian literary figures over the last century and a half and to suggest the continuity of the role of literature in Russian life over that period. The description 'literary attitude' was chosen deliberately to indicate that we were concerned more with a writer's attitude of mind, his vision of life, than with the special characteristics of his craft, though always within the context of his literary achievement and his place in Russian literature as a whole. The choice of the six writers to which we have limited ourselves was governed by two principal considerations. Firstly, that we should treat individual literary figures rather than literary movements or periods. Secondly, that we should choose the most varied, but necessarily the firmest, stepping stones in the history of Russian literature from Pushkin to the present. The omission of Gogol, Lermontov, Turgenev, Goncharov and Chekhov from the nineteenth century or Blok, Mayakovsky, Sholokhov, Aleksey Tolstoy and Yevtushenko from this, not to mention so many others who might well qualify for inclusion, is due to the simple exigency of limited choice.

The aim of the lecture series, as of this book, was to appeal to all those people who might have encountered one or another Russian writer's work in English translation and might wish to know more of that writer's achievement and place in his own literature. It was assumed for the lectures that members of the audience would have read the major works. The same assumption has been made for this symposium, so that the retelling of novels or the defining of character roles has been kept to a minimum. It can of course never be avoided completely. In each writer's case biographical facts have been emphasised to explain a writer's evolution and sometimes this has meant using a psycho-historical approach. Chiefly the object has been to use biographical data as aids to literary evaluation and to set the evaluation very loosely in an historical frame.

Each contributor's approach and manner in dealing with each writer will show individual preference and no doubt some degree of bias. The same has to be said of such formal matters as notes and transliteration. Editorialising has not been strict, but the aim has been consistency in both approach and form (not always achieved and never enforced for its own sake). Latinised Cyrillic has been avoided wherever possible. All translations are the work of the individual contributors unless otherwise indicated.

The initiative for the series of lectures belongs to Winifred Bamforth of the University of London Department of Extra-Mural studies and for the short studies in this symposium to Mr T. M. Farmiloe of Macmillan. The contributors are deeply grateful to both.

Pushkin's 'The Prisoner' (pp. 20–1) and 'The Coach of Life' (pp. 21–2) are reprinted by permission of Faber and Faber Ltd from *Poems from the Russian*, chosen and translated by Frances Cornford and Esther Polianowsky Salaman (London, 1943). Pushkin's 'I thought my heart had lost the power' translated by V. de S. Pinto (p. 24) is taken from *A Book of Russian Verse*, edited by C. M. Bowra (Macmillan: London, 1943).

1 Russian Literary Attitudes from Pushkin to Solzhenitsyn

As Alice remarked in *Through the Looking-Glass*:

'What curious attitudes he goes into!'
'Not at all,' said the King. 'He's an Anglo-Saxon Messenger – and those are Anglo-Saxon attitudes. He only does them when he's happy.'

Between English and Russian literary attitudes there is a similar looking-glass difference: they may appear to be the same thing, save that, if the Anglo-Saxon attitudinises when he's happy, then the Russian usually does so when he's not. But the fact remains that every literary attitude involves some degree of attitudinising. The chief difference between one cultural response and another to literary attitudes is often no more than a degree of seriousness. The Russian response to literature demands of the writer that his social commitment should be manifest and his political position unambiguous. Russian literary attitudes are frequently surrounded by fierce public debate and far from disinterested official concern. They are never frivolous. They are often tragically enmeshed with government policy. In certain notorious cases they have become the pretext for persecution, exile or death.

We have grown used to expecting Russian writing to encroach on areas of learning and experience which are not, strictly speaking, the concern of literature. Politics, sociology, philosophy, psychology, religion, not to mention history or economics, are areas of knowledge which Russian literature has readily assimilated. It is arguable that the history of the Russian intelligentsia, perhaps even the history of Russian national consciousness, was first chronicled in the pages of the Russian novel. What has therefore chiefly excited Russian sensibilities in determining standards of literary excellence has been not how such-and-such is written, nor whether it should be written in this way or that, but its relevance to living experience, its concern for reality. As mere Anglo-Saxons we may have our own preferences and dislikes in assessing the greatest representatives of Russian writing, and we may assume that historical and geographical distance makes it relatively easy for us to pass objective judgement on the phenomenon, but it is still essential for us to realise that attitude as well as

expertise separates Dostoevsky from Gorky, say, or Pushkin from Pasternak. The attitudes are part of a history and tradition alien to us, yet by
no means irrelevant to our experience in the final quarter of the twentieth
century. We like to be pragmatically sure that literature is 'fiction' and
in making such a distinction we may be in danger of overlooking the
essential truths that literature alone can properly enshrine. Such a distinction is hardly recognised in Russian critical writing. In the Russian
attitude to literature there is a tendency to assume that it, and it alone,
is a repository of truth, that eternity is its birthright and the immortality
of the soul its rightful subject. To Solzhenitsyn, for example, in his Nobel
speech, one of the great attributes of literature was the way in which
it could transmit condensed experience from generation to generation:
'So it becomes the living memory of a nation. It sustains within itself
and safeguards a nation's missing history – in a form which cannot be
distorted or falsified. In this way literature together with language pre-
serves the national soul.'

Solzhenitsyn's tone, or manner of expression, in this statement may
seem too bold, out of keeping perhaps with the soft, ingratiating apolo-
getics which we are accustomed to expect from English writers when they
speak about their role. Indeed, he assumes something about literature
which may seem exaggerated and a trifle old-fashioned. There is no
doubt at all that he believes sincerely in the truth of his view of literature, but as Anglo-Saxons, despite our own attitudes, we can hardly
speak of our literature today with that degree of conviction and commitment. The tone belongs, one suspects, to another age and clime, when
our literature aimed to preserve national values against the industrialism
and imperialism of Victorian England. In this sense it resembles the tone
of Thomas Carlyle and it has something of his attitude in it. When he
delivered his lecture on 'The Hero as Poet' on 12 May 1840 and posed
his fundamental query about the English view of the hero as poet, he
was speaking in an idiom which would be familiar to Solzhenitsyn:

> Which Englishman we ever made, in this land of ours, which million
> of Englishmen, would we not give up rather than the Stratford Peas-
> ant? There is no regiment of highest Dignitaries that we would sell
> him for. He is the grandest thing we have yet done. For our honour
> among foreign nations, as an ornament to our English household, what
> item is there that we would not surrender rather than him? Consider
> now, if they asked us, Will you give up your Indian Empire or your
> Shakespeare, you English; never have had any Indian Empire, or never
> have had any Shakespeare? Really it were a grave question. Official
> persons would answer doubtless in official language; but we, for our
> part too, should not we be forced to answer: Indian Empire, or no
> Indian Empire, we cannot do without Shakespeare! Indian Empire will

go, at any rate, some day; but this Shakespeare does not go, he lasts forever with us; we cannot give up our Shakespeare!

Solzhenitsyn is similarly saying: 'Soviet Union, or no Soviet Union, we cannot do without Russian literature!' To be more precise he is saying, as one feels a Russian Carlyle might say if he were honestly seeking to describe a Russian hero-as-Poet: 'We cannot do without Pushkin! The Soviet Union will go, at any rate, some day; but this Pushkin does not go, he lasts forever with us; we cannot give up our Pushkin!' Because Alexander Pushkin, though some two and a half centuries closer to our time than Shakespeare, bears the same seminal, monumentally influential relationship to Russian literature of the last century and this as did Shakespeare to the literature of Victorian England. In some ways Pushkin's relationship to the literature that came after him is more intimate and enduring than that of any English writer to his successors. The grounds of such a claim can provide a means of understanding both why Pushkin is accorded such a lofty place at the beginning of nineteenth-century Russian literature and why his literary attitude – one cannot really call it more than an attitude – establishes standards of literary excellence and intellectual honesty which so much of later Russian literature tried to emulate and yet only occasionally matched.

Pushkin's life, like the history of nineteenth-century Russia, was profoundly affected by an event that occurred in St Petersburg on 14 December 1825. This was the so-called Decembrist Revolt. It was differentiated from the type of palace revolution so common in eighteenth-century Russia by the sincere commitment to change which inspired the educated, officer-class plotters in their attempt to overthrow the ruling dynasty. A desire for liberty, for a constitution and for the rights of man certainly inspired the Decembrists; but the most important of the changes on which they were generally agreed was the need to abolish serfdom. Educated in the ideas of the French Revolution, the Decembrists were serf-owners who planned to make a revolution in order to lose their rights. In fact, their 'revolt' was little more than a modest show of dissidence which occurred when officers of some of the most distinguished guards' regiments quartered in St Petersburg, called to swear allegiance to the new Tsar, Nicholas I, marched their men out on to the Senate Square. After a certain amount of parleying had failed, the new Tsar ordered up cannon, the insurgents were dispersed, five of their ringleaders were hanged the following year and more than a hundred were sent off into Siberian exile. Despite the relatively small scale of the event, it had profound repercussions on Rusian history. It meant, for one thing, that the educated members of Russian society had to abandon their hope of altering the political and social scene in Russia by direct political means. It meant also that the dissemination of ideas and opinion –

matters so essential to the development of a free society – had to be achieved by indirect means, through word of mouth, through salons and, above all, through literature. It also meant that the Decembrists themselves quickly acquired the legendary glamour and remoteness that attaches to all who achieve martyrdom in the name of freedom, and their example soon enough called into being a younger generation – and then succeeding younger generations – of an intelligentsia dedicated to changing Russia by revolutionary means.

Pushkin was of the Decembrists' generation, though he did not participate in the Decembrist revolt. As a boy, as a member of the first generation of students at the famous Lycée in Tsarskoe Selo (now Pushkin), he played with political ideas, discussed them with friends and even wrote one or two pieces – one of them an ode to freedom – which showed a passing fondness for revolutionary ideas. He was too much of a free spirit, Ariel-like, too vital, too epicurean, too delighted by the sheer variety of life's pleasures to want to limit himself to anything so arduous as the pursuit of revolution for its own sake. Politics were a feature of his life, no more, and even though he suffered bouts of exile, to the south of Russia and to his family estate, for what were ostensibly political motives, no one could seriously suppose that this charming, part Ethiopian, tender, lively, brilliantly precocious and versatile, dandified figure, more adept at conquering hearts than empires, represented any kind of serious threat to the *status quo* in imperial Russia. He was a threat only to pomposity, hypocrisy and falsehood. But because he seemed to know the secret of truth he was naturally suspected of deceit and mistrusted, so that towards the end of his life, under the insensitive patronage of the Tsar himself, he became scarcely more than a court hanger-on, humiliated by the more powerful, obliged to earn more and more from his writing but hardly succeeding, until the humiliation could go no further; he challenged one of his wife's admirers, fought the inevitable duel and died from his wounds at the age of thirty-seven, in 1837.

For Dostoevsky, in his famous speech at the unveiling of the Pushkin memorial in June 1880, Pushkin's claim to greatness was his universality. It was the universality of a genius who, though identifiable through the power of his own creativity, somehow contrived never to be more than a faithful, almost an exact, echo of the real world. The 'Mozartian' element in Pushkin's work is not only its musicality, which is everywhere discernible, but its remarkable true pitch as well. He took his themes from everywhere; he tried his hand at practically all the genres of the day. It was not that he was a better lyric or nature poet than his contemporaries, but he contrived to suggest what perfection in these modes could mean, what sentiment – in its classical perfection – should resemble when offered in poetry, what beauty flourished at the source of his art even though it remained always the tantalising secret essence. He refined the language of literature and renewed it, so that, in his hands, it was a tool both splendidly made from the artefact of language and exactly suited to the literary artificer's needs. There is always about Pushkin's work a sense of the natural that suggests artlessness in the purest meaning of that word, although one always knows that it is the artificer's skill which creates this impression. Throughout his life, despite the gradual move towards prose and an increasing sense that his powers were no longer quite as vital and spontaneous, he made it seem that he wrote casually, with a lightheartedness bordering on frivolity, an ease that suggested simultaneously inexhaustible enjoyment of life and a sophisticated respect for its mysteries and powers. In everything Pushkin had a discernible aloofness, a capacity for distancing that miniaturised while never diminishing the inherent value of the experience, and an aristocratic, almost royal, prerogative of being above the mundane world while never losing the common touch. It is hard, nevertheless, to illustrate these generalised claims for Pushkin. He had too soft a voice, as it were, for it to carry loudly across frontiers, as did Shakespeare's through the theatrical medium in which he wrote. Pushkin's was too natural, too intimate a genius for it to achieve successful expression by theatrical means. His *Boris Godunov* was a failure as theatre, but became magnificent opera when orchestrated. So too perhaps, for Western sensibilities, his greatest work, *Eugene Onegin*, makes better opera than it does poetry, chiefly for the simple reason that the virtuoso quality of the verse, its delicate music and intricate rhymes are barely appreciable in translation.[1]

Everything said so far is general, and perhaps vague, as a definition of Pushkin's literary attitudes, To define the seminal quality of his influence for Russian literature, it is paradoxically necessary to define what he was not, for it is in what he *did not do* that so much of his literary influence seems to reside. He did not offer panaceas or morals or anything faintly resembling a coherent body of ideas. He set in motion all manner of themes – the contrast between Russian town and country, the moral superiority of the Russian woman (in the heroine, Tatyana, of his *Eugene Onegin*), the problem of egoism, or self-will, in the hero (Onegin, Hermann), the nature of political power – which he sketched out brilliantly, as it were, but left to succeeding writers to develop. He expressed no Christian beliefs. There is a marked paganism in his attitude that employs the idea of Fate to explain the fruitlessness of human hopes and the doomed character of human endeavours. He oversimplified, both in the manner and the matter of his writing, especially in his prose, so that his creations are not Hamlets or Othellos or Macbeths, they do not tend to presuppose that the human condition is at the centre of the known universe, but appear in Pushkin's hands to be creatures dominated by lack of choice, that most obvious token of human freedom, and therefore obliged to accept the idea that some fate or other dwells in the very air around them. In this perhaps negative view of the human condition Pushkin still never abandons his basically commonsense view of the realities of life and his conviction that, of its many joys and compensations, none is more important than respect for truth to oneself, to one's own conscience. His heroine, Tatyana, exemplifies this truth more clearly than any other character created by him, whereas his *Eugene Onegin* expresses his concern for the realities of Russian life more fully than any other of his works.

It is commonplace to say that Pushkin was a realist. But realism as the dominant literary manner of nineteenth-century Russian literature greatly surpassed, technically and thematically, what Pushkin achieved. The realists also assumed things about literature which Pushkin would have found too grandiose – chiefly that literature had not only the power to reflect the truth of human experience but also to legislate on the morality of it. The identity crisis between writer and moralist implicit in this problem is seen to greatest effect in Nikolay Gogol (1809–52), Pushkin's immediate successor as Russia's leading writer. His exuberantly rich, ornate, complex prose style, which demonstrated the wealth of the Russian literary language as a medium for prose in a way Pushkin never did, reflected an equally complex and ambivalent personality which united a unique gift for comic satire with an increasingly bizarre religiosity of tone and purpose. Russian realism owes as much to Gogol as it does to Pushkin, especially in the serious, if misguided, effort made by Gogol to offer his work (particularly *Dead Souls*) as a means of spiritual guidance to the Russia of his time. There was a danger here that opened literature to exploitation, and that danger has tended to cramp and inhibit the development of literature in Russia since the revolution of 1917.

Of those who succeeded to the legacy of Pushkin and Gogol in Russian literature no one is more important than Dostoevsky. Dostoevsky explored the limits to which realism in literature can be taken more fully than any other Russian writer. His literary attitude, from the very beginning of his career, presupposed that human beings were not strictly speaking amenable to rational interpretation. What fascinated him – and has perhaps given him an unjustified reputation as excessively morbid – were abnormal states, both psychological and emotional. In both his themes and his characterisation he owed much to romantic influences, to concepts of character which emphasised emotional extremes – highly strung, volatile women, men given to emotional lacerations, as they have been called, driven by compulsions, consumed by ideas as if addicted to them. Psychologically he was fascinated by the concept of the Double with its romantic associations and derivative features. Such preoccupations are reflected in his earliest studies of the poor copying clerk overwhelmed and destroyed by his infatuation for a young and unattainable girl or of the government official whose personality disintegrates when he gradually becomes convinced that he is being persecuted by his double. These romantic or simply melodramatic themes would be poor, shopworn things in literary terms were it not for the powerful dramatic sense and the profound compassion which Dostoevsky brought to their creation. He has the distinction of being the first Russian writer to probe the problem of man alienated by his urban environment. This probing led to the creation of character portraits which often resemble brilliantly perceptive psychiatric reports cast in the form of stories or literary anecdotes. For what is remarkable and unique in the Dostoevskian view of the world is the sudden lightning flash of understanding with which he illuminates the intricacies and profundities of human motivation. From his twenties he apparently suffered from the divine malady of epilepsy and this disease, though causing him great stress and suffering, helped him to achieve precisely such illumination. The divine malady perhaps gave his life the character of a search for some divine light.

His life certainly reads like a Calvary – early startling success followed by arrest, penal servitude, service in the rank of the Tsarist army in Siberia, then attempts to rehabilitate his literary reputation, terrible indebtedness, bouts of destructive gambling, the deaths of his first wife, his beloved brother, his closest friends, finally a second exile, this time to Western Europe and married to a girl twenty-five years his junior, eventually his return to Russia in the 1870s and slow painful attainment of respectability, solvency and an accumulating reputation, despite growing epilepsy and the tragic early deaths of some of his children. From it all came a doctrine of the acquisition of happiness through suffering and a conviction, never entirely assured but often declared, that mankind could only be redeemed through commitment to Christ and the ideal of the God–man. Together with this were a messianic view of Russia's role in regard to Europe, a certain mildly extravagant xenophobia, a political conservatism that has remarkably radical elements in it, and anti-Catholic bias which was really part of a larger, vaguer, but more comprehensive suspicion of the rationalist and utilitarian bases of Socialism.

It is difficult to talk about Dostoevsky as a writer with a fixed view, not because he changed his views but because he had so many. The abundance of his powers as a writer lends a vertiginous, dynamic character to the way he presents his ideas. All his mature work is dominated by a concern for the state of Russian society which he invariably expresses in terms of the opposition between attitudes – between egoism and altruism, nihilistic free will and subservience to an all-merciful deity, the *pro* and *contra* of the man–God, of the *advocatus diaboli* and the *advocatus dei*. The more one considers the complexity of motive and structure in Dostoevsky's mature fictional work, the greater difficulty one has in assert-

ing that Dostoevsky believed this or that, or held one view to the ex-
clusion of all others. His greatest fictional creations – Raskolnikov, Prince
Myshkin, Stavrogin, each of the Karamazov brothers – may seek to find
solutions to the questions which they have posed about the meaning and
purpose of their own lives but they are never granted more than momentary answers at best. Suicide or madness, sickness or oblivion are the
common ends that meet his characters' endeavours. On the face of it
Dostoevsky's view of the world is pessimistic. Studied with an awareness
of the depths of meaning and a proper understanding of his unusual
psychology, Dostoevsky's picture of human life is more deeply felt, more
inspiring and ultimately more reassuring than any in Russian literature
and possibly in all European literature since the picture we have of re-
naissance man in the work of Dante and Shakespeare.

Even he, though, deferred to Pushkin, and one feels that the deference
was genuine. He offered more painful truths about mankind than any
we can find in Pushkin's rather innocent but by no means childish world.
He was a teacher, a *vlastitel' dum*, in the Russian phrase, in a way that
Pushkin could never be. One can live vicariously in Dostoevsky's work,
be utterly transformed by it, as one can never be by Pushkin's, but notwithstanding the power of his realistic manner Dostoevsky is in the end
no more successful at telling the truth in art than was Pushkin. He has
a tendency, which our Anglo-Saxon attitude may resist as unmannerly,
of seizing the reader by the neck and bullying the truth into him.
Dostoevsky was one of the great masters of importunity in literature
and it has become normal to expect high seriousness, together with an
importunately didactic manner, from Russian literature.

There is no more importunate a writer than Tolstoy. Apparently more
lucid, more balanced, more rational, seeming to create fictional worlds
which are so easily entered and shared by his readers, Tolstoy is always
obsessively moral in his view of the laws which govern human conduct
and it is never hard to discern the didactic tone with which they are
declared to us. He lacked Dostoevsky's diabolical humour and consequently took himself too seriously. It could hardly be otherwise: if you
are by nature endowed with divine gifts, you must inevitably regard
yourself with a certain awe.

Portraits of Tolstoy, just as memoirs of him, emphasise the penetrating brilliance of his eyes, and there is no denying that it is the selective
penetrating clarity of Tolstoyan vision which must strike a reader as
one of the predominant aspects of his art. There is the natural rhythm
of the sentence structure, the purity of style which is really exceedingly
artful, and seemingly the effortlessness of it. It was a magnificent means
for expressing something at which Tolstoy excelled – the animate, vibrant
surface of life. The heart-beat of the Tolstoyan sentence is signalled by
the verbs: they have a natural range of expressiveness in the Russian

which cannot be captured in its entirety by English equivalents. They are, for Tolstoy, the dynamic means of suggesting a world of movement, and movement is essential to the Tolstoyan view of things. Think how cinematically we are moved from scene to scene in *War and Peace* and *Anna Karenina*, how we see the movements and gestures of the characters and recognise them by such means, how what suggests the deeper, historical meaning of the fictions is the movement toward age and change which is worked in the hearts and spirits of such figures as Andrey Bolkonsky and Pierre Bezukhov, of Natasha Rostov and her brothers, of Anna Karenina and Konstantin Levin. Flux, contrast, changeability are, to all appearances, what seem to govern Tolstoy's vision. This, of course, and the splendidly exact detail of the picture, just enough to suggest clear likenesses, artfully conditioned by viewpoint. But in the very instant of witnessing the moment-by-moment concatenation of happenings and scenes in a Tolstoyan novel, we must simultaneously become conscious of the way in which the moments seem to come to us frame by frame or at least in a manner which inevitably and rightly suggests that we are permitted to witness only so much, that there are limits to perception and consequently that there are limits to human conduct.

Here the morality enters ubiquitously into Tolstoy's picture of the world. It is this which differentiates him more sharply from Dostoevsky than any other feature. Though he seems to record the passage of time with an innate ability to register its ever-changing, successive instants, his fundamental ideas about life have a fixed and static absoluteness which seem entirely inappropriate to a writer who could so expertly express 'the dialectics of the soul'[2] in his characters and almost always displays such great powers of psychological understanding. The contradiction between these opposed functions in Tolstoy is mirrored in the divide which separates the pre-1880 Tolstoy from the religious philosopher and cult leader which he became in the last thirty years of his life. His powers as literary artificer were such that they tended inevitably to struggle free of the limitations imposed by his moralising, even in those works of his last years that were specially designed as vehicles for his ideas. In his earliest works devoted to his experiences in the Caucasus or reconstruction of the emotional and psychological ambience of his own childhood, he succeeded in evoking an enduring freshness that so illuminates ordinary reality as to make it appear unfamiliar and this 'making strange' became, both technically and partly in terms of theme, a pervasive, characteristically Tolstoyan feature of the great novels of his maturity. His genius ensured that in practically every subject he treated and every character he created we should always feel the engagement of a serious mind determined never to accept received opinion, always prepared to question, even out of a kind of aristocratic impiety deliberately to court mischief and censure. The personality of the man outshone the often rather preposterously rigid views of the aspiring saint. He proclaimed non-opposition to evil by violence and moral self-improvement through physical labour under the general umbrella of a religious attitude to life, but he never ceased to have the twinkle in his eye that proclaimed his own disobedience, his personal naughtiness. Maxim Gorky, whose picture of Tolstoy in his *Reminiscences* is astonishing for its apparently total recall, exclaimed in admiration that 'no one was more complicated, contradictory and great in everything – yes, in everything,' so that he could indeed claim: 'Look what a wonderful man is living on the earth!' The living Tolstoy was a great human being who elicited devoted love from the majority of his literary contemporaries, Chekhov and Gorky not least among them, and a form of surety, akin to divine providence, that all would be well so long as he lived. As the poet Alexander Blok said on the occasion of Tolstoy's eightieth birthday in 1908: 'I often think nothing matters, everything's still simple and relatively unfearful, so long as Lev Nikolaevich Tolstoy is alive.' The finest testament to that vital force is the enduring power of Tolstoy's reputation.

Maxim Gorky himself was the most important inheritor of Tolstoy's place as the leading Russian writer of his time, although he differed fundamentally from Tolstoy in background and in his themes. As his autobiographical trilogy shows, his background had much squalor in it and taught him at first hand the privations and indignities of life in the 'lower depths' of Russian society in the last quarter of the nineteenth century. His early stories combine dramatically colourful, realistic treatment of such lower depths with themes that emphasise the need for some form of romantic escape from the bondage of money and unrelenting physical labour. Gorky sought all his life for an image of freedom that would suit his vision of man as unfettered, greater than his circumstances, in revolt against social and economic conformity. He once stated that all he could remember of his very first work, a long poem which he took with him on an early pilgrimage to see Tolstoy at Yasnaya Polyana, was a line to the effect that 'I came into this world to disagree.' He tended to be something of a maverick in all he did and no amount of later official hagiography by Soviet critics can detract from the plain *ozornichestvo* or 'mischievousness' in Gorky's literary attitude.

Maxim 'the bitter' (his real name was Alyosha Peshkov; he adopted Gorky, meaning 'bitter', as a literary appellation) expressed his nonconformist attitude in his early literary work chiefly by depicting the free man in bourgeois society as one who was an outsider – the gipsy, the thief, the barefoot one (*bosyak*) wandering in search of work. There can be no doubt about the bitterness that inspired his writing, but he endeavoured through the use of fairy tales, allegories and types of parable to illustrate his conviction that man could achieve an heroic freedom. The fable of the hero Danko, who tore his heart out of his breast so that by its burning light his people might be led out of the dark forest into the open steppeland, is probably the most celebrated of these romantic idealisations.

Gradually the mischievous spirit of revolt in Gorky became channelled into service of Social Democracy and Bolshevism. The commitment was never entirely orthodox and rarely all that explicit. The politics took the form of attacks on liberalism quite as much as they constituted arguments for socialism. Whether in his first novel *Foma Gordeyev* (1899) or in his first play *Smug Citizens* [*Meshchane*] (1902), he continued to deal principally with the problems posed by the bourgeoisie and the illusory truths with which Bourgeois liberalism comforted itself. This idea of the 'comforting lie' is one that Gorky exposes most forcefully and tragically in the greatest of his plays, *Lower Depths*. At the time of the 1905 Revolution he committed himself overtly to the Bolshevik cause and illustrated this commitment most obviously in the most 'revolutionary' of his works, his novel, *Mother* (1906). This work and its message have come to be regarded as a cornerstone of the doctrine of Socialist Realism just as Gorky himself has been declared a champion of the proletariat.

Forced into exile on Capri after the Revolution of 1905, he devoted himself to researching his past, both in the sense of creating a series of works describing the pettiness and extreme philistinism of Russian provincial life as he had known it and in the more personal sense that he began composing the autobiographical trilogy which was to become his most famous work. His picture of his boyhood and education is the real story of escape to freedom, from the squalor of his grandparents' home to his eventual discovery of a university of learning in a bakery at Kazan. Maxim Gorky's own experience exemplifies the revolutionary change which he sought to embody in the heroic figures of his fiction. He endowed literature with the special, revolutionary purpose of demonstrating how men could live better. Allied to this was a disdain for the pathology of Dostoevsky's Karamazovism, for the exploration of the darker sides of man's nature. Nor did he believe that evil was necessarily incarnate. Evil for him was a product of social maladjustment and could be eradicated.

The power and appeal of Gorky's writing lie not in his relatively simple intellectual attitudes, but in the slow, cumulative, harshly coloured effects which he achieves in his pictures of provincial life and in the remarkable fecundity of his characterisation. His major fictions are as organically powerful, but also as fluid, as the river Volga, which was central to his childish experience and which flows like a broad connecting thread through so much of his work. In the same way, his finest work has a sure autobiographical basis. It has a formless, but teeming character, as well as enormous energy and range, born of that gregarious, footloose experience of his early wanderings. After 1917 and his quarrel with Lenin, particularly over the question of the technological intelligentsia, Gorky went into a second exile in Italy. When he returned to the USSR in 1928, he came to assume the pose of a grand old man of Soviet letters and it is in this pose, cast in bronze or concrete, that he so frequently appears in the reverential statuary to be seen throughout the Soviet Union. But he was far more vital as a genius than the official statuary would suggest and if, to English sensibilities, he may not have the intimate, provocatively irreverent appeal of D. H. Lawrence, he has a similar irresponsible, fertile vigour of manner in his best work that will always prevent him from becoming mummified into the statuesqueness of an establishment figure.

All of Russian literature, from Pushkin to Gorky, tends to subsume that at some future point a change will occur, be it simply of heart or a trip to Moscow or a revolution. When revolution and civil war destroyed the Russia of landed gentry and the old liberal intelligentsia, the effect on literature was just as traumatic. Though it may be possible to see certain generally conservative, or non-experimental features in Soviet writing which suggest that it maintains a continuity of tradition, usually through the abiding vitality of Tolstoy's influence as a writer, the literature of the early Soviet period abundantly illustrated the discontinuity of life in its themes and its technical virtuosity. When Socialist Realism became the official doctrine of Soviet literature after the first Congress of Soviet Writers in 1934, at which Zhdanov for the Politbureau and Gorky for the writers made the keynote speeches, continuity between past and present, the preservation and nurturing of links with the nineteenth-century traditions, were acknowledged as part of official policy. In the last two decades of Stalin's rule this meant little more than official oppression of any literary work that suggested experimentation or bourgeois decadence and the virtual silencing of the most gifted literary figures.

Continuity as the real preservation of standards of past excellence in literature is to be witnessed principally in the career of Boris Pasternak. He made his reputation as a poet before Stalinism forced its own terrible orthodoxy on the Soviet literary world; he survived it and lived to celebrate that survival in his greatest work, *Doctor Zhivago*. Pasternak's novel is concerned with survival beyond revolution and civil war, a bridging of the gap between the question-asking intelligentsia of pre-revolutionary Russia and the question-answering commissardom of the Soviet period. It is one of the great stepping-stones in literature, perhaps more valuable to the West as a means of illustrating the trauma of change than to Soviet readers (where the book is not officially available), for they have memories as well as other means of knowing how vital are such stepping-stones between one literary epoch, one literary attitude and another. Boris Pasternak, like his hero Yury Zhivago, could not adjust to the ephemeral demands of political expediency and suffered neglect and censure as a consequence. He was concerned above all with the eternally rejuvenating, elusive, but essentially simple sources of poetic expression in language.

For Ilya Ehrenburg 'the magic of Pasternak lies in his syntax' and there is no doubt that he had a power of magical conjuration with words – the magic of the alchemist who succeeded in making gold out of the dross of average words. There is a superabundance of objects in Pasternak's world, of imagery in his poetry, as if, as Yury Zhivago put it in writing about his own: ' . . . the air, the light, the noise of life, of real substantial things burst into his poetry from the street as through an open window.'[3] Because it is a poetry of things, it is, for all its apparently complex images and associations, no more complicated than a song duel between two nightingales. Zhivago – and one feels that Pasternak himself shared the opinion – grew to like best in the whole of Russian literature what he called 'the childlike Russian quality of Pushkin and Chekhov, their shy unconcern with such high-sounding matters as the ultimate purpose of mankind or their own salvation'.

There is this private or subjective quality about Pasternak's literary attitude. He is concerned by the demands of his art, but art for him has no plurality, it is all of a piece, as it were, nor is it really divisible into epochs, just as 'there are no nations, only persons'. Art is to be conceived, so Zhivago would have it, as a particle which outweighs all other ingredients in a work: it is the essence, the heart and soul of a work, just as Yury Zhivago is in his novel, as the poetry is in his life. The imagery of some alchemical activity neatly summarises the way in which art acted upon Pasternak's vision of the world: it was pervasive, precious, enriching, secret, transforming. It was its own revolution, more powerful in its potential to change than any historical revolution, though Pasternak's work is shot through by revolutionary facts, by the tearing asunder of things and relationships.

The most potent alchemical agent in Pasternak's case was the concept of Christ: 'It was not until after the coming of Christ that time and man could breathe freely. It was not until after Him that men began to live in their posterity . . . they died [after Christ] at home, in history, at the height of the work they devoted to the conquest of death, being themselves dedicated to this aim . . .' Christ's importance was that, like Pasternak's own poetry, 'he speaks in parables taken from daily life, that he explains the truth in terms of everyday reality. The idea that underlies this is that communion between mortals is immortal, and that the whole of life is symbolic because the whole of it has meaning.' Yury Zhivago, the doctor, is symbolic of this life-working, resurrectional principle in Pasternak's work, in the same way as there is a principle of renewal continually at work in everything that he wrote, in themes involving coincidence, the meeting of people after long and tragic separation, a supposition that a kind of immortality is to be realised in the durability of artefacts and human memory, as Yury Zhivago's poems became his memorial and his life a form of holy pilgrimage. When Yury Zhivago thinks to himself, shortly before his death, in the company of his friends Dudorov and Gordon: 'The only bright and living thing about you is that you are living at the same time as myself and are my friends!', he is, not arrogantly, but in imitation of Christ's admonition to his disciples ('Because I live, ye shall live also,' St John, 14:19), indicating his own promise of resurrection and immortality, and in this he might be said to be fulfilling the role which he himself assigned to art and language as transforming powers, particles outweighing all others, devoted to the conquest of death. But of the many images which Yury Zhivago leaves us in his poems none is more haunting than that of Hamlet as Christ, obliged to play his role on the stage of history. In like manner, despite himself, Pasternak was obliged to play the role of Hamlet, the introspective, sensitive man, no maker of history himself, who knew the role and audience but asked that his cup should pass from him; it did not and he was persecuted to the very end.

The decision of the Soviet authorities to prevent Pasternak's receipt of the Nobel Prize for literature may have seemed a minor injustice, but it served to emphasise the often arbitrary character of Soviet administrative procedures and the much deeper injustice which could be inflicted on those who were considered dangerous to the Soviet state. When Pasternak died in 1960, Soviet literature had made no mention of the gravest of these injustices, the slave camps which had proliferated under Stalin. It was not until 1962, on the insistence of Nikita Khrushchev, that public acknowledgement of this injustice was made in Soviet literature, and the acknowledgement took the form of the publication of the first work of an unknown author, Alexander Solzhenitsyn. The appearance of his *A Day in the Life of Ivan Denisovich* in the leading 'liberal' Soviet journal *Novy mir* provoked a wave of shock and delight throughout the Soviet Union and the Western world. On the face of it, if only perhaps to the most optimistic, it seemed as though Soviet literature had achieved something akin to the freedom which it had enjoyed during the New Economic Policy in the 1920s. With the ousting of Khrushchev in 1964 and the gradually increasing hostility of the authorities towards Solzhenitsyn, this impression soon evaporated. Like Pasternak, Solzhenitsyn was also to be deprived of the opportunity of receiving his Nobel Prize and was finally, in early 1974, exiled to the West, but the graver injustice was the deliberate obliteration of his literary existence in the Soviet Union, not only through the virtual banning of his first published work but chiefly through the refusal to publish any of his subsequent major works. *The First Circle, Cancer Ward* and *August 1914* have appeared only in the West. His reputation as the greatest writer of the post-war period has been made precisely where it is least needed – in a non-Soviet world where writers are not exiled for their defence of justice. In the Soviet Union, to which he has always sought to speak, his reputation exists clandestinely. No doubt in due course he will come to be numbered among those who 'have saved the honour of the name of Russia', as the greatest of nineteenth-century Russian political exiles, Alexander Herzen, put it in describing his own struggle against Tsarism.

To an Anglo-Saxon way of thinking Soviet ideas of justice may well appear to be the products of a grotesquely arbitrary looking-glass world. One Soviet dissident has defined the problem in the following way:

> The idea of justice is motivated by hatred of everything outstanding, which we (Russians) make no effort to imitate, but, on the contrary, try to bring down to our own level, by hatred of any sense of initiative, of any higher or more dynamic way of life than the life we live ourselves, This psychology is, of course, most typical of the peasantry and least typical of the 'middle class'. However, the peasants and those of peasant origin constitute the overwhelming majority of our country.[4]

Injustice is not exclusive to peasant societies, but it is obvious that a society which has to be protected against literature exhibits the kind of bigotry that one associates with extreme sectarianism, racial prejudice and religious intolerance. Although Solzhenitsyn himself has seemed in some of his utterances almost as narrowly biased as those he condemns, he has never been fearful of speaking out for what he regards as justice. 'Justice exists', he said in October 1967, 'so long as there exist at least a few people who can feel it.' His literary work is living witness of his own feeling for justice. As Musa suddenly asks, looking up from her book while she is reading in the girls' hostel in *The First Circle*: ' "Have you ever noticed what makes the characters of Russian literature different from those in Western literature? In the West they have no time for anything except their careers, money and fame. But in Russia, they don't even need food and drink – all they want is justice. Don't they?" '[5] 'Don't they?', we may be inclined to repeat. And what kind of justice? At least, one supposes, the kind of justice which should banish for ever from Russia the abominations that Solzhenitsyn has exposed in his picture of the first and other circles of hell.

Solzhenitsyn's literary work springs directly from his own experience in all its principal ingredients and is at its most powerful when the auto-biographical impulse is central to it. His 'Soviet' novels are a series of biographies and episodes of confrontation with no heroic centre apart from a chorus-like, semi-autobiographical figure (Nerzhin, Kostoglotov). In formal terms their action is concentrated in one setting over a relatively short time-span. He has allegedly confessed that the literary genre which most interests him is 'the polyphonic novel with precise indication of time and place'; and he has defined polyphony in this connection as quite simply the way in which 'each character becomes the principal character upon entering the field of action.' His manner reflects Tolstoy's both in its God's eye view of life and in its concern for the moral bases of human relationships.

Georg Lukács claimed that 'Solzhenitsyn's significance as a novelist rests above all on the fact that he gives clear and convincing compendia of the inhibiting after-effects of the Stalinist period.'[6] These 'compendia' involve the portrayal of human beings institutionalised by environment in a society dominated by mutual suspicion. The source of this suspicion is Stalin himself, depicted in *The First Circle* as a man who has institutionalised himself as well as his subordinates, who in their turn institutionalise the rest of society. The picture is by no means as monolithic as this necessarily compressed description may suggest, but it is precisely the injustice created by this institution-consciousness that Solzhenitsyn exposes. The exposure is always based on the novelist's sensitive awareness of the psychological and spiritual uniqueness of individuals, the privacy of their experience and the survival of their human dignity in circumstances that have systematically dehumanising or degenerating effects. Solzhenitsyn's confined, pressure-cooker worlds of prison camp and cancer ward highlight more powerfully than Dostoevsky's record of his prison experiences or Tolstoy's account of his spiritual anguish the inexhaustible resilience of the human spirit and the never-ending pressure towards freedom experienced by all men under restraint.

His pleas are those of an Antigone against the authoritarianism of a Creon. Yet he seems to have stared long into Creon's eyes and read the meaning in them. For all his remarkable powers of empathy in character-creation, the long experience of prison camp and later harrassment by the Soviet authorities have had a hardening effect on both his style and his literary attitude, appearing on occasion to make his views as inflexibly authoritarian as those he opposes. Perhaps his mathematician's training can justify the necessary tension and attraction between opposites which comprise the equation of his world-view. Always and deeply a patriot, with convictions of the need for love between human beings which match and outshine even those expressed by Tolstoy, endowed with mythologising powers as a writer and the oratorical powers of a Burke as a publicist of his political views, he can still dismay admirers with his phobic obsessions, magisterial rigidity of outlook and truculent disparagement of liberal attitudes. There is no doubt, though, that his witness as a writer has already earned itself an enduring place in the Russian literature of this century. His work may have little of Pasternak's poetry in it; it can seem prosaic, utilitarian in style, despite frequently brilliant imagery; yet it is durable, and informed by a sense of the eternal purposes of literature that catches the spirit of Carlyle's words on Shakespeare. As Solzhenitsyn himself expressed it in the Secretariat of the Union of Soviet Writers, in September 1967, when he was defending the truthfulness of his picture of the cancer treatments given in *Cancer Ward*:

> In general a writer's tasks are not to be reduced to defending or criticizing one or another means of distributing the social product, or to defending or criticizing one or another form of state system. A writer's tasks are concerned with questions of more general and more eternal significance. They concern the secrets of the human heart and conscience, of the conflict between life and death, the overcoming of spiritual sorrow and those laws extending throughout all humanity which were born in the immemorial depths of the millenia and will cease only when the sun is extinguished.

Russian literary attitudes lay claim to be based on this kind of knowledge of the secrets of the human heart and conscience. In modern times, meaning in the century and a half since Pushkin set his seal indelibly on Russian literature, it is Russian literature of all great world literatures which has come closest to offering us visions of man's dilemma comparable to those which may be found in Shakespeare. The conflict between life and death, the conquering of sorrow and the revelation of those universal laws which identify human beings to each other, given meaning always in respect for the truth of private experience rather than the expediency of public utterance, are ever-present issues in the greatest works of Russian literature, treated with a seriousness that never shirks their raw, unappeasable challenge to complacency and falsehood. The harshness as well as the exuberant warmth of Russian life, the Russian winter as well as the summer, pervade the literature, but in its humanism and compassion it is a literature that transcends the local and temporal, outlasts ephemeral policies and derives enduring strength from its independent search for truth and justice.

NOTES

1 When a work does translate well, it illustrates the charm, compounded of wistfulness, nostalgia, low-key effects, articulation of feeling so remotely recollected as to be almost dispossessed, that, for a moment at least, is what Russian sensibility finds in his Shakespeare, his Pushkin:

> I loved you; and the feeling, why deceive you,
> May not be quite extinct within me yet;
> But do not let it any longer grieve you;
> I would not ever have you grieve or fret.
> I loved you not with words or hope, but merely
> By turns with bashful and with jealous pain;
> I loved you as devotedly, as dearly

As may God grant you to be loved again. (1829)
Walter Arndt, *Pushkin Threefold* (London, 1972) p. 37

2   The term was first used by the leading radical publicist of the 1860s, N. G. Chernyshevsky (1828–89) in a review of Tolstoy's *Childhood, Boyhood* and *Military Tales* in 1856.
3   This and later passages are taken from the translation of *Doctor Zhivago* by Max Hayward and Manya Harari (London, 1958).
4   Andrey Amalrik, *Will the Soviet Union Survive until 1984?* (New York, 1970) p. 35.
5   *The First Circle*, trans. Michael Guybon (London: Fontana, 1970) p. 341.
6   Georg Lukács, *Solzhenitsyn* (London, 1970) p. 79.

2 Pushkin

Alexander Pushkin was born in the last year of the eighteenth century – 26 May 1799[1] – and died at the age of thirty-seven. His life coincided for a quarter of a century with the reign of Alexander I which started in a comparatively liberal mood, witnessed the Napoleonic wars, and led to the abortive and tragic Decembrist revolt. It ended under the intensified reactionary policy of the reign of Nicholas I.

The landmarks of Pushkin's life are known well enough not to be retold in any detail once again. Much of his precocious childhood was spent in the literary salon of his uncle and in the French library of his father. From the age of twelve, his home was the Lycée of Tsarskoe Selo where his life-long friendships were formed and his occasional verses encouraged. Gifted, vain, irreverent, unindustrious, and rather *un enfant terrible* – this is how his friends remembered him at the time. Already lionised in this very restricted milieu for his largely derivative verse, he soon became a literary idol among the rich St Petersburg society into which he plunged with relief after the boredom of the school years. Despite his life of dissipation, he found time to write and to cultivate his literary acquaintances. Anthology pieces, fashionable elegies, and witty epigrams followed one after another, with an ease and elegance that overshadowed his comparative immaturity, and culminated in 1820 in his first major work, *Ruslan and Lyudmila*, a narrative mock-heroic poem which was received by the critics as an epoch-making event.

A few months before the publication of *Ruslan and Lyudmila* Pushkin was sent into exile. He was not a revolutionary and had neither the vocation nor the tenacity of a real political conspirator. But he was always sensitive to the life around him, and certainly was not devoid of patriotism and liberal feelings; these, added to a certain aggressive daring, resulted in a number of poems which, in the atmosphere of the day, were considered politically dangerous. His ode on 'Freedom' [*Vol'nost'*] (1817) directed against tyrants; his epistle 'To Chaadayev' [*K Chaadayevu*] (1818) – the best of his 'freedom-loving' poems animated by a truly patriotic spirit and recalling a genuine friendship; 'Noel' [*Skazki. Nöel*] (1818) which treated the Tsar's political promises as fairy tales for children in the form of eighteenth-century French satirical songs; his elegy

'The Village' [*Derevnya*] (1819) which brought up the question of serf-dom from the point of view of eighteenth-century enlightenment; and his sarcastic epigrams against Arakcheyev and others circulated in numerous manuscript versions all over St Petersburg (*Samizdat* did not start in the twentieth century). The revolutionary content of most of these poems does not seem to be very serious, but Pushkin just escaped from banishment to Siberia. Thanks to the intercession of his influential literary friends, he was merely sent to the south of Russia.

Pushkin's exile in the south coincided with his youth, with romanticism, with his brief Byronic period, and was almost a fairy-tale background provided by fate. Convinced that his exile would be of short duration, the twenty-one-year old Pushkin was not unhappy at first. When the months lengthened into years, he gradually became despondent.

The first Byronic elegy written on the way to the south, 'The orb of day has died' [*Pogaslo dnevnoye svetilo*] (1820), opened a new chapter in Pushkin's creative life. He described himself in it 'in search of new impressions'. Indeed, new environments produced new themes, southern nature came to be contrasted with the north, Crimea was seen through the prism of classical associations, at first buoyantly, later in a minor key. Associations with Ovid brought about several short poems, as well as the 1821 epistle 'To Ovid' [*K Ovidiyu*] in which we get a moving picture of one exiled poet by another, and where Ovid the southerner is contrasted to Pushkin the northerner. The basic theme of the poem is banishment, but it links in one whole a personal theme, a historical theme and a contemporary theme. This breadth of associations combined with a dual perspective will become one of Pushkin's distinctive marks and will reach its perfection later in *The Bronze Horseman*.

One of the major themes of romanticism, and the one that reverberated most loudly in Eastern Europe – the striving for freedom, associated with protest against prevailing social and political norms – evoked sympathetic echoes in Russia and held a special appeal for Pushkin in his southern exile. This, together with the purely literary attraction of Byronism, represented then by the Byron of the eastern tales, found its expression in the series of southern tales which, of all Pushkin's works, proved to be the most popular in his lifetime: *The Prisoner of the Caucasus* (1821), *The Robber Brothers* (1822), *The Fountain of Bakhchisaray* (1821–3), and *The Gipsies* (1824). Among the numerous lyrics of the period we find such strikingly romantic ones as 'To the daughter of Karageorgy' [*Docheri Karageorgiya*] (1820), 'The Dagger' [*Kinzhal*] (1821); or 'The Prisoner' [*Uznik*] (1822), much more successful despite the conventionality of its theme:

> In a damp cell behind the bars sit I,
> An eagle young, and proud, and born to fly;

Outside, the sad companion of my day
Flutters his wing and pecks his bleeding prey;

Then pecks no more, but through the window stares
As though we thought the same thing unawares,
As though with look and cry his heart would say:
'Brother, the time is come to fly away.

We are free birds together, free and proud;
Fly where the mountains whiten through the cloud
To that sea country blue beneath the sky
Where only walks the wind, the wind and I'.

(trans. Frances Cornford)

Pushkin's contemporaries appreciated the political flavour of this poem —
whether intended or not — as well as of such innocent poems as 'The little
bird' [*Ptichka*] (1823) which, in its delightful simplicity, defies translation. By 1823, a note of disappointment and doubt in the possibility of
freedom both on a personal and on a political level can be heard in 'The
Demon' [*Demon*] and 'Sower of freedom in the waste' [*Svobody seyatel'
pustynny*] in which Pushkin asks: 'Do herds need freedom?'

Despite the importance of the Byronic apprenticeship, the diversification of Pushkin's interests and forms of expression can already be seen
in the southern period: next to romantic lyrics we have poems of purely
classical inspiration such as 'The Nereid' [*Nereida*] (1820) and the whole
cycle of short 'sculptural' pieces; next to the exuberant, indecent 'Tsar
Nikita and his forty daughters' (1822), ballads on historical themes like
'The Song of Oleg' [*Pesn' o veshchem Olege*] (1822) and such 'philosophical' anthology favourites as 'The Coach of Life' [*Telega zhizni*]
(1823):

The swaying coach, for all its load,
    Runs lightly as it rocks;
Grey Time goes driving down the road,
    Nor ever leaves the box.

We jump into the coach at dawn,
    Alert and fresh and free,
And holding broken bones in scorn,
    'Go on!' shout we.

By midday all is changed about,
    Our morning hearts are cool;
We fear the steep descents, and shout:
    'Go slow, you fool!'

> By dusk we're used to jolt and din,
>   And when the light is gone
> We sleep before we reach the inn.
>   As Time drives on.
>   (trans. Frances Cornford)

Above all, in Kishinev and Odessa Pushkin began *Eugene Onegin*. By 1824, exile in the south ended, and the poet spent the following two years in his family country place at Mikhaylovskoye, a remote corner of northern Russia, still under police surveillance. The only form of freedom he could aspire to was the freedom to write. And on this point, he would never give in.

Freedom to create, to heed only his inspiration, to be his own ultimate judge in artistic matters was vital to him. He had to have the right to believe in the 'absolute essentiality of the inessential'[2] as well as the right to chose loftier commitments. The latter alternated, and we can find various images of the poet in Pushkin's work – the aloof figure impervious to crowds and utilitarian demands, the prophet who burns men's hearts with his word, or the poet who stirs kindly sentiments by his lyre; the one and only commitment which never changed was to 'the free play of the creative imagination'. In 1825, Pushkin wrote to his brother: 'They are saying that in verse the verse is not the main thing . . . That heresy must be eradicated . . .', and to a friend who was wondering about the aim of *The Gipsies*: 'The aim of poetry is poetry.' In 'The Dialogue of Poet and Bookseller' [*Razgovor knigoprodavtsa s poetom*] (1824) which Pushkin had written in Mikhaylovskoye and which was at first intended as a preface to *Eugene Onegin*, the bookseller urges the poet to write for the public; the romantic poet resists the idea, defending the independence of art from material interests and the encroachment of a materialistic age, but the bookseller realistically reminds him that without money there is no freedom. Finally they strike a bargain: the poet's inspiration cannot be sold, but one can sell a manuscript. This down-to-earth solution without any compromise over essentials is characteristic of Pushkin's attitude throughout his life. He never wrote to order and never accepted any patronage; he wrote regardless of censorship, regardless of whether there was any chance of publishing his work or not. At the same time, he had to live on the proceeds of his work: he was not writing any more like his predecessors for 'literary amusement', his was no longer merely a 'gentlemanly' occupation. And thus we have the curious case of a professional writer who refused to write for money – the very idea paralysed him, he said. Ironically, by sending his resignation to the authorities in 1824, he found himself in a situation in which he was forced to become a professional writer. The situation was new not only in the life of Pushkin but in the literary profession in Russia as a whole.[3]

Pushkin wrote some of his best lyrics in his new environment, at first reminiscences of the south he had just left: 'To the sea' [*K moryu*] (1824), 'To the Fountain of the Bakhchisaray Palace' [*Fontanu Bakhchisarayskogo dvortsa*] (1824). He poeticised his southern memories in a minor key in 'The dismal day is over' [*Nenastny den' potukh*] (1824), universalising an intensely private feeling.[4] Somewhat later he drew his inspiration from his new Russian setting, immortalising his nurse and the folklore themes he associated with her in 'Winter Evening' [*Zimniy vecher*] (1825):

> Sing to me of how the titmouse
> O'er the sea in peace did dwell;
> How the maiden in the morning
> Went for water to the well . . .
> (trans. Walter Morison)

Several of Pushkin's love lyrics date from that time: the cycle connected with Vorontsova to which belong also the later 'The Talisman' [*Talizman*] 1827) and 'Farewell' [*Proshchaniye*] (1830); the famous 'I remember a wonderful moment' [*Ya pomnyu chudnoye mgnoveniye*] (1825) dedicated to Anna Kern; and some others in a lighter vein. Lyric strains combined with politics in the historical elegy, 'André Chénier' (1825); reading of Shakespeare resulted in the same year in *Boris Godunov* and *Count Nulin*.

In 1826 Pushkin was summoned to Moscow by Nicholas I who granted him an illusory freedom. In a moment of trust, the poet exhorted the new Tsar to follow in the footsteps of Peter the Great ('Stanzas', 1826), and later answered his critics: 'No, I am no flatterer when I sing free praise of the Tsar' ('To Friends' [*Druz'yam*] 1828). At the same time he courageously wrote a whole series of poems dedicated to the memory of the Decembrists among whom he had so many friends: 'In the depths of the Siberian mines' [*Vo glubine sibirskikh rud*] (1827), 'Arion' (1827), and the moving short poem commemorating the anniversary of the Lycée, '19 October 1827', which starts with the words: 'God preserve you, my friends . . .' As usual with Pushkin, the sentiments expressed are universal, but they stem from a concrete reference to the exiles in Siberia.

By the end of the 1820s a tragic tone enters many of the lyric poems. Tormented by censorship, interrogations and suspicions, Pushkin writes 'The Foreboding' [*Predchuvstviye*] (1828), starting with the line, 'Silently above my head / Clouds have massed again . . .' The 1828 'Casual Gift' [*Dar naprasny, dar sluchayny*] with its poignant question 'Casual gift, oh, futile gift, / Life, why were thou given me?' contrasts sharply with the 'comfortable' philosophy of the earlier 'Though life may conspire to cheat you / Do not sorrow or complain . . .' (*Esli zhizn' tebya obmanet*, 1825). An echo of Pushkin's restlessness at the time can be found in 'Laments on the road' [*Dorozhnye zhaloby*] (1829). His lyrics become increasingly more compact, his language more exact, his descriptions even more realistic; it is enough to read 'It is winter. What shall we do in the country?' [*Zima. Chto delat' nam v derevne?*] (1829) to realise how simplified his language has become, how closely it corresponds to everyday modern Russian, and how close to the rhythm of prose it is.

Most of the end of the 1820s was devoted to *Eugene Onegin*; *Poltava* was written in 1828; and the Boldino autumn of 1830 was the most creative in the whole of Pushkin's career. The range of major works is almost incredible: in three months Pushkin wrote five prose works (*The Tales of Belkin*), a comic narrative poem (*The Little House in Kolomna*), and four dramatic investigations in blank verse which are among his very best works.

1831 was the year of Pushkin's disastrous marriage to Natalia Goncharova. His relations with the authorities were as difficult as ever, he had serious financial problems, everything seemed to be against him: the public which ceased to understand him, the authorities, his mother-in-law, the expensive tastes of his wife, the Tsar, the courtiers. Quantitatively, Pushkin's lyric output in his last years was small, qualitatively — of the very highest order. Pushkin was writing mainly for himself. He felt that his lyrics were too personal, too intimate to be published. Among them we find the tragic 'God grant me never to be mad' [*Ne day mne Bog soyti s uma*] (1833) and the unfinished lyric to his wife:' 'Tis time, my friend, 'tis time . . .' [*Pora moy drug, pora*] (1834) which so characteristically renders Pushkin's awareness of the passage of time and his longing to work which he equated with peace and freedom. Less intimately, Pushkin's idea of happiness was stated in 'From Pindemonte' (1836) where he spoke of the poet's right 'to live without giving account to anyone, to serve and please no one but oneself'. And on the rare occasion we have a spark of the old Pushkin again, responding once more to life and beauty:

> I thought my heart had lost the power
> Of suffering love's gentle pain:
> I said, 'The past, the fleeting hour
> Comes not again, comes not again.
>
> 'They've gone, the raptures and the longing,
> The flattering dreams that shone so bright . . .'
> But as I spoke, they came back thronging,
> Called up by Beauty's sovran might.
> (*Ya dumal serdtse pozabylo* (1835))
> (trans. V. de S. Pinto)

Among the major works in this last period of Pushkin's life is his greatest narrative poem, *The Bronze Horseman* (1833), his most important prose works, *The Queen of Spades* (1833) and *The Captain's Daughter* (1836), and three long folk poems. Pushkin could only find happiness and peace in work. The last years of his life were troubled by wounded pride, extreme jealousy, fear of ridicule, the pettiness of human behaviour. The unavoidable end of it was the duel in which he was mortally wounded. He died two days later, on 29 January 1837.

One of the reasons why Pushkin's lyric poetry has never made much of an impact outside Russia lies in the very nature of his poetry which combines simplicity with expressiveness. Pushkin's poetic language is noted for its few metaphors, for the seeming absence of any adornments; not a word can be moved or substituted, however, without destroying the perfectly balanced pattern of language, verse, metre and rhyme. The depth of Pushkin's poetry is not due to any philosophy of life or any subjective self-revelation; his 'wisdom' has little to do with intellect, but rather with an instinctive and artistic ability for pin-pointing the essence of things, reactions, feelings. The universality of his poetry does not only stem from the wide range of subject-matter, forms, and idioms – his lyrics include love poems, metapoetry, fugitive poetry, political poetry, folk poetry, philosophical meditations, nature descriptions, echoes of various moods and experiences; and his tone ranges from frivolous to biblical, from intimate to majestic, from prosaic to elevated. It also stems from the characteristically Pushkinian sublimation of his personal experience into a general and universal one. Despite the uniqueness of the poet's mood behind the lyric, the reader finds in it something familiar, something that his range of experience can cover, however different his background may be to that of Pushkin's. Pushkin's genius for sublimation and distance, his ability to see everything *sub specie aeternitatis* make him a classic who will always transcend the complexity of our modern visions. Pushkin's art of expressing this 'natural universality' does not travel well: it is Pushkin's feeling for language and proportions that make any translation disappointing.

However perfect many of his lyrics are, Pushkin is not primarily a lyric poet. From his earliest years he gravitated to narrative poetry and the dramatic form. The long *poema* is central to his work, but it is only for classification purposes that one tends to treat it in isolation. In reality, Pushkin's narrative poems are inextricably bound up with his lyrics – they are both rooted in the real world and in the poet's experience.

The main novelty of *Ruslan and Lyudmila* (1820) was its mixture of genres. A narrative mock-heroic poem, it shook the critics by introducing an ironic, playful and parodic vein as well as a fantastic element into a heroic context, and the verse itself – the four-foot iambic which was to determine the form of the Russian narrative poem in the future – was

B

new in the sense that it had never before been applied to a non-lyric genre. Entirely alien in spirit to the classical poem, *Ruslan and Lyudmila* was free from moralisation and didacticism. But though it marked a break with tradition, it was to a great extent derivative – indeed, it was almost a kind of a literary collage of heterogeneous elements including Push-kin's own Lycée lyrics, held together by the constant presence of the narrator whose light, bantering manner corresponded to the image of himself projected by Pushkin in his early poetry. At the same time it looked forward to the fairy tales and the historical scenes of *Boris Godunov* and *Poltava*. There is no notion of character as yet in *Ruslan and Lyudmila*, and Pushkin's heroes are mere puppets whom no one can take seriously because the poet who manipulates them at his whim does not himself take them seriously. The poem as a whole is unmistakably Pushkinian in tone. A delightful fantasy, it is no more than the poet claims in the epilogue – just a plaything of his imagination.

Pushkin's southern poems were variations in the new idiom of the early nineteenth century. Patterned on the lyric Byronic epic, they illustrate Pushkin's ability to respond, absorb, and transform.

Already in *The Prisoner of the Caucasus* (1821), Pushkin's romanticism is checked by a concreteness that is absent in Byron. The strange and the exotic are held in close restraint; experience in some form or other always intrudes. Pushkin cannot fully identify himself with his hero, though there are parallels between their respective situations, and between the narrative poem and several lyrics of the time; he observes him, and the notion of character is already there in embryo. This is not accidental – Pushkin said later that he had intended to show in his nameless hero 'that indifference to life and its pleasures, that premature ageing of the soul, which have become characteristic of nineteenth-century youth'. He may not have entirely succeeded, but he did point to the essential self-centredness of the Prisoner. An amusing comment which reveals something of Pushkin's 'workshop'[5] may be found in a letter to Vyazemsky: 'Others are disappointed that the prisoner did not plunge into the river to drag out my Circassian girl – well you just try: I have swum in Caucasian rivers – one can drown there sooner than find a soul . . .' The centre of gravity of Pushkin's first romantic poem lies more in the realistic setting than in the love drama. The picture of the Circassians' manners and way of life is the best and the most Pushkinian part of the poem.

If *The Fountain of Bakhchisaray* (1821–3), with its more sustained lyric mood, its exotic and dream-like visions, and its beautifully melodious verse, is the most Byronic of Pushkin's poetic tales, *The Gipsies* (1824) firmly marks his tendency to free himself from Byron and romanticism. The character of Aleko is a further development of the Prisoner, and in a sense a forerunner of Onegin. A poem of love and jealousy, it also raises deeper problems without solving them, points to the ambiguous nature of freedom, and brings out with some force the conflict between man and society. Civilisation as well as inability to conform are consciously criticised. Whatever Aleko may stand for, he personifies the bankruptcy of romantic egocentricity, the inability of civilised man to run away from civilisation, or, even more, from himself, or ultimately perhaps from fate. His influence on Russian literature, and especially on Dostoevsky, was considerable.

In character drawing, in content, and in form, *The Gipsies* marks a serious development in Pushkin's art. Extremely compact in structure, the work is polyphonic in mood. It has a variety of styles, with the conflict dramatised, real dialogue replacing the lyric monologues of the Prisoner and the heroine no longer merely antithetic, since the action advances from her initiative; the lyric elements play a role in the development of the story and descriptions are part of the motivation. Concrete details of time and place and even prosaic touches are interspersed in the basically romanticised picture of gipsy life.

John Bayley – in the most serious book on Pushkin in English – rightly stresses the importance of *The Prisoner of the Caucasus* and *The Gipsies* for the evolution of Pushkin's hero and shows to what extent Pushkin uses the romantic idiom while remaining detached from it. The dethronement of the romantic hero initiates the process of portraying contemporary man. Merely suggested in the romantic poems, this process will be found completed and canonised for the Russian novel in *Eugene Onegin* (1823–31).

Written over a period of eight years, *Eugene Onegin* in every sense occupies a central position in Pushkin's work as a whole. Written 'freely', without a preconceived idea of the final shape it was to take, this novel in verse gradually changed, developed and matured side by side with its author. At first, Pushkin contemplated writing something in the manner of Byron's *Don Juan* or *Beppo*. The first three chapters were written at the same time as *The Fountain of Bakhchisaray* and *The Gipsies*, and in 1824 Pushkin still called his work 'a romantic poem'. His manner at the beginning recalls that of *Ruslan and Lyudmila*: the frivolous chatty tone is familiar. But as the work advances, digressions become fewer and more controlled, descriptions more concrete, romantic metaphors disappear, the style becomes simpler and the tone more objective. Onegin who at first seems to be tied to the narrator, gradually emerges as conditioned by his education, reading and the fashion of the time. He is of the society and background that formed him, and at the same time above it. Because he reacts against his milieu, we see him in unfamiliar surroundings where he stands out for us to observe him better. His relationships with the other characters, and with Tatyana above all, make us aware of his private personal experience which makes him a unique individual as well as a type. The shifting points of view add further depth to his characterisation. The same is true of Tatyana, and their unfulfilled romance is not really due to missed opportunities, but to two encounters at different times of their development both as typical products of their age and background and as individual human beings.

By chance rather than design, added to Pushkin's natural propensity for *seeing* and recording the concrete detail – or, in deference to Russian critics, due to his 'sense of history' – the author of *Eugene Onegin* discovered something that is at the very basis of the nineteenth-century novel, namely the placing of the character in a recognisable, authenticated background. The authenticity of background gives authenticity to the character, and if one adds to it the assurance that a multiplicity of points of view gives us, the contrasts in settings and characters, the impression of reality produced by the presence and interaction of several characters and groups of characters, each typical and individual, as well as the sense of movement and of the passage of time – most of the elements of the realistic novel are there. Within its own tradition and time, the work is entirely original in this respect, as is the dual perspective and the inconclusive solution of the romance.

To think of *Eugene Onegin* however *only* in terms of a novel of sentiment, or in terms of a novel *tout court*, is not only to impoverish our understanding of it, but to misinterpret it entirely. *Eugene Onegin* is not a novel, but a novel in verse – 'the devil of a difference', in Pushkin's own words, and the difference that makes of it a unique work. It is as much a poem about Pushkin as a poem about Onegin and Tatyana or a picture of Russian life. We can trace through the work the phases of Pushkin's life as well as the phases of his literary career. We get a stylised projection of the poet who participates in the story in the first person but who, as Nabokov remarks, enjoys all the rights of expression and confession that the third person characters have. But we also get nearer to Pushkin the man for – as in his lyrics – the most universalised of his moods is based on his experience. Moreover, the autobiographical allusions and references to real events and real people recreate cumulatively not only the age in which Onegin lived but the world of Pushkin the man and Pushkin the writer. The more attentively we read this extraordinary novel in verse, the fuller it becomes. No work in Russian literature has produced, fruitfully, so many textual commentaries on practically every line as has *Eugene Onegin*. This does not mean that the work cannot stand by itself without an array of scholarly apparatus. Indeed, most people have enjoyed it and will continue to do so without any specialised knowledge of Pushkin's life and times. But how many of us are so familiar with Russian literature, for instance, as to realise that the very first line of Chapter 1 contains an allusion to Krylov's Fable 'The Ass and the Peasant' in which the ass is a creature of the highest moral principles and therefore is entrusted with guarding the vegetable garden, ruining the whole place in the process of doing so? Referring to Onegin's uncle as 'the soul of honour', Pushkin introduces lightly a parodic element, a comic and irreverent element, and at the same time fills in the social profile of the uncle who reappears briefly in Chapter 2, stanza 3. This example, for all its relative insignificance, discloses a network of associations which constantly enrich the narrative and must have been obvious to Pushkin's contemporaries.

Above all, in his digressions on professional matters and in his literary allusions Pushkin addresses the narrow circle of his friends who are able to appreciate the scintillating variation of his stanza which organises and keeps in control the effervescence of styles and poetic techniques. For there is not one style but a variety of styles in *Eugene Onegin*,[6] and Pushkin uses them not only as an additional method of characterisation, not only to speed or slow down the narrative, or to structure it invisibly, seemingly retreating from the text to vouch for the reality of his protagonists, or deliberately intruding to puncture that reality and add another dimension to it. He also effortlessly manipulates his styles to show proudly and confidently his peacock's splendid poetic plumage, and we are deliberately drawn into and made aware of his creative process. He seems to conduct a never-ending dialogue with literary modes, fashions, models, and primarily — with himself as a poet, testing his poetic art, brilliantly improvising, proving to himself and to the world the deceptive ease of his mastery over word and verse, and revealing for posterity his only life-long commitment — to his art.

The importance of Pushkin's novel in verse for subsequent Russian fiction cannot be overemphasised.[7] Within Pushkin's own development, this most 'poetic' of his works contained the seeds of his prose — both in its language and in its sobering transition from the romanticism of youth to the realism of maturity. Pushkin's introduction of the 'prosaic' into poetry can also be seen, on a miniaturised scale but more consistently, in *Count Nulin* (1825), a by-product of his interest in Shakespeare which resulted in the same year in *Boris Godunov*, a truly magnificent failure conceived as an attempt to apply the principles of Shakespearean drama to the Russian stage. A parody of *The Rape of Lucrece*, *Count Nulin* is none the less a typically Pushkinian anecdote about a volatile provincial wife, written in two days, full of life and verve and ironic twists. Its realistic, deliberately prosaic background with its village pond, dogs, ducks and washing line became almost a pattern for Russian prose, and was brilliantly echoed by Gogol. The critics of the day immediately condemned the use of 'low themes' in poetry, and behaved — in Pushkin's words — like an awkward country girl on a visit to a St Petersburg *grande dame*.

Somewhat similar in spirit in its central anecdote is *The Little House in Kolomna* (1830), a narrative poem in octaves, written at the time when

Pushkin had nearly completed *Eugene Onegin*. In its opening *Art poétique*, Pushkin defiantly, though at unusual length for him, professes to be bored by the four-foot iambic line and proceeds to tell in five-foot iambics the tale of a widow, her pretty daughter and the daughter's lover who settles in their house disguised as a female cook until the girl's mother finds him shaving. John Bayley singles out *The Little House* as Pushkin's only poem in which modification and paraphrase of a source, in this instance Byron's *Beppo*, does not yield a commensurate gain. Though not a masterpiece by Pushkinian standards, the tale is an apposite illustration of Pushkin's art of the anecdote. The *pointe* comes with the moral: 'In my view, it is dangerous to engage a cook for nothing. If you are a male, you have no business to don a skirt. Sooner or later you will have to shave, and this is incompatible with the nature of a lady . . . Nothing else can be squeezed out of my tale.' A spirited answer to the critics who objected to the 'insignificance' of his themes in poetry, it clearly shows Pushkin's attitude; a story is a story, and it would be foolish to pretend that it merits any deeper treatment. The potential of this mere anecdote is limited, but it is realised.

Between the two 'prosaic' tales, Pushkin wrote *Poltava* (1828), a longer work of much greater importance in his development, but one which usually confounds the reader by the presence of two distinct themes, one – the love story – seemingly a step backwards towards romanticism, the other – the historical drama culminating in the battle of Poltava – which looks forward to *The Bronze Horseman*. Though the personality and the treason of Mazepa links thematically the lyric and the epic elements, there is a lack of overall balance in this hurriedly written work. Despite the romantic and at times even melodramatic theme of the first two cantos, the style is concentrated, and with one or two exceptions, entirely objective, impersonal and sober. The heroine who is seen at first in a folk-tale context becomes a romantic melodramatic figure and does not gain by it, but Mazepa, and to some extent Kochubey, who are also introduced in the typical set manner of folk songs, do acquire psychological depth. The interrelation of people's fate with history, traceable to Walter Scott, and at the centre of *The Captain's Daughter*, is already touched upon here, and Pushkin brings out the personal motivations of his characters behind the political drama. The third canto, with its superb scene of the battle which decides the historical destiny of Russia, makes of *Poltava* a heroic and national poem. It is notable for its apotheosis of Peter the Great who comes to the fore after the personal drama is over. His isolation outside the plot, and the high style of the traditional ode that surrounds him, seem to underline his semi-God-like figure. The epilogue of *Poltava* is characteristically Pushkinian: both the love tragedy and the historic drama are shifted into the distant past. A hundred years have gone, and the strong passions of the heroes as well as the ravages of war are forgotten; only the hero of Poltava has raised a monument for himself. The way is now open for the prologue to *The Bronze Horseman*.

Unlike *Poltava*, *The Bronze Horseman* (1833) blends perfectly into one memorable whole all the disparate elements that go into its making. As nearly all Pushkin's work, it has at its basis a whole mosaic of concrete details and personal associations: literary polemics with Mickiewicz, contemporary accounts of the floods of 1824, possibly the Decembrist rising, an anecdote which may have given rise to the idea of the statue coming to life, Algarotti's description of St Petersburg as a window through which Russia looks at Europe; among the personal associations, the themes of marriage, money and even madness being the more obvious ones. It also has a network of links with other Pushkin works, among which *Ezersky* and *My Genealogy* are the most important. At the outset, Pushkin's presence is established as the narrator who tells us a real story, as the author of *Eugene Onegin*, and in the prologue as the poet in love with his city and as the Russian patriot.

The whole poem is based on antithesis. Even Peter the Great is presented at two historic moments – at the beginning of the Swedish war when he decides to lay the foundations of a new town, and a hundred years later, during the floods of 1824 – as a statue. In the prologue he is a real historical figure, though raised on a pedestal; in the main narrative – a statue come to life, in Evgeny's deranged mind. The basic contrast of course is the opposition of the Tsar and the poor clerk Evgeny, but his conflict with Peter is unreal and exists only in his imagination. Evgeny's non-entity is relative: if he is 'a little, wronged man', he is a little man with a great soul.[8] But he has no chance when faced with either the uncontrollable forces of nature or with the mighty of this world. The nature antithesis is doubled, for even 'tsars cannot have mastery over the divine elements'. The antithesis of an earlier lyric, 'Splendid town, wretched town' [*Gorod pyshny, gorod bedny*] (1828) is further developed in the contrast between Peter's splendour and the poverty of his surroundings, between his grandiose plans and the pitiful reality. Stylistically, the contrast between the heroic poem and the realistic narrative is supported by the odic form and Slavonicisms whenever Pushkin speaks of Peter the Great or of his creation, St Petersburg, and by the simple, intimate, almost prosaic language when he speaks of Evgeny. Both the heroic poem and the realistic narrative with its built-in fantastic element are supported by an extraordinarily developed sound instrumentation and Pushkin's most ambitious 'orchestration'.[9]

Being a poem on several planes, *The Bronze Horseman* suggests a variety of interpretations. Some will seek in it political symbolism, a reflection of contemporary events, the struggle against despotism and autocracy, the opposition between 'ruled' and 'ruler', between the individual and the state. Belinsky saw in the figure of Peter the Great the expression of historical determinism, the incarnation of a historical idea, and in the poem as a whole a contrast between two poles of human activity which are in the nature of the historical process. The great impact of the poem is due to the absence of any judgement on the part of Pushkin, and perhaps even more to his ambivalent, almost equivocal attitude: he undoubtedly admires Peter the Great and yet seems to accuse him; he is genuinely sorry for Evgeny and yet implies that however unfortunate his case, it is in the nature of things. Who is guilty of the human tragedy? Is it the elements, the splendidly personified river, the 'Neva tossing like a sick man in his restless bed'? Is not nature stronger than both Tsars and individuals? Or is it ultimately fate, as in *The Gipsies*? Pushkin does not draw any conclusions, he just presents – from a multiplicity of viewpoints – the tragic, unavoidable contradiction between the many and the few, between progress and the price of it. St Petersburg, Evgeny, Peter the Great – they all seem to be there merely as material for Pushkin's thoughts on history, on Russia, on fate. There is no ideological commitment, only poetic commitment. Pushkin instinctively understood that great art has to remain 'incomplete' in order to contain within itself the power of infinite suggestion and infinite renewal. *The Bronze Horseman* is a great poem because it will always reverberate in the imagination of successive generations, constantly acquiring new dimensions, superimposing new connotations on the old ones, constantly enriching and renewing itself. The theme of St Petersburg and the myth of *The Bronze Horseman* haunted the imagination of Gogol, Dostoevsky, and the Symbolists. It was most spectacularly exploited in Andrey Bely's brilliant novel *Petersburg*.

The Bronze Horseman was the last narrative poem of Pushkin, his last great poem. After that he wrote almost entirely prose.

In turning to prose, Pushkin was motivated by several considerations. As early as 1822 he expressed his opinion on contemporary Russian prose, criticising in particular the prevalent periphrastic style:

> What are we to say of our writers who, deeming it too low to write plainly of ordinary things, think to liven up their childish prose with embellishments and faded metaphors! These people will never say 'friendship' without adding 'that holy sentiment, of which the noble flame, etc.'. They want to say 'early in the morning', and they write 'hardly had the first rays of the rising sun irradiated the eastern edge of the azure sky'. How new and fresh all this is! Is it better simply for being longer?

In the same draft article he mentioned Voltaire as the best example of sensible style, and saw the prime virtues of prose in precision and brevity, the two qualities which were to distinguish his own prose works.

Thus Pushkin reacted against contemporary standards. He reacted also to the mood of the reading public which by the 1830s was satiated with poetry: novels and tales were the best-sellers of the day. Above all, anticipated in the development of his poetry, prose presented Pushkin with a new artistic challenge. His first completed prose work, *The Tales of Belkin* (1830–1), bears all the marks of being an experimental work. The five stories which go into its making were written in the autumn of 1830, and the figure of Belkin – the fictitious modest narrator – was added a year later in an introduction which forms a sort of a 'sixth tale'.[10] Pushkin's decision not to own up at first to having written the stories was partly due to the uncertainty of their reception: whereas he had an instinctive sense of poetic form, prose was new territory made more forbidding by his very insistence on keeping the two entirely separate. The introduction of Belkin and of multiple narrators within the stories was the result of a self-conscious search for a satisfactory structural solution to an unfamiliar exercise.

The Tales of Belkin are basically anecdotes on well-worn sentimental and romantic themes, which – on careful reading – acquire the dimension of miniaturised novels. The proviso of careful reading points immediately to the basic quality of Pushkin's prose – its extreme compactness allied with a 'suggestiveness' which makes the work grow in the imagination of the reader who is prepared to contribute to the process. In a curiously paradoxical way, the effort demanded is similar to that required by modern poetry, but the reason for it is not to be found in bold metaphors but in Pushkin's determination 'not to spell it out' and in his use of the *mot juste*. Thus the romantic elopement in *The Station Master* is central to the story only in so far as it affects the girl's father; his individual world is related to and enriched by his social world; the subsequent fate of the daughter and her feelings are merely hinted at: life goes on despite the death of the station master, in a way unanticipated either by convention or literary models, or by the father, or the symbolism of the Parable of the Prodigal Son pictures on the wall. The whole story is some 2,000 words long but it encompasses a whole life, a social background, human relations, human behaviour, a reality which ironically, does not follow the pattern. Morality does not come into the question. Pushkin does not judge the girl: she is frivolous and susceptible to riches and rank; neither does he judge the station master who accepts money from his daughter's seducer, throws it away in disgust, has second thoughts and returns to pick it up only to find that it had disappeared. The father does not die of a broken heart but his downfall is accelerated by his taking to drink.

The truth of human behaviour is shown 'in action', dramatically. The presence of the narrator helps to cut down on descriptions, to solve problems of structure and time sequence. The device of multiple narrators, an element of literary parody, the simplicity and clarity of Pushkin's laconic narrative manner are typical of the *Tales* as a whole. If to a great extent they end sentimentalism and romanticism, they do so not merely by the ironic handling of the banal plots, but also by the realistic manner with which these are presented. Pushkin is determined to prove that any subject can be treated soberly. We may be conscious of his mastering a new form, but we are witnessing the creation of Russian prose and of the literary language of Russia. By the time *The Queen of Spades* was written (1833), Pushkin was in full control of the art of pure narrative.

The Queen of Spades is incomparably richer, deeper and more concentrated than any of *The Tales of Belkin*. The interest of the reader is entirely centred on the development of the story; its 'architectonics' are built-in, without distracting the attention of the reader. Mirsky claimed it was no more than 'a glorified anecdote'; John Bayley attributes to it 'the weight of a novel'. Both claims merely show how pointless it is to encompass any work of Pushkin within a given genre. The anecdote is undoubtedly at the centre of the work in a double sense: for not only may the whole narrative be seen as an extended anecdote, but a real anecdote triggers off the plot. It is Pushkin's tense compactness which prevents us perhaps from unhesitatingly calling it a miniature novel. *The Station Master* might have conceivably lent itself to a more leisurely treatment; an epic manner would have ruined *The Queen of Spades*. Yet its background and its various ramifications certainly belong to the world of the novel, to a much greater extent than in the earlier work. The social setting against which the story evolves is defined at the very beginning as the world of high society whiling the night away at a game of cards. Hermann, the German engineer, is an outsider: the plot will be centred on him. A few paragraphs later the setting is extended: Tomsky tells his friends of his grandmother's Paris days some sixty years earlier, when Richelieu himself courted 'la Vénus moscovite'. The past breaks into the present, and the momentary intrusion of the second setting into the first sparks off an idea in Hermann's mind which will provide the tension of the story. This tension is merely an extension of the one which already exists in Hermann: fascinated by the game, he does not dare to touch a card, for he cannot afford risking the necessary in the hope of acquiring the superfluous. The interplay of the two settings is a backcloth for the interplay of reality and fantasy throughout the story. The world of the old Countess, as introduced by Tomsky, may both be real and unreal. Hermann is the first to dismiss it as fiction, yet it is he who takes it seriously. At the same time, it is recreated in all its precise reality when we witness with Hermann the secrets of the old Countess's bedroom. Similarly, the firmly established contemporary world which broadens and takes in even social comment is imperceptibly manipulated to include a world of fantasy. The superbly handled pure narrative embraces the workings of a mind: there is no psychological analysis but sheer action and suspense reveal the development of an obsession. The conclusion which, so uncharacteristically for Pushkin, ties up all the ends – brings us back to reality. Now that Hermann is disposed of, life goes on: some social patterns remain unchanged, some are rearranged to begin a new cycle.

The texture of reality in *The Captain's Daughter* (1836) is of an entirely different kind. City gives way to the country, contemporary social setting to eighteenth-century history, the rapid and tense narrative to a more leisurely epic manner. The work owes much to the tradition of Walter Scott, though certainly not its manner of narration. Unlike the *walterskotiki*, the 'little Walter Scotts' of Russian literature who lavishly imitated some formal characteristics of Scott's novels, Pushkin was attracted to Scott's historicism, as he says, 'not through the *enflure* of French tragedies, not through the primness of sentimental novels, not through the *dignité* of history, but in a contemporary, domestic manner'. The unheroic and insipid character of the first-person narrator, the young country squire Grinyov who despite himself gets involved in the two opposing camps, enabled Pushkin to give both an intimate close-up and a wider, more objective view of the historical events. It also enabled him to embody in Grinyov a divided allegiance which reflected the ideological conflict between heroic rebellion and traditional law and order without fully resolving it. Grinyov may be the organising principle of the whole picture and the prime mover of the plot, but the truly memorable characters are those of Captain Mironov and his wife, and of Savelich, the old man-servant. Gogol was surprisingly close to the mark when he wrote:

> In comparison with *The Captain's Daughter*, all our other novels and short stories are like sickly-sweet watered porridge. In it, purity and artlessness attain such heights that reality itself seems artificial and caricatured. For the first time, we have truly Russian characters: a simple officer commanding a fort, his wife, a lieutenant, the fort itself with its one lone cannon, the confusion of the period, the modest grandeur of ordinary people. Not only is it truth itself, but something even better.[11]

What Gogol did not or could not notice was the powerful attraction of Pugachov's figure whose reckless courage Pushkin could afford to admire in the novel through Grinyov in a way which he could not in his *History* of the Pugachov Rebellion which he had just completed.

Donald Davie felt that *The Captain's Daughter* was hardly a novel, but rather 'like the Platonic idea of the perfect novel'. Yet Pushkin's 45,000-word work has all the ingredients of the novel: a romance, a broad historical canvas, and characters who are ultimately more important than either. Plot, history and the socially differentiated characters are so 'inevitably' interrelated that no detail is superfluous or accidental. Pushkin's feeling for composition and his almost severe concentration on a single line of interest are truly classical. But if it is true, as Ortega y Gasset remarks, that the novel is and must be 'a sluggish form', that it must depend on the cumulative effect of minutiae to be able to recreate life in all its wealth and endless ramifications, then Pushkin's terseness – however admirable – is a flaw. Curiously enough, in a somewhat different context, Pushkin himself wrote: 'A novel demands *chat*; everything must be expressed . . .', but for him 'everything' was strictly limited to 'everything relevant' – in prose more so than in poetry. This explains perhaps the apparent paradox of why *Eugene Onegin* in which the poet allows himself a lavishness he would have considered inappropriate to prose – despite its verse form or indeed *because* of it – proved to be the greater influence on the Russian novel.

The form that suited Pushkin temperamentally best was perhaps that of the *Little Tragedies* (1830). Poetry and not prose was Pushkin's 'natural' medium, and the blank verse of *The Stone Guest, The Covetous Knight* and *Mozart and Salieri* is one of his greatest triumphs. Much more pliable than in *Boris Godunov*, it responded to every mood and is as memorable for its colloquial ease in the rapid exchanges between Don Juan and Laura, as for its sustained rhetoric in the monologues of the Baron or Salieri. Pushkin hardly ever surpassed the language of the *Little Tragedies*, its simplicity, its poetry, its suggestive power to convey the respective geographical, historical and cultural settings. Structurally, inner and outer contrasts, parallelisms, symmetry are all used in a most unobtrusive but entirely 'inevitable' way. *The Stone Guest* in particular, the most perfect of the *Little Tragedies*, is a model of Pushkin's innate sense of balance, proportion and precision. Ranging from 560 to 230 lines in length, from four to two episodes, from ten to two characters, with a corresponding curtailment of scenic time, the *Little Tragedies* are truly miniature dramatic sketches, but their size is not due to simplification but to compression without the slightest loss of complexity. Indeed, each of the *Little Tragedies* raises some of the most complex themes that Pushkin ever treated: the nature of love, the power of money, the conflict between talent and genius. Any attempt at formulating the themes of the *Little Tragedies* points immediately to the difficulty of defining and circumscribing the multiplicity of meanings: *The Covetous Knight* contains within itself an investigation into the nature of avarice, freedom, lust for power, and father–son relations; *Mozart and Salieri* is as much a study of envy or justice as of the tragedy of genius; *The Stone Guest* is as much a study of a passion as of retribution. The thematic richness of the contents is inextricably bound up with the complexity of characters. Pushkin achieved in the *Little Tragedies* what he had only partially succeeded in doing in *Boris Godunov*. The characters in the *Little Trage-dies* are many-sided individuals, and the sketches are primarily dramatic investigations of the incongruity of human nature. The Baron is not only a miser but also a knight; Albert subconsciously wishes the death of his father but is revolted by the proposition of the Jew; Salieri kills Mozart but is the first to cry over his death; Don Juan is far from being a mere adventurer. Shakespearean undercurrents of emotion, which are absent in *Boris Godunov*, are beautifully rendered in the sketches, and are especially poignant in the second scene of *Mozart and Salieri*, which culminates in the final blow to Salieri when Mozart says: 'Genius and villainy are two incompatible things.'

The development of situation is foreshortened to give weight to the *dénouement* and thus provide the tension in which the characters are revealed in all their complexity. The concentration on the climax of the conflicts makes every line, every word loaded and pregnant with meaning. Diversification is achieved by dramatic irony, by theatrical effects, by the role of inanimate categories, by the Pushkinian endings which do not solve anything. Mozart may be dead, but the problems raised by Salieri continue to reverberate; and we will never know whether Don Juan was really in love or merely a cynical seducer. As John Bayley rightly remarks, it is impossible to pin Don Juan down, for his role consists in not being open to interpretation.

One of the most remarkable features of the *Little Tragedies* is the constancy with which the dramatic situation – and only this – reveals the psychology of the characters. And yet Pushkin's individual private experience is at the very basis of all the three sketches: they are the most lyrical of all his works and at the same time the most objective. The element of autobiography does not touch dramatic objectivity: personal experience has been sublimated into a perfectly realised art form.

Even the most cursory review of Pushkin's work reveals a constant artistic movement: Pushkin never stands still. Whatever concept he approached, he saw it primarily as a theme to be evaluated in terms of its aesthetic potentialities; every new genre was a new artistic challenge. Pushkin learnt from others and from himself, and one can observe a constant process of cross-fertilisation within his works. He seems to have played with ideas, genres and modes of expression; he learned by experimenting, rejected what he did not need, and absorbed what he wanted to perfect. The ideal of perfection was constantly in front of him, and the standards of excellence – his only preoccupation. Direct experience was the common background of all his works: the artist seems to have been constantly testing the truth of his creations against the truth of reality itself. Both had to coincide, for Pushkin not only felt that it was artistically wrong to spell things out, but also that there was no one answer to anything, no single point of view. Hence the ambivalence, the open-endedness, the lack of commitment of much of his work. Poised between two centuries, Pushkin transmuted the tensions between disparate values into an equilibrium that was entirely a result of his art. A few decades later he might not have been able to keep his independence. It is Gogol perhaps who summed up best Pushkin's literary attitude: 'Pushkin was given to the world to show in himself what a poet is, and nothing more . . .' But that was enough.

NOTES

1   O.S., i.e. Old Style, meaning according to the Julian Calendar, adopted in Russia in the eighteenth century, being twelve days behind the Gregorian (New Style) Calendar in nineteenth-century Russia and thirteen days behind in twentieth-century Russia. In this book all dates before 1918 are given Old Style.
2   See Victor Erlich's essay on Pushkin's metapoetry in *The Double Image*, Baltimore, 1964.
3   There is a most interesting study on the subject of André Meynieux, *Pouchkine homme de lettres et la littérature professionnelle en Russie* (Paris, 1966).
4   See John Bayley for an excellent analysis of the poem.
5   The expression is that of Tatiana Wolff whose excellent translations of Pushkin's letters and articles have been frequently used in this chapter.
6   John Fennell has recently elaborated this point with much insight.
7   See Richard Freeborn's most valuable study in *The Rise of the Russian Novel*.
8   The point is made by Slonimsky.
9   See John Fennell's study in *Nineteenth-Century Russian Literature* (London, 1973).
10   See Jan M. Meijer, 'The Sixth Tale of Belkin' in the collection of essays by Jan van der Eng *et al.*, (The Hague, 1968).
11   *Selected Passages from Correspondence with Friends*, Essay xxxi.

3 Dostoevsky

It is a convention – readily understandable in the light of his evolution as a writer – to emphasise that Dostoevsky's career began and ended with moments of personal triumph. His career as a writer opened in 1846 with the resounding triumph of his first original work, *Poor Folk*; it ended with the resounding applause that greeted his famous Pushkin speech at the ceremony in Moscow to mark the unveiling of a memorial to the poet in June 1880. A little over six months later, on 28 January 1881, Dostoevsky died and on 2 February his body was followed to its rest in the cemetry of the Alexander Nevsky Monastery in St Petersburg by a vast gathering of mourners, the beginning of what was to become a world-wide following that has brought him increasing fame since his death.

No other Russian writer has exerted the universal appeal of Dostoevsky. Significantly, it was precisely the 'universality' of Pushkin's genius that Dostoevsky emphasised in his speech, allied to what he also referred to as Pushkin's 'prophetic' character. If one is to generalise in the vaguest terms about Dostoevsky's genius, then one must stress its combination of universality and prophecy which transcend national boundaries and epochs and make his work seem as contemporary now, in the final quarter of the twentieth century, in the universality of its psychological understanding and the relevance of its prophetic vision, as it had been in his lifetime, a century ago. This said, it is equally true that Dostoevsky's vitality as a writer springs from his own deep concern for the problems of his own country and his own age. He is as 'national' a writer as was Pushkin and as fully conscious of the prophetic, educative role which literature and life demanded of him. As he said at the beginning of his Pushkin speech:

Pushkin appeared on the scene at the precise moment when we began to make a correct assessment of ourselves as a nation, a process which had only just begun and taken root in our society after a whole century since the Petrine reforms, and his appearance contributed greatly to illuminating our dark way forward with a new guiding light. In this sense Pushkin was a prophet and guide.

In a similar sense, though at a later and more complex stage in the evolution of Russian national consciousness, Dostoevsky was a prophet and guide.

Being born in 1821, Dostoevsky was alive at the beginning of the process of Russian national self-discovery and an inheritor of the ideological disputes and obligations to which the initial stages of the process gave rise. During Pushkin's lifetime the process had been embryonic, although he had contributed more than the Decembrist Revolt of 1825 or the policy of Official Nationalism promulgated in 1833 to defining what the idea of nationality – *narodnost'* is the Russian term – should mean in the context of Russian interpretation of her history, her political institutions and the moral bases of her society. By the time of Pushkin's death an intelligentsia was beginning to establish itself. Independent of, and practically always opposed to, the government, claiming always to think and act in the name of the Russian people, the Russian intelligentsia was initially drawn from among the educated nobility, but in the course of the 1840s, when Dostoevsky reached maturity, it was already becoming dominated by intellectuals of lower social origins drawn from the professional classes and artisans. Of these the most representative and influential was the literary critic Vissarion Belinsky. His pro-Western, anti-religious, utopian-socialist idealism, with its passionate defence of freedom and the individual and its equally passionate belief that literature should be committed to exposing the injustices in society, exerted a profound guiding influence on Russian thinking and on all the Russian writers who first came to prominence in 'the forties'. Among those opposed to him were various apologists of Russia's *status quo*, like the small but articulate group of theorists known as the Slavophiles who sincerely believed that Russia should seek her future identity rather in her own indigenous culture and religion than in the progressive and revolutionary ideals of nineteenth-century Europe; or like the writer Nikolay Gogol (1809–52) who believed in a patriarchal Russia largely of his own imagining that would be purified by greater religiosity and charitable effort.

Central to the Russian intelligentsia's humanitarian concerns was the question of poverty – the poverty induced by the social injustice of serfdom, by metropolitan capitalism, or that poverty of spirit which sprang from inadequate education, patriarchalism, religious cant and narrow political tyranny. By a trick of providence Dostoevsky received this central concern with poverty as a birthright: he was born the second son of a doctor at the Marinsky Hospital for the Poor in Moscow. The tiny apartment where Fyodor Dostoevsky spent his childhood, from the age of two to the age of sixteen, sharing a room scarcely larger than a cupboard with his elder brother Mikhail, is now a museum devoted to his memory. It can explain as well as anything the confined, obsessive, neurotically

sensitive states of mind which Dostoevsky bequeathed to his 'dreamers'
– those of his literary creations who fashion identities and ambitions
for themselves out of their own solitariness. Dostoevsky's was a confined
childhood, though not an unhappy one. His father, Mikhail Andreevich,
was a dour man, hard-working and by the standards of the time successful, for in 1827 he obtained entitlement to hereditary nobility – which
meant that his son, Fyodor, was a member of the Russian nobility, a
dvoryanim – and he thereby acquired the right to own land and serfs. He
bought two run-down village settlements in the province of Tula where
Dostoevsky was to spend several childhood summers. The memory of
that rural world remained with Dostoevsky to the end of his life and
is immortalised in *The Brothers Karamazov* in certain place names (e.g.
Chermashnya) and the fact that fire destroyed both the settlements in
1832, which presumably supplies the source for Dmitry Karamazov's
dream of the peasant woman who has lost her home in a fire and stands
helplessly at the roadside with a famished baby crying in her arms.
Apart from such glimpses in his writings, Dostoevsky has left little firm
witness to his boyhood experiences. There were Bible-readings in the
Dostoevsky household, the study of Latin, discussions of Pushkin and
Zhukovsky, and eventually, when the young Dostoevsky learned to read,
Karamzin, Walter Scott, Anne Radcliffe, Schiller, the Book of Job – these
and many others provided the heady brew which formed his early literary
consciousness. On his own admission, nothing affected him more deeply
than a visit to the theatre at the age of ten to see Schiller's *The Robbers*.
Such experiences, clearly more related to the enrichment of his inner life
than to greater sociability, were largely the consequence of his father's
insistence that the Dostoevsky children should not associate with other
children in the neighbourhood, least of all with the children of the poor.
But the Moscow poor were daily to be witnessed in Dostoevsky's childhood. They were the single most conspicuous fact of his early life.

The Dostoevsky family was not poor, but Mikhail Andreevich was a
tight-fisted man. After the mother's death in 1837, the two oldest
Dostoevsky children, Mikhail and Fyodor, were sent off to St Petersburg to enrol in the Military Engineering Institute. Their education to
that date had been at local Moscow schools, though in Fyodor's case it
had more likely been a process of self-education through vicarious
reading, and this process continued at the Military Engineering Institute
where he is supposed to have read much Romantic poetry and such
characteristically Romantic writers as Hoffmann, Cooper and de Quincey.
Throughout his cadetship at the Institute he was kept short of money
by his father and consequently, for this as well as for other reasons,
Dostoevsky's attitude towards money was always characterised by an
almost perverse impracticality and a wilfully prodigal disregard of its
value. His writings are similarly filled with money, just as so many of

his fictional characters are preoccupied to distraction by the absence of it; but nowhere in Dostoevsky's view of the world is money subsumed to palliate or remedy as it would appear to do in the work of Dickens. There were other, deeper preoccupations for Dostoevsky at this time. In 1839 his father was murdered by peasants of one of the settlements in Tula province, perhaps – so it was rumoured – in revenge for his corruption of two teenage peasant girls. Whatever the true cause may have been, for Dostoevsky the relationship between an elderly man and a young girl was to be a continually re-examined theme, from the first of his works to the last, just as the theme of parricide was to provide the obsessive, ideological as well as judicial, centre of his final, and greatest, novel. His father's death may have been what prompted him to remark in a letter to his brother Mikhail of August 1839: 'Man is a mystery. It is necessary to solve the mystery, and if you should go on trying to solve it all your life, then don't say you've wasted your time; I'm preoccupied with this mystery, because I want to be a man.' These words by the seventeen-year-old Dostoevsky can be read as an epigraph to his life's work.

His years at the Military Engineering Institute undoubtedly taught him to appreciate the need for 'architecture' in his writing, meaning planning and composition. Judging by the surviving notebooks, no Russian writer planned his major fictions as fully as Dostoevsky, even though his actual jottings appear often to be little more than thought-balloons dotted haphazardly about the page. The architectural proportions, as well as the essential paradox, of St Petersburg left its profound mark on his sensibilities and his attitudes as a writer. In one recollection, no doubt deriving from his early years as a cadet at the Institute, he had the following vision of St Petersburg (or so he recalled in his 'St Petersburg Dreams in Verse and Prose' of 1861) which perhaps reveals the very source of that partly unreal, fantastic, mystical apprehension of the city which is shared by so many of his fictional characters, particularly Raskolnikov:

I remember once, on a wintry January evening, how I was hurrying home to the Vyborg side. I was very young. Coming to the Neva, I stopped for a moment and threw a penetrating glance down river towards the smoky frost-dark distance which had suddenly become crimson in the last blood-red rays of the sunset as it burned out on the mist-filled horizon. Night was settling over the city, and the entire vast emptiness of the Neva, a swelling landscape of frozen snow, was sprinkled with endless miriads of sparks of prickly hoar-frost illuminated by the final glow of the sunset. There were already twenty degrees of frost . . . A freezing steam rose from tired horses and from the people rushing by. The ice-hard air rang quiveringly with the least sound, and just like enormous giants there rose and hung in the air

above the housetops on both embankments columns of smoke, inter-
weaving and unweaving in such a way that it seemed new buildings
were arising above the old, that a new city was being built in the
air . . . It seemed, finally, that the whole of this world, with all its
inhabitants, its strong and its weak, with all their dwellings, the hovels
of beggars or the gilded palaces, bore a resemblance at this twilight
hour to a fantastic, magic vision, to a dream which would vanish instantly in its turn and disappear in a cloud of smoke into the dark blue
sky. I suddenly had a strange thought. I shuddered, and my heart was
flooded in that instant with a hot uprush of blood that suddenly boiled
up in me from the access of a powerful but unfamiliar sensation. It
was as if I'd understood something in that instant that had previously
been stirring in me but had not been comprehended; as if I'd had a
vision of something completely new, a completely new world, unfamiliar to me and known only through some obscure rumours, through
some mysterious signs . . . Tell me, good readers, was I not given to
phantasies, was I not a mystic from my earliest years?

The answer to the question was given by Dostoevsky himself years later,
when he wrote of his own 'penetration of reality', for it is this 'penetrating glance' at the urban world, whether of St Petersburg or the many
townships which serve as his fictional locales, which distinguishes Dostoevsky's vision as a writer and helps to explain his never-ending, seemingly addictive interest in the boundaries between the real and the surreal,
reality and dream, phenomenal and noumenal, the squalor of present
human existence and the utopian ideal of a golden age, most paradoxically of all between the necessary obligations of conviction in life and
the metaphysical freedoms offered to man by the glamorously nihilistic
act of suicide. Much that Dostoevsky brought to his illustration of these
paradoxes derived from his reading. He entered Russian literature at the
moment that Romanticism was yielding to Realism or, to put it in a
simpler form, when the literary influence of Pushkin was already receding
before the dominance of Nikolay Gogol.

For Dostoevsky Romanticism meant both a literary heritage and an
emotional experience. The two combined and, in their respective ways,
remained enduring influences in Dostoevsky's life and work. His friendship, for instance, with a young poet, Shidlovsky, some five years his
senior, was a deeply felt, romantic experience which simultaneously
awoke in him the need to discover an identity of his own and consciously
broadened his experience of the meaning of literature. Partly through
the passionate friendship with Shidlovsky he came to discover the richness and variety of literature, from Schiller, Hugo and Hoffmann to
Racine, Shakespeare and Homer. His letters to his brother speak ecstatic-
ally of his discoveries. Equally, though in a different way, he encountered

in his friend something of the duality which was present in himself — a duality which, put at its crudest, can be equated with the contrast between romanticism and realism. Other friendships were to be less deep, it seems, but were similarly to reinforce Dostoevsky's awareness of the essential paradoxicality of human beings (his friendship with the 'Mephistophelian' Speshnyov, a member of the Petrashevsky group and supposed prototype of Stavrogin in *The Possessed*, is a case in point). Yet all his friendships at the Military Engineering Institute seem to have had a literary connection, so that by 1844, when he applied for release from army service, he was already determined on a literary career. He began it with a translation of Balzac's *Eugénie Grandet*. Though Dostoevsky borrowed from Balzac the theme of money for his first original work as a writer, a far more potent source of inspiration was the ostensible realism of Gogol's *The Greatcoat* and its study of the poor clerk Akaky Akakievich.

Poor government officials had become respectable themes in Russian literature since the appearance of Pushkin's study of the pathetic Samson Vyrin in *The Station Master* (the longest of his *Tales of Belkin*) in 1831. Gogol's study not only emphasises the pathos of Akaky Akakievich; it also tends to lay bare the 'spiritlessness' or sheer mediocrity (*poshlost'*) of the wretched clerk who seeks to give himself a semblance of personal individuality through purchasing a new greatcoat. Dostoevsky acknowledges the purely literary inspiration for his own study of the type of poor clerk by making his hero Makar Devushkin repudiate Gogol's portrait of Akaky Akakievich. In so doing, Dostoevsky turned his first literary work into a polemic with Gogol, into a challenge to all the prevailing standards in Russian literature. Equally, he exactly caught the tenor of the times by making his hero not only pathetic but also a mouthpiece for the dispossessed, the humble, the meek, for all those in Russian society who had no voice apart from that which literature might be said to permit them. Whether consciously or not, Dostoevsky instantly acquired a reputation which suited 'the forties' perfectly: he displayed a humanitarian concern for the deprived 'poor folk' of St Petersburg and thus contributed to the growth of a socially committed or realistic literature.

Vissarion Belinsky had no doubt that this was Dostoevsky's principal role. He was percipient enough as a critic to realise the young Dostoevsky's great potential on first seeing the manuscript of *Poor Folk*, but he grew dismayed later by Dostoevsky's further evolution as a writer. In fact, the essentially personal, obsessive, even pathological aspects of human character which Dostoevsky was to explore so profoundly later are present in his first work as fully as elsewhere, though they may appear to be disguised by the epistolary form and the many derivative features. The title itself is misleading. Although *Poor Folk* (1846) is about an ostensibly poor clerk and the apparently equally poor girl with whom he falls in love, their relative impoverishment seems thematically irrelevant when compared with the plight of the Gorshkov family, for instance, or the beggar boys who ply for alms in the St Petersburg streets. The central story is inherently sentimental: the lengthy, rather one-sided correspondence between Makar Devushkin and his Varenka, which ends when Varenka marries a wealthy merchant. Of greater depth and import is the astonishing empathy with which Dostoevsky creates the character of Makar himself through a series of confessional, highly idiomatic, histrionically effusive letters that resemble the blurted out-pourings of a psychiatric report. What becomes apparent finally is that Makar Devushkin's identity as a human being is inseparable from his ability to express himself, that he is to this extent a surrogate of Dostoevsky's own essential dilemma of identity as a writer, that the relationship which can be said to exist between Dostoevsky and his characters is almost that between equals, but that Makar himself is eventually overwhelmed by his 'love' for Varenka, to the extent at least – his final letter demonstrates this – of finding that his personality itself is beginning to disintegrate under the threat of her absence.

Many elements of the later Dostoevsky can be discerned in this first work, among them, though covertly, the notion of human free will or caprice as a fundamental assertion of the human paradox and the equally assertive idea that, as Makar puts it, 'poverty is always insolent' [*Da i vsegda bednost' nazoyliva*]. The insolence or importuning insubordination of the smallest towards the greatest, of the poor towards the rich, of Makar's button towards the General in whose presence it falls from its thread and goes spinning across the floor, or – on a different plane, though one that appealed to Dostoevsky – the insolence of the devil towards God is a theme examined in many paradoxical ways throughout Dostoevsky's work. The insolence of the insubordinate is at the heart of the masochistic embarrassment with which Dostoevskian characters find themselves 'shown up', 'scandalised', publicly shamed, for no matter how apparently genuine the embarrassment there always seems to be a relishing of the covert insolence which sustains the embarrassed soul. Insolence and all its impious, irreverent, scandalous connotations which had a special meaning in the oppressive social climate of nineteenth-century imperial Russia was to be the impulse behind so many of Dostoevsky's studies of the humiliated and insulted. Added to which was his abiding interest in the pathology of the persecuted and the barely distinguishable, but quite real, boundary between the real and the fantastic, the real and the ideal.

It is not known exactly when he began to show signs of the epilepsy that was to be the scourge of his life, although he did not suffer regular attacks until after penal servitude. His medical adviser and close friend,

Dr Yanovsky, has left testimony to Dostoevsky's often nervous condition in the late 1840s and his interest in pathology as well as social questions, religion and spiritualism. His second work, the long novella *The Double* (1846), is a study of the pathological state of Golyadkin, a government official, who finally relinquishes all hold upon his sanity and is taken off to an insane asylum. Golyadkin is persecuted by an insolent usurper of his own identity in the shape of Golyadkin Junior and endures several publicly shaming *skandal* scenes which are presented, as is much of this work, in a manner that combines ostensibly serious realistic narrative with a proneness to comic, even bizarre, exaggeration. The theme of the double, like the whole question of human identity, whether related to individuals or societies or nations, derived from Dostoevsky's preoccupation with antinomic forms of thought and reflected his deeply paradoxical character. There is no doubt, though, that Dostoevsky's intention was to discover the harmonising and reconciling truths which would lead to a single identity of interest and brotherhood between all men.[1] If he concerned himself with such pathological conditions as the disintegration of personality, as in the figure of Golyadkin, or the dream-consumed state of his garrulous dreamer-hero [*mechtatel'*] of *White Nights* (1848), or his heroine's perversely erotic, even Lesbian, relations in his unfinished novel *Netochka the Unnamed* (1849), he was simultaneously concerning himself – although we do not know exactly how seriously – with the Petrashevsky group discussions about Utopian Socialism, especially Fourierism, and talk of changing society by revolutionary means. He had been brought to these interests chiefly by Belinsky, whose socialism and atheism strongly challenged Dostoevsky's own belief in Christ and the moral bases of human conduct, but there is little doubt that the purely literary value of such ideas rather than their political meaning most interested him. It was because he read aloud Belinsky's *Letter to Gogol*, the critics's most candid and angry proclamation of his sociopolitical views, at one of the meetings of the Petrashevsky group that Dostoevsky was arrested and imprisoned along with other members in the spring of 1849. After four months of judicial investigation, during which he defended himself courageously and rightly refused to admit to any sedition, without even conceding that Belinsky's *Letter* had for him more than literary interest, he was sentenced to public execution. At the last moment, on the Tsar's orders, the sentence was commuted to four years' penal servitude followed by service in the ranks.

For ten years, 1849–59, Dostoevsky was cut off from European Russia. The four years of penal servitude in Siberia (1850–4) are powerfully evoked in his own record of them, a classic of prison literature, *Notes from the House of the Dead* (1860–1). They describe the anguish of his isolation as a political prisoner among common convicts or – to put it in class terms – of his role as a 'gentleman' [*dvoryanin*] in a hostile, predominantly peasant environment. Though he was later to argue the need for the Russian intelligentsia to learn from the peasantry, an idea that was crucial to his 'philosophy of the soil' [*pochvennichestvo*], probably the most traumatic aspect of his prison experience was the lack of personal privacy.

After release from penal servitude he attempted to re-establish his reputation as a writer by reopening the polemic with Gogol. In the longest of his Siberian works, *The Village of Stepanchikovo and its Inhabitants* (1859–60), he indirectly poked fun at many of the ideas in Gogol's highly sententious *Selected Correspondence* (1847), to which Belinsky's *Letter* had been a reply. This is a comic, in part satirical, work which demonstrates, firstly, Dostoevsky's new found interest in portraying societies or groups of persons and, secondly, how much significance he now attributed to ideological polemic in his fiction. The experience of penal servitude and subsequent exile in Siberia had forced him, it seems, to realise the need for relationships, whether in the personal sense of his own need for love and companionship – at the time he married Marya Dmitrievna Isaeva, widow of an alcoholic, herself a consumptive, after an agonising courtship – or in the philosophical sense of the relatedness between ideas, no matter how seemingly opposed.

As soon as he was finally given permission to return to European Russia in 1859, he at once set about reconstructing his literary reputation by joining his brother Mikhail in the launching of a new journal *Time* [*Vremya*]. From January 1861 until May 1863 this journal became the vehicle for advocating his quasi-Slavophile doctrine of *pochvennichestvo* and a means of publishing his own original work – the record of his prison experiences was published here in part and his first novel *The Injured and Insulted* (1861). Such journalistic work, however arduous, brought him an immediate new audience and gave him contact with what he most wanted – the topical, the day-to-day. All his major fiction was to spring from his profound and prescient interest in topical events and ideas. As one of the leading contributors to his journal N. N. Strakhov put it, Dostoevsky '*felt ideas* in an extraordinarily vital way' and it is to the same source that we owe the following verbal portrait of Dostoevsky at this time:

> When I recall him, I am struck by the inexhaustible vivacity of his mind, the inexhaustible fertility of his spirit . . . He exhibited with quite extraordinary clarity a particular kind of double character, which consists in the fact that a man can give himself very enthusiastically to certain ideas and feelings but still retain in his soul a sure and firm point from which he can look down on himself, his thoughts and

feelings . . . Fyodor Mikhailovich always astonished me by the breadth of his sympathies and his ability to understand different and opposed points of view.

Unfortunately the Tsarist censorship was less magnanimous and closed down his journal on account of an article on Russo-Polish relations written by the same Strakhov. That was the end of Dostoevsky's first attempt to rehabilitate his reputation.

In 1862 he went abroad for the first time. His pictures of Western Europe (in his *Winter Notes on Summer Impressions*, 1863) betray both his intense xenophobia and the culture shock of the experience, especially his first sight of the squalor of metropolitan capitalism. His encounter with a child prostitute in the Haymarket is more dreadful than anything in Dickens:

> In the Haymarket I noticed mothers offering their small daughters for gain. Little girls of up to twelve years of age would seize you by the arm and beg you to go with them. I remember once, in a street crowd, I saw a little girl, no more than six years old, all in rags, dirty, barefoot, hollow-cheeked, and with signs of having been much beaten: the skin shining through her rags was covered in bruises. She wandered as if she'd forgotten all about her state, aimlessly roaming about for God knows what reason in the crowd; perhaps she was starving. No one noticed her. But what struck me most of all was how she wandered with such a look of sorrow, such hopeless desperation on her face, that to see this little creature, already having to bear such a burden of perdition and despair, was somehow contrary to nature and terribly painful. She went along shaking her dishevelled head from side to side, as if reasoning out something, all the while spreading out her little hands, gesticulating with them, then suddenly entwining them together and pressing them to her bare chest. I turned round and gave her sixpence. She took the little silver coin, then looked at me wildly, with fearful astonishment, directly in the eyes and at once dashed off as fast as her legs could carry her, as though frightened I might take my money back.

On the other hand, he also saw for himself the most powerful symbol of bourgeois 'progress', the Crystal Palace, which was to represent the ideal of a socialist future for the radicals of the 1860s and for Dostoevsky was to epitomise the 'ant-heap' of a rationally ordered society. Yet added to this first experience of Western Europe was the disaster of the closure of his journal, the incurring of serious debts, his passion for a much younger woman, Apollinaria (Polina) Suslova, desperate bouts of gambling at European resorts in an effort to recoup his losses, and then, as if these misfortunes were not enough, there came Dostoevsky's 'terrible year' – 1864.

In April of that year his wife died and in July his beloved brother Mikhail. Overwhelmed by a grief and indebtedness greater than any before, he worked desperately to make a success of a second journal *Epoch* [*Epokha*]. He may have introduced into it sensational criminal reports – an interest which he was shortly to use as the basis for his major fiction – and he may have begged such famous contemporaries as Turgenev to contribute to it in order to boost circulation, but this second, and last, of Dostoevsky's journals is chiefly famous for the publication of his own most important work to date, *Notes from the Underground*, which was to open the way to his grandiose studies of nihilism and free will in his greatest novels.

Notes from the Underground derived directly from his first experience of Western Europe. It was an attack on the view of man as an essentially rational creature which had been advanced by the Russian radical and materialist thinkers of the 1860s, particularly by N. G. Chernyshevsky in his novel of 1863, *What is to be Done?* Through the mouth of the masochistic and paradoxical 'man from the underground' Dostoevsky argues that mankind does not seek what is rationally advantageous but will always prefer the 'elevated sufferings' associated with individual free choice to the 'cheap happiness' promised by the social utopians. In a form of rhetorical question-and-answer confession the seedy forty-year-old 'underground man' insolently sticks out his tongue at the so-called laws of the natural sciences which are supposed to govern his life. So Dostoevsky, ever the polemicist, both mocked European rationalist views of man and simultaneously, in the second part of his *Notes*, revealed the 'underground man's' essential inability to assert his own free choice over others. A third part was to have contained – as his notebooks and correspondence reveal – statements about Christ and immortality, but the censorship may have prevented their publication.

The catastrophes of 1864 drove Dostoevsky into working for money-lenders in order to escape from creditors – in other words, into the world of *Crime and Punishment*. In June 1865 *Epoch* finally failed, leaving him with debts of 15,000 roubles and no choice but to go abroad. He strove unsuccessfully to win at roulette and eventually became stranded in Wiesbaden. It seemed that he had reached the limit of his hopes and resources. In desperation he wrote to Katkov, editor of the famous journal *The Russian Messenger*, seeking an advance for a new work of his which he described as 'the psychological report of a crime' and which he outlined in remarkable detail. The proposal was accepted. From these desperate circumstances emerged the desperate plight of Rodion Raskolnikov, the twenty-four-year-old drop-out from St Petersburg University, whose murder of a money-lender and her sister was to be the crime that provoked the intricate and profound psychological study of motive in Dostoevsky's first great novel *Crime and Punishment* (1866).

The novel has remarkable structural coherence both in the sense that it is centred in Raskolnikov and in its concentration of all the principal events into the space of two weeks and into one relatively limited area of St Petersburg around the Hay Market. Despite deliberately obscured features of his character and motivation, Raskolnikov emerges as a startlingly vital personality from the novel's opening moment when he sets out 'at the beginning of July, in extremely hot weather', to rehearse the crime which he is to commit finally at the end of the novel's first part. In its central theme the novel is concerned with gradual revelation of the motives for Raskolnikov's crime. Though he can be said to confess them, in carefully graded stages, to Porfiry Petrovich, the official investigator, it is doubtful whether they actually explain his conduct. Briefly, a two-fold motivation can be discerned: on the one hand, Raskolnikov supposes that by killing the money-lender he will be performing a socially useful act and will save others from falling into her clutches; on the other hand, he will be proving that he can actually 'overstep the barriers' which divide the ordinary mass of humanity from the extraordinary, from the lawgivers, from those who establish what might be said to be the norms of right and wrong in human conduct. The second of these two sets of motives is the more significant in that it emphasises the question of free will and the necessary corollary of man's relationship to God or some higher law.

The choices implicit in these motives are embodied for Raskolnikov in Sonya Marmeladov, the young prostitute, who urges upon him the need to accept the idea of an all-merciful God, and in the sinister Svidrigaylov, ostensibly a suitor for Raskolnikov's sister, who represents in caricature form the essential aimlessness of human claims to free will and a freedom above the moral law. The choices are ultimately nihilistic, represented by Svidrigaylov's eventual suicide, or religious, in the sense that, on Sonya's insistence, Raskolnikov should turn aside from his challenge to God's authority and bow down and confess his guilt. Raskolnikov does not kill himself, but confesses and is sentenced to Siberia. Whether or not he finally acknowledges his guilt remains in doubt right to the end of the novel, though it is intimated, as had been suggested earlier by Sonya's reading of the story of the raising of Lazarus, that his love for Sonya will help to achieve his moral resurrection.

The novel may be interpreted as an examination of the false premises of nihilistic thought and the extent to which men's minds may be possessed by such falsehood in the name of rationality. It poses the question whether or not man has the right to usurp the role of God and aspire to be a man–god. But in all its ideas, as in its characters and its settings, the novel is rooted deeply in its own time and place, in a contemporary urban Russia dominated by an incipient and oppressive capitalism, by extreme poverty, by talk of socialist remedies and concern for the moral bases of society and the family. Equally important is the novel's pervasive air of insecurity and tension, as if all life depended upon one expulsion of breath, one instant of desperate action, one throw of the dice.

Significantly, as if enclosed within the womb of this great novel, during the course of its composition Dostoevsky devoted three weeks, in October 1866, to composing a short novel called *The Gambler* concerned with precisely this problem of staking all on the spinning of a roulette wheel. He dictated it to a young stenographer, Anna Grigoryevna Snitkina, in order to meet a deadline imposed by an unscrupulous publisher. In this case Dostoevsky staked all and won. Not only did he meet the deadline, but Anna Grigoryevna was also to become his second wife. Although there was a quarter of a century's difference in age between them it was to prove a marriage of extreme happiness and to guarantee him increasing peace of mind and gradual freedom from indebtedness. But practically immediately after their marriage in February 1867 the newly-weds were obliged to flee abroad to escape the creditors of the failed *Epoch*. They remained abroad for four years, from 1867 to July 1871.

Insulated to some extent from the immediately pressing problems of Russian life, though by no means protected from the day-to-day cares of living, Dostoevsky was to have the freedom to scrutinise the question of Russia's future and to project this question into both the great novels written during his second exile – *The Idiot* (1868) and *The Possessed* (1871–2). The problem of Raskolnikov's possession by nihilistic ideas casts its shadows over both works and may be said to provoke the crimes and mayhem that seem, in Dostoevsky's view, unavoidable in the growing chaos of a Russia assailed by Western ideology, atheistic socialism, erosion of Christian values and the disruptive demonology of the man–god syndrome. As an antidote to such a vision of mankind he sought to depict a 'positively beautiful man', though he had to admit that, if this was intended to be the principal idea of his novel *The Idiot*, 'the beautiful is an ideal, but an ideal far from worked out either by us or by civilised Europe. The world knows only one positively beautiful person – Christ, so that the coming down to earth of this immeasurably, eternally beautiful man is, of course, forever miraculous' (letter of 1/13 January 1868). As his notes show, he took almost a year to work up the conception of his new hero who initially, and in later stages of the novel's preliminary drafting, bore a strong resemblance to Raskolnikov. It was only when he saw through the comic aspects of his new creation to the character's *innocence* that he was able to achieve the memorable figure of his 'idiot', Prince Myshkin.[2] In an illuminating jotting in his notebook, he wrote that 'if Don Quixote and Pickwick as good characters are sympathetic to the reader and successful, it is because they are comic. The hero of the novel, the Prince, though he isn't comic, has another sympathetic trait: he is *innocent!*' Shortly after this jotting Dostoevsky apparently came to the conclusion that Prince Myshkin, in his humility and innocence, was to be identified with Christ as a positively beautiful man for his own time. *The Idiot* is the first of Dostoevsky's novels to offer the image and ideal of Christ as means for achieving the salvation of both Russia and the West.

The novel tells of the return of Prince Myshkin from Switzerland to Russia. His innocence is partly due to his 'idiocy', a condition of which he has temporarily been cured, but it is also due to his child-like simplicity, aggravated by epilepsy, and his ignorance of worldly ways. On his train journey to St Petersburg he meets Rogozhin who represents all that is darkest, most arbitrary and libidinous in Dostoevsky's vision of contemporary Russia. Rogozhin is to become Myshkin's rival and malevolent 'brother' – a fateful destroyer of Myshkin's innocence of mind and heart. Immediately upon arriving in St Petersburg Myshkin is plunged into a tumultuous world of wealthy Russian generals, their families and hangers-on, of merchants and their mistresses, of money and libertinage and high passion. If Virginia Woolf is to be believed in her claim that 'the novels of Dostoevsky are seething whirlpools, gyrating sandstorms, waterspouts which hiss and boil and suck us in,' then the opening of *The Idiot*, with its descriptions of the Epanchin household and the Ivolgins, the proud nature of Totsky's mistress, the beautiful Nastasya Filippovna, and the recklessness of Rogozhin, tends to suck the reader into its large-scale *skandal* scenes, until the climax to Part I comes with Nastasya Filippovna flinging Rogozhin's packet of 100,000 roubles into the fire in a challenge to her erstwhile suitor Ganya. The first Part of *The Idiot* is one of the most remarkably sustained dramatic *tours de force* in Dostoevsky's writing.

Parts II and III have splendid episodes in them, but the ramifications of plot and sub-plot tend to slow up the impetus of the novel. It is clear that Dostoevsky increasingly uses his novel as a vehicle for expressing his own ideas. These include attacks on nihilism as a doctrine which cannot accept belief in Christ as well as attacks on Russian liberalism. The consumptive student Ippolit's justification of suicide in his 'Necessary Explanation' arises from his sense of horror – one shared by Dostoevsky himself upon seeing Holbein's 'The Corpse of Christ' – at the thought that 'if death is so awful and the laws of nature are so powerful, how can one overcome them?' To him all that matters is existence, so he concludes that suicide, the law of self-destruction, is the only act which he can successfully begin and end of his own volition.

If Part III dwells on the idea of self-destruction as a law, the final part of the novel develops the idea of the Russian Christ in Myshkin's attacks on atheism and Roman Catholicism and his proclamation of himself as saviour of all whom he has known. But the novel ends on a murderous note which belies the prince's optimism. On the eve of the prince's marriage to Nastasya Filippovna she is spirited away by Rogozhin, the rival for her love, and murdered by him. In a final memorable scene he and the prince, returned now to his former idiot state, spend a night's vigil by her bedside.

Despite such positive affirmations as those made by Myshkin to his fellow princes, Dostoevsky's view of Russia's future remained at best sceptical and at worst diabolically pessimistic. He illustrated his pessimistic diagnosis in the darkest of his novels *The Possessed*, an anatomy of the sickness which, in his view, had attacked the body of ideas to which the Russian intelligentsia was heir. It tells the story of another member of the Russian nobility, Nikolay Stavrogin, who returns similarly to his home, a provincial town, where he meets two of his so-called disciples and thereby reacquaints himself with his former ideas. For this novel explores, through character relationships, the evolution of the Russian intelligentsia as Dostoevsky saw it, from its beginnings among the 'men of the forties', represented here by Stepan Trofimovich Verkhovensky, to its present state as we see it in the figure of Stepan Trofimovich's son Pyotr, the amoral nihilist and revolutionary. But Stepan Trofimovich is also the ideological tutor of Stavrogin; he is the first generation of the Russian intelligentsia, out of whom the 'devils'[3] of Western ideology have gone to possess the minds and hearts of the next generation, meaning Stavrogin and the disciples of his, Kirilov and Shatov, who have in turn become the possessors of his ideas.

Kirilov and Shatov may be said to represent the choices facing the Russian intelligentsia at the beginning of the 1870s. Kirilov's possession by the idea of suicide as a means of releasing man from God and the fear of death is paralleled by Shatov's paradoxical assertion of Russia's messianism in the concept of the Russian people as 'God-carrying' [*narod-bogonosets*] and, simultaneously, of his own shakiness of belief. When questioned by Stavrogin, the progenitor as it were, of his idea, Shatov declares that he *will* believe in God, but his present state is not that of the convinced believer. Both Kirilov and Shatov are fated to die as victims of the revolutionary intrigues organised by Pyotr Verkhovensky. Stavrogin himself, the man chosen by Pyotr to be the figurehead of the planned revolution, turns out to be a false God, one who not only plays at nihilism, but who is also a latter-day Antichrist, with a demonology of man–god-hood, child-violation and heartless egoism as his hallmark. He ends by hanging himself.

A novel composed of such melodramatic deaths by murder and suicide, to which may be added other violent events, including widespread arson, factory riots and general comic mayhem, must seem to spring from gothic romanticism and to have features of the Victorian penny dreadful. It transcends such gutter literature, though retaining all its excitement, by integrating serious ideological problems into a narrative which gathers momentum on a tide of *skandal* scenes peopled by remarkably vivid, eloquent characters. Dostoevsky's attitude towards the revolutionaries is a blend of satirical censure and sneaking approval. His picture of the Russian establishment, particularly in his malicious caricature of Turgenev in the person of the famous writer Karmazinov, has about it a sense of the grotesque which seems to endow even his monstrously sinister revolutionaries with a febrile dignity by contrast. In the final reckoning, his picture of Russian society is censorious and dark. Only the birth of a child to Shatov's wife, Kirilov's glimpse of eternal happiness in a yellowing, wind-blown leaf, and the final discovery of Stepan Trofimovich, have an affirmative meaning. After his son has done his murderous work in the provincial town, Stepan Trofimovich goes on a kind of holy pilgrimage among the peasants in the outlying countryside. With his dying breath, he confesses exultantly to a conviction about Christ as the Great Idea:

'The entire law of human existence resides in man's ability always to bow down before the immeasurably great. If people are deprived of the immeasurably great, they will refuse to go on living and will die in despair. The immeasurable and eternal are just as essential to man as this little planet which he inhabits . . . My friends, all of you, long live the Great Idea! The eternal, immeasurable Idea! Everyone, no matter who he might be, has to bow down before the Great Idea!'

In its affirmation of belief, especially due to the absence of a single positive figure,[4] the novel is inevitably weak; its strength as a brilliant example of polemical literature is in its prophetic insight that the revolutionary aspiration towards political freedom, without conscience or divine sanction, will lead all too easily to more dreadful and untamed tyranny of the few over the majority. The European totalitarian governments of the twentieth century have abundantly justified Dostoevsky's hellish vision.

Though the murder of Shatov in *The Possessed* was based on the actual murder of a student at the Moscow Agricultural Academy on the orders of Nechaev,[5] and the provincial town which is the novel's setting bears a strong resemblance to Tver, the realism of Dostoevsky's novel as a picture of contemporary Russia is not to be taken at its face value. It was only after his return to Russia finally in 1871 that he was able to take a more balanced and coherent view of Russian problems. It was a process which evolved over several years, despite the fact that the plans for his final, and greatest, novel were ready in embryo at the beginning of the decade. The seventies were to be the period when Dostoevsky ultimately consolidated his reputation, both as a publicist and as the dominant literary figure.

Despite initial hardship, the deaths of some of his children in infancy, increasing epilepsy, the home circumstances of Dostoevsky's life under his wife's efficient management offered a generally serene and lovingly attended atmosphere for his writing. It had become his habit to write mostly at night. He would rise at about eleven o'clock each morning, do some exercises and then dictate to his wife what he had prepared in the early hours. As a method of working it proved exceedingly fruitful. By this means, and with his wife undertaking the duties of his publisher, he began to issue a publicistic work *The Diary of a Writer*, which appeared initially in 1873 and continued, with interruptions for major fictional work, right up to his death. It contained his personal views on contemporary topics, personal reminiscences and the occasional short story or sketch. In political terms its flavour was conservative – though never as ultra-conservative as was Prince Meshchersky's *Citizen*, a journal which Dostoevsky briefly edited in 1873 and 1874. It was the litmus paper with which he tested Russian public opinion and on which he in turn registered his reaction to it. A highly idiosyncratic and formless publication, it offered jingoistic opinions which can still outrage Western sensibilities, but it also demonstrated in such remarkable short works as *A Gentle Girl* [*Krotkaya*] and *The Dream of a Foolish Young Man* how deeply pessimistic, yet uncompromising, was Dostoevsky's view of human frailty and the possibility of human redemption other than by Christian means. In his major fiction of the period he was less outwardly despairing, though his study of an 'accidental' family in *A Raw Youth* (1875) is hardly comforting either for its message or for its excellence as an example of his art. The climate of violence present in so much of his mature work finally became a part of the reality of Russian social and political life with the attempted murder of the governor-general of St Petersburg by the young terrorist Vera Zasulich. Dostoevsky attended her trial in 1878, at which she was acquitted. But her act of violence was merely a reflection of the large-scale violence of the Russo-Turkish War of 1877–8 and the violence practised by the Russian government against the many young Populists who had been arrested for attempting to promote change among the peasantry in the so called 'pilgrimages to the people' [*khozhdeniya v narod*]. Vera Zasulich's bungled pistol shot was to set in motion the terrorism of The People's Will. It was also to be a principal impulse in the writing of Dostoevsky's final novel.

The Brothers Karamazov (1878–80) is concerned with an event which occurred supposedly thirteen years before the present time of the fiction – the murder of Fyodor Pavlovich Karamazov. At the trial which forms the climax of Part iv of the novel a miscarriage of justice leads to the indicting of the eldest Karamazov brother, Dmitry, on the charge of parricide. The first three parts of the novel, occupying approximately three days, describe the events and motives which actually led to the murder. The novel's interest, then, lies in the exploration of motive, the discovery, as it were, of the many paradoxes which form a part of human and divine justice. If, for Dmitry, the victim of an injustice, what matters above all is a Schilleresque affirmation of the joy of living, then for Alyosha, the youngest and most spiritual of the brothers, justice is to be brought down to earth in the fulfilment of the Christian injunctions of his spiritual mentor, Father Zosima. Yet neither of these brothers, though indirectly implicated, is as guilty of the parricide as is Ivan Karamazov. His doctrine that 'everything is permitted' in the moral sphere is a supreme justification of free will. By infecting the illegitimate Smerdyakov with his doctrine, he can be said to have provoked the murder of his libidinous and venal father, though in the end he will argue that all men desire the death of the father, whether biological or spiritual, in the name of total nihilistic freedom. To Ivan Karamazov are given the most masterly of Dostoevsky's atheistic arguments in the famous chapters entitled 'Revolt' and 'The Grand Inquisitor'. Though, in the *pro* and *contra* pattern of the novel, Ivan Karamazov can be said to have his opponent and answer in the person and teaching of Father Zosima, there is little doubt that Ivan's is the more glamorous and memorable doctrine. Unfinished though it may be, this novel is the most complex and profound of Dostoevsky's works, in its characterisation as well as in its ideas, and in the many layers of interpretation – judicial, financial, ideological, sociopolitical – that may be identified in its realistic blend of detective novel and philosophical drama.

For Dostoevsky the novel was intended both as his answer to the growing reputation of his leading contemporary Tolstoy and as an analysis of the forces which he felt were impelling Russia towards her destiny. The three brothers may have been, in the eyes of the prosecuting counsel at the trial, the sons of a father who 'apart from licentious pleasures sees nothing in life and teaches his sons likewise', but they also epitomised the influence, inevitably dangerous, of European rationalism on Russian life (Ivan), Alyosha's 'popular nationalism' and of Dmitry's common mean of sensuality and idealism. In their totality the brothers and the crime in which they are implicated are declared by the prosecuting counsel to be symbolic of Russia, just as the verdict of the jury will be made to have the character of a universal judgement on Russia's future role. Echoing the final vision of the Russian troika racing towards the future in Gogol's *Dead Souls*, the prosecutor says, addressing the jury:

'Remember that you are the defenders of our truth, the defenders of our holy Russia, of her fundamentals, of her family, of all that is sacred to her! You represent Russia at this moment, and your verdict will resound not only in this hall but throughout Russia. . . Do not torment Russia and her expectations, for our fateful troika rushes ever onward, perhaps to perdition. And for a long while now throughout Russia hands are reaching out and calls are made to stop the frenzied, unpardonable race into the future. And even if other nations still stand aside from the wildly racing troika, then this is perhaps not out of respect for it, as Gogol thought, but simply in horror – take note! In horror, perhaps, and in revulsion they may still stand aside, but there may come a time when they'll stop standing aside and will form a strong wall against this onrushing vision and will put a stop to the mad race of our unruliness, in order to save themselves, their culture and their civilisation!'

The bombast of these words cannot be divorced from Dostoevsky's self-imposed role as prophet and guide, one who sought to make his literary work a vehicle for promoting the growth of Russian national consciousness. So much of his major fiction had this impulse to it that efforts to deny it, or to argue that his work is fashioned from 'the stuff of the soul', from a 'dream world', from a Russia of the mind, have no real basis in fact. Dostoevsky was always deeply involved in the reality of his own time. His literary attitude always presupposed that there were norms of reality, just as there were norms of health, through which the fantastic, perverted or sick could ultimately be identified. His concern for human aberrations was symptomatic of his deeply felt awareness of human breadth and variety, just as his awareness of ideas forced him to acknowledge the deeps of the human psyche from which they derived and to which they were attached by bonds of mythic strength.

Dostoevsky's universal appeal derives chiefly from his analytical approach to human problems. His analytical manner must account for the dramatic intensity of his novels, his posing of ideas and emotions in sharp *pro* and *contra* relationships, his seeming penetration of reality, his proneness to offer fictional characterisations by means of extended confessional monologues. Analysis, as the principle or purpose of his literary attitude, presupposes both stasis and a concern for discovering the secret to which the analysis will finally penetrate. The emphasis in Dostoevsky's elaborately plotted novels consequently falls on revelation of motive rather than on detection of the criminal and on the relating of past emotional and ideological conflicts to the brief present moment of the fictional enactment. All of which implies a remarkable, and essentially novel, concentration upon intensity of experience, the magnification of time so that minutes pass as hours, days like eternities, and whatever is emoted or intellectually felt assumes the proportions of intensely engaged experience that must seem to have reached its highest pitch, unrepeatable and seemingly in open challenge to the evanescence of human life and endeavour.

c

In one of his final jottings he declared that he was not a psychologist, but 'only a realist in a higher sense, i.e. I depict all the depths of the human spirit.' This remark shows how hard it is to 'essay' a genius of Dostoevsky's intense humanity. Practically everything that he wrote demonstrates his consciousness of the prolific abundance which life meant to him – an abundance which has led the famous Soviet critic Bakhtin, for example, to describe Dostoevsky's teeming novels as 'polyphonic'. From the ever-shifting, multitudinous, predominantly urban worlds of his fiction there emerge certain positive delineations of the human spirit that may perhaps offer promise of redemption. Of these the 'positively beautiful man' is the most easily identifiable, even though Dostoevsky's idea of beauty was complex. For him the redemptive power of the ideal of beauty was closely associated with his conception of the role of Christ as Saviour. But he was also ready to acknowledge, particularly through what Dmitry Karamazov says, that beauty encompasses the whole spectrum of emotion from the ideal state, the Madonna image, to the basest, the uttermost degradation of Sodom. Man as intellectual or aesthetic louse or as lustful insect conveys the baseline of Dostoevsky's thinking, whereas man as Christ-like, as one who takes upon himself the sins of all others and suffers to achieve redemption, is the peak of his conceptualisation of man's ideal. Even so, these were not isolated, but essentially dynamically related extremes of the same human spectrum. For Dostoevsky conceived man not only as deep but also as broad – too broad, and he wished he were narrower, yet all his work is testimony to his profound understanding of the torments and exultations to which the broad and unfathomable nature of mankind is prone.

NOTES

1 Among those who have a right to speak of the meaning of 'the double', both in a personal and a literary sense, none is tragically more qualified than Sylvia Plath. During her senior year in college she wrote an undergraduate Honours thesis entitled 'The Magic Mirror: A Study of the Double in Two of Dostoevsky's Novels', in which she concluded by saying: 'Although the figure of the Double has become a harbinger of danger and destruction, taking form as it does from the darkest of human fears and repressions, Dostoevsky implies that recognition of our various mirror images and reconciliation with them will save us from disintegration. This reconciliation does not mean a simple or monolithic resolution of conflict, but rather a creative acknowledgement of the fundamental duality of man; it involves a constant courageous acceptance of the eternal paradoxes within the universe and within ourselves.' From 'The Theme of the Double, Sylvia Plath, and Dostoevsky' by George Gibian in his edition of *Crime and Punishment* (N.Y.: W. W. Norton, 1975) p. 639.
2 Myshkin means literally 'little mouse'.
3 The novel's title in Russian, *Besy*, means literally 'The Devils' and refers directly

to the story from St Luke's gospel about the man possessed of devils which Christ suffered to enter into the herd of swine.

4 The chapter which contained such a positive figure, the priest Tikhon, was omitted from the final version of the novel because it also contained the highly controversial 'Stavrogin's Confession', describing his violation of a little girl who eventually kills herself.

5 Nechaev (1847–83), of peasant background, collaborated with the anarchist Mikhail Bakunin in composing the most violently revolutionary document of the period, *The Catechism of a Revolutionary*, and in the autumn of 1869 he apparently put his violent ideas into effect by engineering the murder of the student Ivanov who had begun to question Nechaev's authority. Though Nechaev escaped abroad, the trial of his collaborators became a *cause célèbre*.

4 Tolstoy

When John Bayley, in his excellent *Tolstoy and the Novel*, says with a ring of desperation: 'As no other author, Tolstoy makes the critic feel how superfluous his office can be,'[1] he expresses a feeling shared not only by the critic but by every conscientious reader of Tolstoy. Tolstoy's work appears to mirror life so accurately that comment on it seems almost as superfluous as comment on the fact of life itself. Life *is*; Tolstoy *is*. To say more is to become speculative and artificial. This is one measure of Tolstoy's greatness, of his appeal to so many millions of readers and of the challenge that he presents to anyone foolish enough to attempt to interpret his work.

It is easy enough to draw a reasonably accurate but disparaging picture of Tolstoy as a hypocrite and profound egoist. For all his attempts to simplify himself and lead the life of a common peasant, he was never less than aristocratic in his attitudes and his circumstances. He lived approximately seventy of his eighty-two years on his country estate of Yasnaya Polyana, surrounded chiefly by women. Circumstances can be said to have helped him to indulge his aristocratically eccentric predilection for the simple life, for Rousseau and for a 'Tolstoyan' vision of the way to God. When he was simple Count Lev Nikolaevich Tolstoy, he had no scruples about the army of servants and peasants who worked to support his aristocratic way of life. When he became the first apostle of his own religion, he had few scruples about being the aristocratic democrat whose way to God was supported by an army of disciples. This picture of Tolstoy invokes the hypocrisy in much of Tolstoy's posture as prophet and seer and may also suggest the self-indulgent egoism of the aristocratic and well-heeled writer who sought to alleviate human suffering while suffering so little material discomfort himself.

The cynicism of this view is opposed by the testimony of those who experienced the infectious sincerity of the man, just as his writings have the power to infect us with the sheer truthfulness of his vision of life. The painter Repin, for example, seeing Tolstoy in his maturity, gave the following word picture:

> Awesome, overhanging eyebrows, penetrating eyes, he is without doubt a giant among men. No one has the stupid brashness to ap-

proach him off the cuff or to adopt an irreverently mocking manner. But he is the kindest of souls, the most delicate of men and a true aristocrat in his manners and the special elegance of his speech. How fluently and exquisitely he can speak foreign languages! How courteous, generous and unaffected he is in his treatment of people! And how much vitality, how much passion there is in this hermit! Never before in my life have I met a man with a more infectious laugh.

Lenin described him as 'A Mirror of the Russian Revolution', but Tolstoy, if hardly conscious of the political meaning of what he mirrored, was always conscious of the mirror-like effect that art should achieve if it were to be accounted art at all. This is the Tolstoy whom one must seek beneath the layers of extra-literary reputation which have adhered to his portrait. His role as religious thinker, seer, moralist or, quite simply, as personality (especially in the last twenty-five years of his life) has acquired a patina of legend. This is not to suggest that as a writer Tolstoy was not always concerned with the same questions of religion, morality and his own personality, but within the confines of literature we can more easily recognise his uniqueness and explain his literary attitude.

Tolstoy's uniqueness in literary terms is best discerned by comparing him with Dostoevsky. Both writers were realists in the use of metonymy, emphasis on character motivation and verisimilitude of background; both were in their own ways equally preoccupied by the urgent problems facing Russia in their time. To dissociate them as writers is necessarily to exaggerate special features in their work which can only explain superficial and general differences. In such general terms, then, it can be said that Dostoevsky was a novelist who turned his greatest works into dramas, was more certain of the nightmarish reality of ideas than of the rationality of man, loved paradox, exhumed in anticipation of Freud and modern psychology the violent depths of inner human conflict, held sacred the moment when the all-revealing truth becomes apparent but was uncertain of practically all else. Tolstoy, by contrast, aspired to an epic manner in his work, presumed that all human experience formed part of a historical continuum, that man was a predominantly rational creature who could discover morality and God through an awareness of the absolute laws governing human life; but most of all he celebrated the tangibility of the real, the corporeal reality of human experience, deeply mysterious in its very sensuousness and always animate, animal-like and defiant of death in its sentient richness. This is the Tolstoy who, despite his aristocratism and his religiosity, acquired respectability in Soviet eyes sooner than any other great pre-revolutionary Russian author and whose popularity in the Soviet Union has never ceased to grow.

The earliest of the Russian critics to make a serious comparison between Tolstoy and Dostoevsky was Dmitry Merezhkovsky (1865–1941).

He rightly emphasised the 'earthiness' of Tolstoy, his role as 'seer of the flesh' and the vividly pictorial strengths of Tolstoyan realism:

> Pushkin's descriptions remind one of the light watery tempera of the Florentine masters of antiquity or the murals of Pompeii with their even, faded, airily translucent colours which do not obscure the drawing, like an effect of early morning mist. Lev Tolstoy's are much heavier, crude, but also vastly more powerful oil colours like those of the great northern masters: along with the profound, impenetrably black, yet vivid patches of shadow there are rays of sudden, blinding light which penetrate through and through and suddenly ignite and highlight out of the darkness some separate item – the nakedness of a body, the fold in some item of clothing caught in an instant of headlong movement, part of a face contorted by passion or suffering – and endow them with astounding, almost abhorrent and frightening vitality, as if the artist were seeking to represent in the natural world taken to its extreme limits some supernatural quality or in the humanly corporeal taken to its extreme limits some suprahuman essence.

The pictorial analogue in this statement is useful, but it has deeper implications than Merezhkovsky suggests. The notion that the Tolstoyan vision, however seemingly concerned with exact and detailed appearances, always penetrates like the rays of a sudden, blinding light is an invaluable reminder that there is more to the Tolstoyan picture of the world than pictorialism. There is always a hint in the Tolstoyan view, sometimes quite deadpan or unemphatic but rarely unapparent, that the seeing eye is limited both by the frame of its own vision and by the moral evaluation which accompanies the act of viewing. In the masterly way that he animates his fictional worlds by adopting towards supposed reality the viewpoint of one or another fictional character, Tolstoy appears to be objective, but is often doing no more than act the reader's part. He invites us into his fiction through the eyes of the observer–narrators who are both Tolstoyan *personae* and archetypally human, sympathetically objective participants in the Tolstoyan narrative. By emphasis on outward appearance, gesture, bodily movement, dialogue, tone of voice, colour and expression of eyes, the characters observed by such Tolstoyan *personae* and observer–narrators acquire startling and enduring vitality, but they are also simultaneously judged in terms of their moral worth and in those cases where such moral worth is dubious or absent Tolstoy deliberately suggests their limitations by such devices as zoomorphic similes, emphasis on the clockwork-like character of their movements and gestures, specially unappealing physical characteristics like white hands or large ears, that have a repetitiously Homeric identifying stamp.

In all this Tolstoy exhibits his habit of importuning the reader. He knew this was his weakness. He could never wholly abandon the didactic manner. Comparing himself once with Pushkin, he is reputed to have said: 'Pushkin, in describing an artistic detail, does so lightly and doesn't care whether or not it is noticed by the reader; whereas he (Tolstoy) would, as it were, importune the reader with this artistic detail until he had explained it to him fully.' He is being a little unfair on himself in saying this, for Tolstoy is rarely capable of boring the reader with his descriptions even though he never possessed a Dostoevskian degree of intense involvement in his characters' lives and experience. Tolstoy had to preserve a distance between himself as fictional pantocrator and the fiction that he created, which means that he appears to know less about his characters than Dostoevsky. He liked to think that art was necessarily artificial. What he strove for was truth in his representation of reality. We may debate whether or not Tolstoy has any right to claim that his 'fiction' enshrines the truth, but we cannot dispute that he aspired to persuade the reader of *his* truth. What he always aimed to achieve in his art was 'infectiousness' – the infecting of the reader with his, Tolstoy's, feeling, his vision of life. When the spontaneity of that experience and vision began to yield to a pondering on the meaning of what was experienced, and therefore what should be seen, not only did morality enter in but there occurred a change of tone, just as there occurred a change of tone in Tolstoy's own life at the point where he underwent conversion from his natural, spontaneous receptivity to life's infectiousness to a state in which he allowed the didactic element to dominate and curb (although never completely) the spontaneity of his splendidly lucid response to the external world.

Writing of the last of Tolstoy's important fictional works, *Hadji Murat* (published posthumously), the Soviet writer Isaac Babel has expressed as well as anyone the electric effect of Tolstoy's 'spontaneity':

. . . the electric charge went from the earth, through the hands, straight to the paper, with no insulation at all, quite mercilessly stripping off all the outer layers with a sense of truth – a truth, furthermore, which was clothed in dress both transparent and beautiful.

When you read Tolstoy, you feel that the world is writing, the world in all its variety. In fact, people say, it's all a matter of devices, of technique. If you take any chapter of Tolstoy's, you will find great heaps of everything – there is philosophy, death. And you might think that to write like this you need legerdemain, extraordinary technical skill. But all this is submerged in the feeling for the universe by which Tolstoy was guided.[2]

Again, if writers can be said to have antennae, then Tolstoy's were extraordinarily sensitive, both in their perception of the links between the apparently irreconcilable elements in reality and in their consciousness of the spiritual meaning of physical phenomena. But they were sensitive principally to the apparent novelty of the familiar and the mundane, for if Tolstoy electrifies anything it is ordinary life, ordinary experience which, by a psychologising process, he 'makes strange', he projects as newly witnessed.[3] The most obvious instances of such 'making strange' occur when Tolstoy is deliberately concerned to deflate the pompous or contrast the natural with the artificial. The least obvious instances occur perpetually in Tolstoy's work and are inseparably part of the 'Tolstoyan' freshness of viewpoint.

Tolstoy's biography explains the causes of his 'naturalness' as a writer to some extent, though it can hardly explain his genius. He was born the fourth son of Count Nikolay and Countess Marya (née Volkonsky) Tolstoy, at Yasnaya Polyana, the Province of Tula, on 28 August 1828. Yasnaya Polyana was a Volkonsky estate supported by some 800 serfs. For all practical purposes it could support itself as a viable ecconomic entity. This can explain Tolstoy's later conviction that men should all work at rural pursuits, but it must also have had a conditioning effect on his attitudes towards the city and such evil manifestations of nineteenth-century industrialism as railways. To the very young Tolstoy the secret of happiness was written on a little green stick (or so Nikolay, the eldest Tolstoy brother, had insisted) and at the age of eighty Tolstoy dictated that he should be buried within the grounds of Yasnaya Polyana at the place of the little green stick. Yasnaya Polyana meant to him the secret of happiness, the natural source of love from which he viewed an outside world that always fell short of his Tolstoyan ideal.

But Yasnaya Polyana was also associated with tragedy. The first such tragedy was the death of Tolstoy's mother before he was two years old. The last tragedy was the terrible marital conflict which developed between Tolstoy and the mother of his children, Countess Sonya (née Bers), which ended in his escape from Yasnaya Polyana on 28 October 1910 and his death on 7 November at the small railway halt of Astapovo. The death of his father before he was nine years old meant that the Tolstoy children were orphaned early and left in the hands of Aunt Tatyana and their paternal grandmother. Two of his brothers died young. If he was himself later to create a thriving family home at Yasnaya Polyana, where he became father to eight children, he came increasingly to regard this estate of his as the arena where he wrestled not only with his own mortality but with the significance of life and death for all mankind.

Educated at first by tutors, then at the University of Kazan (1844–7), where he transferred from the faculty of oriental languages to the faculty of jurisprudence but never completed the course, he was more successful at setting himself educational tasks, as his diaries testify, than he was at devoting himself to sustained study. Perhaps the fact that he never completed a university course helped to free him from the sense of complacency which can accompany such academic achievement. In any case he soon enough discovered how rich and restless was his own personality, how closely it needed to be regulated and guided in the manner of Benjamin Franklin and how great were the curbs which he needed to apply, never very successfully, to his passionate and errant male nature. He led the conventional licentious life of a young nobleman, having more than one serf mistress, but he always attempted to educate himself morally towards self-improvement. After a particularly dissolute winter in Moscow, 1848–9, he moved to St Petersburg and attempted to embark on more re-education by taking the entrance examinations for St Petersburg University. For approximately three months, during the winter and early spring of 1849, he lived within a few doors of Dostoevsky, but they never met at that or any other time. The Petrashevsky affair was soon to send Dostoevsky into ten years of exile and in 1851, at the age of twenty-three, having abandoned all attempts at a university career and generally without occupation, Tolstoy was to go into another form of exile, this time self-imposed, when he accompanied his brother Nikolay to the Caucasus to participate in the Russian colonial war against the hill tribes. In the Caucasus Tolstoy was to discover himself and his vocation.

His first serious attempt at writing had occurred in 1851 when he wrote a detailed account of an evening spent at the Volkonskys in a manner which anticipated the stream-of-consciousness technique of twentieth-century writing while owing some of its digressions and mannerisms to Lawrence Sterne. It was a fragment called 'A History of Yesterday'. It showed how successfully Tolstoy could 'psychologise' his characterisation and in this respect it pointed the way to the most outstanding features of his first published work, the semi-fictional account of two days from the childhood of a boy of ten, *Childhood* (1852). Tolstoy completed *Childhood* in the Caucasus and sent it off to the famous poet and editor of the *Contemporary*, Nekrasov, who published it at once. Its appearance caused intense interest. N. G. Chernyshevsky perhaps best summarised the reason for such interest when he described Tolstoy's manner of characterisation as 'a dialectics of the soul', for what Tolstoy explored in *Childhood* (as in the later and somewhat less successful parts of what was to become an autobiographical triology, *Boyhood* (1854) and *Youth* (1856)) was the dialectical interaction between the boy's apprehension of surrounding reality and the moral growth which occurred through his gradual understanding of this real world. Though semi-fictional, much of *Childhood* was based on Tolstoy's own experience. The fresh, childish candour of the boy's apprehension of his circumstances, his own psychological and emotional reactions, and his relationships with others act as a kind of lens or filter that makes everything seem strange in its novelty. But the didacticism is also present in the rather obtrusive comments of the twenty-four-year-old nostalgic author and, more surprisingly and morbidly, in the concentration on the death of the narrator's mother which occurs at the close of the work.

The Caucasus itself, with its mountain splendours and its frontier life, as well as the war against Shamil and the hill tribesmen, highlighted for Tolstoy the meaning of death and the nature of martial courage (*The Raid*, 1852, for example). Out of this Tolstoy's work developed thematically in two principal directions, towards further examinations of the extremes of human experience in war and towards a deepening moral scrutiny of the social contrasts in Russian life which were necessarily set in relief by war or alien surroundings or sheer human vanity. The outbreak of hostilities in the Crimea (1854–5) and the siege of Sebastopol, in which Tolstoy participated as an artillery officer, provided the material for such brilliantly evocative and yet deeply sceptical examples of war reportage as *Sebastopol in December* and *Sebastopol in May*. But immediately after his return from the Crimean War to St Petersburg, where he was befriended by Turgenev and lionised in the literary salons, he found the atmosphere of metropolitan life alien to him and the revolutionary–democratic ideas of the *Contemporary* inimical to his own aristocratic attitudes, so that he began to explore in his own independent way the relationship between the generations (*Two Hussars*) and between the serfs and their masters (*A Landowner's Morning*). In a series of short works he set about examining the moral dilemma of an intelligent, sensitive member of the Russian nobility faced by the injustices of serfdom or the disdainful attitude of the rich towards the evidently exceptional talents of the poor (*Lucerne, Albert*). Practically all of this writing had a clear autobiographical basis, whether deriving from the kind of self-scrutiny which he practised in his diary entries or from his first visit to Western Europe (1857), an event that made him profoundly critical of certain features of European life. His conviction that literature should have a higher purpose than the purely utilitarian alienated him from his radical contemporaries and made him in turn contemplate such 'eternal' issues as death – the three deaths of a noblewoman, a peasant and a tree (*Three Deaths*, 1859) – and the question of love as an emotion leading ideally and rather puritanically to marriage and family life (*Family Happiness*, 1859). By 1860 Tolstoy had created a considerable reputation for himself as a writer, but criticism of his most recent works contributed to his decision to apply himself to the more immediate problem of educating the peasant children on his estate. Excited by this new activity and never content to do anything by halves, he made a second trip to Europe (as it turned out, it was to be his last) in order to study at first hand the latest educational methods. The trip was, however, dominated by the death of his beloved eldest brother Nikolay. In anguish Tolstoy wrote: 'Art is a lie, and I can no longer love a beautiful lie.' Though he continued his European trip and met such illustrious figures as Froebel,

Matthew Arnold (it is not known how or when), Herzen and Proudhon, he found little in Europe, it seems, to make him change his mind about the superiority of his own educational ideas. Consequently, when he returned to Yasnaya Polyana he set up his school for peasant children on a formal basis and began issuing a journal. The educational experiment was a brilliant success, judging by some of the results which Tolstoy obtained, but he abandoned it almost as suddenly as he had begun it. In 1862 he gave up his bachelor life finally and, a mature thirty-four years of age, married Sonya Bers, who was sixteen years his junior. Yasnaya Polyana now became the family home where he turned himself into a paterfamilias and a novelist of international repute.

The Caucasus still remained the most important source of his inspiration, despite the many other themes and issues which had occupied him in the ten years since his first experience of it, for during that ten years he had gradually composed what was to be his single most important book to date, *The Cossacks* (1863). It is a study of the shock sustained by a young Russian nobleman, Olenin, when he confronts the primitive, but essentially natural, society of the Cossack frontiersmen in the Caucasus. It illustrates the personal and moral conflict which arises in Olenin as he attempts to adapt himself, in a Rousseauesque manner, to the noble savagery of the Cossack ethos. Olenin, an obvious Tolstoyan *persona*, though interestingly drawn, seems to lack the substantiality and richness of characterisation which Tolstoy succeeds in giving to the Cossack figures, especially the Cossack philosopher Uncle Yeroshka. The most successful aspect of the work is the complex and variegated picture of Cossack society itself. In this respect, Tolstoy achieved more than he had done in any previous work. His skill in evoking the intricate network of relationships which comprises a society was to become an invaluable aid to characterisation, in the sense that his most fully drawn characters were always to belong to particular societies or social groupings and were to be comprehensible only in relation to those groupings. His most accomplished study of peasant society *Polikushka* (1863) illustrates this precept in the figure of the wretched Polikushka himself, but in its power to evoke the money-dominated wretchedness of a whole community this story is among the most effective and terrible that Tolstoy ever wrote.

Until this moment in Tolstoy's career as a writer he had not written a work of conventional form, nor had he entirely succeeded in overcoming a marked autobiographical element in his chief characters. With hindsight one may anticipate some of the developments which were to occur in Tolstoy's evolution as a writer between 1863 and 1869, but it is doubtful whether even Tolstoy himself had a clear idea of the form his work was to take. Like *The Cossacks* it had its source in Tolstoy's experience of war in the Caucasus. Similarly it grew out of his reaction to Russia's defeat in the Crimean War and his distaste for the anti-aristocratic

radicalism of the *Contemporary*, just as his settled way of life at Yasnaya Polyana after his marriage naturally inclined him to emphasise the
importance of the family. These and many other issues may arguably
have contributed to Tolstoy's interest in Russia's victory over Napoleon
in 1812, but the ramifications of possible personal, literary and ideological influences that brought him eventually to complete his epic novel
War and Peace (1869) have a seemingly infinite complexity. He began
writing his new work in 1863, contemplating a reasonably short historical
novel on the first nineteenth-century encounter between Russia and
Napoleon in 1805. Gradually this grew into a vast work embracing the
entire Napoleonic epoch in Russian history and examining some of the
mainsprings of Decembrism and later nineteenth-century sociopolitical
problems. In the course of the writing Tolstoy seems to have allowed the
work to grow by a cumulative process that perfectly suited the apparently
unstrained realism of this historical epic. As a genre *War and Peace* appears to demonstrate Tolstoy's bitterly felt conviction that 'Art is a lie.'
In its elaborate invocation of a past age *War and Peace* fuses art and
history into a type of work which Tolstoy himself described as 'history–
art' – a unique example of creative reconstruction that had no parallel in
Russian or European literature.

War and Peace is of course governed as literature by respect for historical chronology. Volume I occupies approximately six months, from
June or July 1805 until November of that year, during which each of the
principal characters is presented to us in some situation that is critical for
his future life. Volume II occupies as many years, from 1806 to 1811, during which we witness the way in which the main characters develop both
intellectually and emotionally. Volumes III and IV describe the Napoleonic invasion of Russia in 1812, the battle of Borodino, the burning of
Moscow and the French retreat. The work concludes with two epilogues,
the first carrying the story seven or so years forward and the second
offering Tolstoy's theory of history. All is presented of course as Tolstoy
would have us see it, but the viewpoints of individual characters condition us to a viewing of characters and occasions in particular ways. To
this extent Tolstoy adopts a form of method acting in his portrayal of
character and lodges himself within the skin of certain fictional *personae*.
We have to accept that such pychologising is governed by fairly rigid
priorities in Tolstoy's scale of human values and that the characters themselves exhibit a self-sufficiency – what John Bayley has called *samodo-
volnost*'⁴ – which tends to insulate them against change until a dramatic
event obliges them to accept the influences of external forces.

In its fictional aspect *War and Peace* has some resemblance to a
family chronicle on the English pattern. The central family is the Moscow-
centred Rostov family who, especially in the case of the youngest children, show a remarkable intuitive familial unity and tend to symbolise a

sensitive corporateness of experience and attitude. The intense vitality of Natasha is matched by the intense loyalty of Nikolay and the youthful, ultimately tragic, impetuousness of Petya. Their enjoyment of life is the final Tolstoyan yardstick of virtue. Strictly speaking, those who are not touched in some way by the Rostov magic have no claim to goodness. The remotest of such figures, the gravest threat to the ideal of the family, to the Rostovs and to Russia, is of course Napoleon. Closely linked to the Rostovs, and finally bonded in marriage, are the Bolkonskys. They represent through the figure of the old prince the official St Petersburg ideal of imperial Russia. In the figure of Princess Mary Bolkonsky, Tolstoy suggests a tranquil, religious virtue which contrasts with the egotistical, phlegmatic, martial virtue of her brother, Prince Andrey. These representatives of the Russian nobility and their close associates are Tolstoy's vision of an *élite*, a true nobility in human as well as class terms, who have an unquestioned right to own estates and be the masters of their peasants. It is to this ethos that Napoleon is the enemy. *War and Peace* is the story of his defeat and a vindication of their elitist ethos. But *War and Peace* is a great work very largely because it deals with great issues on a great scale. Though, in cinematic fashion, it moves us rapidly from the private intimacies of the study or bedroom to the public grandeurs of the ballroom or battlefield, it suggests the scale of these places and occasions with an equal veracity, so that we are unobtrusively re-educated, as it were, in our understanding of what is truly great, be it the true greatness of the individual soldier's personal bravery or the supposed greatness of a pompous Napoleon inspecting the *beaux hommes* dead on the field of battle. Contrast not only between great and small but also, in a bold, sometimes assertively arrogant fashion, between historical and fictional characters, between war and peace, between cultures, between settings is the essential means of representing the scale of events and issues in this historical fiction. The panoramic portrayal of such battles as those of the Enns bridge or Borodino is intercut with kaleidoscopic glimpses of essentially private moments. In this manner, by using *montages* of historical material, by offering scraps of dialogue and momentary word pictures of the haphazard martial flux, Tolstoy evokes the chiaroscuro effect of wartime experience. That he is the Olympian witness and manipulator of all that happens can never be in doubt, though Tolstoyan invention may frequently leave one wondering whether it may not be more vicariously real than any historical reality could ever be. A fundamental principle of the Tolstoyan picture of war is that it should be framed by the permanencies of nature, so highlighting the follies and vanities of human bravery and carnage in the foreground. But such greatness would be limited to large-scale pictorialism were it not also reinforced by a consuming interest in the issues governing human conduct.

Andrey Bolkonsky and Pierre Bezukhov are the principal means by which Tolstoy explores the great issues of life and death. Andrey Bolkonsky is the only true tragic hero in the work. He has a princely coldness of demeanour which turns his search for fame into a death-wish and a final realisation that God is love, that 'to die means for me, a particle of love, to return to a common and eternal source'. For Pierre God is life and to love life is to love God. Both heroes discover their ideas of God as a result of the pressure of external events upon them, Andrey through identifying God with the limitless sky above the battlefield of Austerlitz and then through an acknowledgement of the force of love on his death-bed after Borodino, Pierre through the traumatic experiences of the French occupation of Moscow, his capture and then, in his captivity, his meeting with the only important peasant figure in the work, Platon Karataev. Tolstoy generally celebrates ideals of acceptance, humility and pietism. The best examples of this are the quietest philosophy of Karataev himself and the wise passivity of the Russian commander, Kutuzov. Although Tolstoy assumes that people grow up and change, there is also a fatalism in his view of life which makes him deny his characters free will in a strict sense. Pierre may discover a means of changing life through what he calls 'active virtue', but Tolstoy presupposes that there are certain governances in life. Such are those which prescribe Natasha's transformation after her marriage into a portly matron or those which dictate that history is created not by the so-called 'great men' but by the mass of men who participate most directly in a historical event. These Tolstoyan assumptions may condition to a great extent the picture of the historical process which we find in *War and Peace*. They do not in any way diminish the astonishing effect of supposedly real experience which Tolstoy has succeeded in giving to his historical epic.

It is not to be wondered at that, after completing the seven-year labour of writing *War and Peace*, he should suffer a form of nervous breakdown. The horrific vision of death that accompanied the breakdown, in a hotel room in Arzamas probably in September 1869, is recorded in his *Notes of a Madman*. It may possibly be that this event marks the beginning of Tolstoy's conversion, which officially dates from some ten years later. There is no doubt that for Tolstoy the entire decade of the 1870s was to be one of continuous self-scrutiny and a growing absorption by an interest in the question of death. At first, however, though he contemplated a historical novel on the time of Peter the Great and toyed with one or two other themes, he devoted himself to his educational projects and produced an ABC book in four parts as an elementary reader for peasant children. Only in 1873 did he turn back to literary work and begin the writing of *Anna Karenina*. This, his second and finest novel, mirrors in a multitude of ways the problems of Russian society in the 1870s and Tolstoy's own problems as he moved towards a crisis in his life.

The epigraph to *Anna Karenina* – 'Vengeance is Mine, said the Lord, and

I will Repay' – explains little more than does the famous first sentence: 'All happy families are alike, each unhappy family is unhappy in its own way,' but both indicate Tolstoy's concern with the morally normative in relation to the fundamental social institutions of marriage and the family. *Anna Karenina* is about three types of marriage and family: the failed marriage of Anna and Karenin, the conventional society marriage of Stiva and Dolly Oblonsky and the true marriage of Konstantin and Kitty Levin. It illustrates, unobtrusively but inevitably, that Tolstoy subsumes certain absolute normative principles in human morality. The deliberate violation of the marriage vows which Anna commits in deciding to give herself to Vronsky is accompanied by a gradual, but tragically inevitable, destruction of her personal happiness, leading eventually to the final act of suicide. Anna enters the fiction by means of the railway lines on which she finally kills herself. Through a repetitious symbolism, a concentration on Anna as a restlessly moving figure, a refusal to explain Anna's past, even the real reasons for her marriage to Karenin, and an unwillingness to allow her to find a religious answer to her problem, Tolstoy gives the impression of illustrating a thesis in his portrayal of his heroine – and this thesis is, quite simply, that Anna must be seen to have violated a divinely sanctioned law for which, as the epigraph obliquely suggests, a vengeance will be exacted. This reading of Anna's problem is partly supported by examining the complementary theme of Levin's search for a meaning to life, which is only granted to him when he has married Kitty and settled down to raise a family. Where Anna fails, as it were, he succeeds. He succeeds in discovering, both through the grace of the married state and through a chance encounter with a peasant on his estate, that his life can be given meaning by realising that good and evil are outside the chain of cause and effect and that by faith in the natural laws of goodness, intuitively known to the mass of the Russian people, he may become reconciled with 'the people' and therefore able to enact a positive purpose in life.

The novel is not as schematic as this description suggests, but it has a conscious architecture based on the complementary strength of the two themes and on an infrastructure of contrasts between town and country, new and old, sky and earth, spiritual and physical. In its more limited, domestic ambience *Anna Karenina* has not the range or 'openness' of *War and Peace*, yet by its very presumption of fixed norms – of social differentiation and the ordered routines of social living – it suggests the realities of ordinary, undramatic existence more effectively while simultaneously conjuring into life a much more mature, adult world than did its predecessor. There is no greater *tour de force* in all of Russian literature than Tolstoy's creation of Anna Karenina. Her portrayal may be hobbled to a didactic intent which never allows her the freedom she ultimately deserves, but still she outpaces Tolstoyan censure and moves with superb feminine vitality from episode to episode of her life, so that in the end, when she has nowhere to turn, when whatever vengeful fate makes her destroy herself, it is not her we blame but the mediocrities and non-entities of a brittle, unfeeling society to which she appears to have fallen victim. Caught in a tragic process, she, like the others affected by the tragedy, loses what she most wants: her lover Vronsky and her son Seryozha, just as her husband Karenin loses his much-cherished further chance of promotion in his official career and Vronsky himself, the social 'upstart' (*vyskochka*, as Levin calls him), loses the deeply felt need to legitimise himself as a family man and pillar of society. For all her vitality, Anna destroys more than she creates. The fault is partly Tolstoy's, for he never succeeds in suggesting the true character of the sexual passion between Anna and Vronsky. Take, for example, Tolstoy's description of the beginning of their affair:

> What for almost a whole year had been for Vronsky the sole desire of his life, replacing all former desires; what for Anna had been an impossible, horrifying and thus all the more seductive dream of happiness – this desire was now satisfied. Pale, with a quivering lower jaw, he stood over her and begged her to compose herself, not knowing himself how or why.
>
> 'Anna! Anna!' he said in a voice that shook. 'Anna, for God's sake! . . .'
>
> But the louder he spoke, the more she lowered her once proud and happy, now shameful, head, and she bent double and fell from the divan on which she was sitting to the floor, to his feet; she would have collapsed on the carpet if he hadn't held her.
>
> 'My God! Forgive me!' she said, sobbing and pressing his hands to her bosom.
>
> She felt herself so criminal and full of blame that she had no choice but to abase herself and ask forgiveness; and in her life now there was no one but him, so she addressed her prayer for forgiveness to him. Gazing at him, she had a physical sense of her abasement and could say nothing more. He, in his turn, felt what a murderer must feel when he sees the body that he has robbed of life. This body robbed of life was their love, the first period of their love. (Part III, ch. 11)

Desire is instantly reduced to moral abasement, masculine sexuality to a kind of murder in this outrageously over-written depiction of the consequences of illicit passion. A cold puritanism seems to bring a tone of disgust to this description and the others which mark the downward progress of Anna's illicit relationship with Vronsky. Similarly, though on a more morbid level, there is a vivid anguish about the Tolstoyan treatment of death, particularly the death of Konstantin Levin's brother, Nikolay (this death is marked by the only chapter heading in the novel). Anna's own death is described in slow-motion inevitability through her experience of it. The imagery of light and dark which accompanies it, culminating in the final image of the guttering and extinguished candle, evokes the light and dark of her own life, the mixture of passionate duplicity and loving care that endow her portrait with such poignancy.

Konstantin Levin is the most opinionated hero in Russian literature. He is not Anna's foil so much as the participant observer–narrator in the fiction who exhibits through the naïve candour of his observation all the directness and naturalness which we associate with 'making strange'. Also, in the most telling confrontation in the novel, it is through his eyes that we see Anna shortly before her suicide and his eyes, like the painter Mikhaylov's before him, see the vitality and poise but cannot, save by guesswork, plumb the depths of her terribly bruised nature or the anguish of deceit and jealousy by which she must live. Levin is none the less the surest witness we have in Tolstoy's fiction and his natural probity makes it easy to accept the soul-searchings that lead him eventually to seek a non-rational purpose to his life. His discovery of faith tells the story of Tolstoy's own conversion and search for a religious alternative more powerfully than does Tolstoy's *Confession* (1879–82). But if Anna's tragedy offers a Tolstoyan view of the question of female emancipation, a question widely discussed in the Russia of the 1870s, then Levin's opinions touch on a range of matters that contributed to the intellectual atmosphere of the decade – his relationship with the peasantry, the organisation of labour, the problem of the individual and society, Panslavism, not to mention the question of art in many forms, especially realism in literature, which is one of the topics he discusses when he visits Anna. Above all, the portrait of Levin shows how much Tolstoy sought to release himself from the burden of being a writer in order to become a preacher. Uniquely gifted though Tolstoy was as a literary artificer, it is hard not to feel on occasion that he could have turned his hand to anything had he chosen, that he was not driven by the literary and publicistic compulsion of a Dostoevsky. He sought and was gratified by fame, but fame was not the real spur to his achievement; the real spur was the little green stick containing the secret of happiness which he dreamed of as a child.

Soon after the completion of *Anna Karenina* the sense of *ennui* which he describes so brilliantly in Levin's attitude to life seems to have overtaken Tolstoy himself. During the writing of his masterpiece he had been distracted by many interests but none more preoccupying and satisfying than his learning of Greek. When he faced the future he found life as unappetising and doomed as it had seemed to him during the traumatic experience in the Arzamas hotel room. His knowledge of Greek was to become the key to a reinterpretation of the Gospels and a reconstruction of his own life.

Confession cannot help reading a little like a salvationist's *apologia*.

The best parts of it are the allegorical illustrations. The worst are the patronising remarks about the intuitive faith of 'the people'. There is some justification in assuming that throughout the 1870s Tolstoy had liked to think of himself as a spokesman of the peasantry. When he came to the point of formulating his religious philosophy, it became axiomatic for him to determine degrees of rightness or wrongness in terms of acceptability to peasant understanding. But there always remained the sophisticated, aristocratic Tolstoy who, as Chekhov said of *Anna Karenina*, liked 'to ask the right questions' and of these the most pertinent that he asked was: 'Is there any meaning in my life that the inevitable death awaiting me does not destroy?' If no science, philosophy or religion could have give him a satisfactory answer, a century of popular acceptance of his literary work in all countries of the world might suggest a clear answer to the intelligent layman. However, it was precisely his literary reputation that Tolstoy sought to put behind him. He sought by moral precept and example in a curiously Victorian way to achieve a form of saintliness and so to inspire a moral rejuvenation in the society of his time.

His life and work in the 1880s were dominated by a proselytising zeal which pervaded both his philosophical and literary writings. The chief among his philosophical works was *What Then Must We Do?* — and it was a question which Russian literature had addressed to its readers in various forms ever since the immediate post-Crimean War period, chiefly, of course, in Chernyshevsky's famous socialist treatise of a novel, *What Is To Be Done?* (1863). Tolstoy's work was directed at analysing the awful disparity between rich and poor and it proposed a simple enough remedy in Tolstoy's own terms: no man should exploit another, all men should earn their living and livelihood by the sweat of their own brow. In the context of a rural economy this might be a practicable answer; in a complex industrial society it made little sense. Tolstoy continuously referred for his answers to his own — frankly rather limited — experience at Yasnaya Polyana and was often belligerently neglectful of non-Russian examples. Yet when he illustrated his stern, moralistic precepts in his literary work, as in *The Death of Ivan Ilyich* (1886) and *The Kreuzer Sonata* (1889), he wrote powerful realistic studies in the long-drawn agony of Ivan Ilyich's morally unprepossessing death or Pozdnyshev's 'crime of passion' in murdering his wife out of sexual disgust.

In the 1890s he became actively engaged in much large-scale charitable effort on behalf of famine sufferers and minorities, especially those opposed to government oppression, such as the Dukhobors, whose emigration to Canada was aided by the proceeds from his last novel *Resurrection* (1899). His most important tract for the times *The Kingdom of God is Within You* (1893) argued very cogently for his major precept of non-violent opposition to evil and, by attacking the power of government, implied support for policies of civil disobedience. In this decade he also enunciated his view of art as a form of infection (*What is Art?*, 1898) and he established a new reputation for himself as a major dramatist with his most important play *The Power of Darkness* (written 1886, first produced in Russia, 1895) about infanticide, ignorance and ultimate repentance in a peasant setting. He had by now become so outspoken and well-known for his attacks on church and state that he was excommunicated by the Holy Synod of the Russian Orthodox Church (1901), an act which merely enhanced his authority and gave him the right to criticise even more strongly such – to him – immoral matters as private ownership of land or such manifestly arbitrary acts as the government executions in the wake of the 1905 revolution. All the time, however, behind the public façade of Tolstoyanism, Tolstoy was engaged in private feuding with his wife and close members of his family over the disposition of publishing rights and jealousies about his relations with his disciples, especially the most prominent and trusted of them, V. G. Chertkov. The atmosphere of bickering and recrimination at Yasnaya Polyana undoubtedly soured Tolstoy's last years and contributed to his decision, long postponed though it may have been, finally to escape from his home in October 1910.

Something of this sourness must have been due to Tolstoy himself. A perusal of the work of the last thirty years of his life can quickly identify certain *bêtes noires* which his puritanical attitudes found abhorrent: modern art, Shakespeare, alcohol, tobacco, revolutionary ideas etc., but the two subjects of science and sex elicited a frostiness bordering on mania. He attacked science for its pretensions very largely, but he attacked sex, it seems, simply because as an instinct it could not be conveniently fitted into the strait-jacket of his morality. D. H. Lawrence, on the centenary of Tolstoy's birth, voiced in his own prejudiced way an appropriately sour estimate of Tolstoy's attitude to male sexuality and the likely reasons for his admiration of the peasantry:

> He envied the reckless passionate male with a carking envy, because he must have felt himself in some way wanting in comparison. So he exalts the peasant: not because the peasant may be a more natural and spontaneous creature than the city man or the guardsman, but just because the peasant is poverty-stricken and humble. This is malice, the envy of weakness and deformity.
>
> We know now that the peasant is no better than anybody else; no better than a prince or a selfish young army officer or a governor or a merchant. In fact, in the mass, the peasant is worse than any of these. The peasant mass is the ugliest of all human masses, most greedily selfish and brutal of all. Which Tolstoy, leaning down from the gold

bar of heaven, will have had opportunity to observe. If we have to trust to a *mass*, then better trust to the upper or middle-class mass, all masses being odious.

All masses were equally odious to Tolstoy, notwithstanding his conviction that the simple peasant, like the noble savage, was nearer to Godliness than other men. Whatever institutionalised men and made them act as automata or parts of a swarm was abhorrent to Tolstoy. For all his scorn of leaders, he believed in heroes and heroism. When we recall the kinetic, detailed brilliance of his fictional art, akin to the cinema in so many of its effects, we are struck by Tolstoy's genius in showing us both the exterior, or visual, complexity of the world and the complexity of his heroes' and heroines' apprehension of it. Andrey Bolkonsky, Pierre Bezukhov, Natasha Rostov, Anna Karenina, Konstantin Levin are the vital personalities who stand out both against the kinetic background and against the crowd. They are heroes and heroines in their unwillingness to conform and in their essentially individual search for happiness. Also, for all their desire to be otherwise, they have a natural aristocratic superiority, an elitist nobility of character. Humanity, in the Tolstoyan view, was always naturally graded into greater and lesser mortals, not according to class hierarchy but rather according to degrees of heroic individuality. After a similar pattern of consistency Tolstoy's career as a writer ended where it started, in the sense that his last novel *Resurrection* deals, through a resurrected early literary *persona* Prince Nekhlyudov, with questions of morality and an aristocratic conscience which Tolstoy had probed so discerningly in his earliest studies. But the full circle traversed by his career is seen to best effect in the finest of his last works, *Hadji Murat*, which derives from Tolstoy's experience in the Caucasus and illustrates his admiration for the heroic individual – in this case, one of Shamil's lieutenants who gives himself up to the Russians but dies bloodily when he tries to escape from Russian bondage. In its superbly lucid and economical style, *Hadji Murat* is a model Tolstoyan work, but in its characterisation of the heroic central figure and in its suggestion of the involvement of so many great and small, from Tsar Nicholas I and Shamil down to the meanest peasant soldier, it evokes in microcosm a world viewed as it were through the eye of God. The secret of Tolstoy's literary attitude is that he sought to view the world as it were through the eye of God. In literary terms he succeeded as nearly as possible in achieving this impossible aim in his picture of Hadji's heroism, but in life he succeeded perhaps in manifesting a divine likeness in the very obverse of the heroic, in an engaging impishness, a kind of roguishness.

The most perceptive testimony to this aspect of Tolstoy is given by Maxim Gorky. He perceived the roguishness[5] in Tolstoy which set him against the crowd. It is fitting to end a brief study of Tolstoy with Gorky's glimpse of him. Quite suddenly, in a roguish way, Tolstoy turned to him one day and asked: 'Why don't you believe in God?' Gorky replied that he had no faith whereupon Tolstoy spoke of the meaning of faith and in so doing displayed his own formidable likeness to divinity:

. . . 'Faith, like love, requires courage and daring. One has to say to oneself, "I believe" – and everything will come right, everything will appear as you want it, it will explain itself to you and attract you. Now, you love much, and faith is only a greater love; you must love still more and then your love will turn to faith. When one loves a woman, she is unfailingly the best woman on earth, and each loves the best woman; and that is faith. A non-believer cannot love: today he falls in love with one woman, and next year with another. The souls of such men are tramps living barren lives – that is not good. But you were born a believer and it is no use thwarting yourself. Well, you may say, beauty – and what is beauty? The highest and most perfect is God.'

He hardly ever spoke to me on this subject, and its seriousness and the suddenness of it rather overwhelmed me. I was silent.

He was sitting on the couch with his legs drawn up under him, and, breaking into a triumphant little smile and shaking his finger at me, he said: 'You won't get out of this by silence, no.'

And I, who do not believe in God, looked at him for some reason very cautiously and a little timidly. I looked and I thought: 'This man is godlike.'

That triumphant little smile and shaking finger are splendid final images of the Tolstoy who always triumphantly proclaimed the joy of living while simultaneously proclaiming the need for moral limits. In his Yasnaya Polyana isolation he could be the militant moralist, archaic perhaps in some of his ideas and indifferent to the political significance that was attributed to his worship of the peasant, but in his insistent proclamation of the need for faith and love, in the high seriousness of his moral intentions, in the profundity of his knowledge of life's secrets he can be said to have acquired the closest likeness to divinity of any human being in the twentieth century.

NOTES

1 *Tolstoy and the Novel* (London, 1966) p. 98.
2 Translated by M. Hayward. From *Leo Tolstoy*, ed. Henry Gifford (Harmondsworth, Middlesex, 1971) pp. 203–4.
3 'Making strange' [*ostranenie*] was a term coined by the leading Formalist critic,

V. Shklovsky, principally in his study of Tolstoy, *Material i stil' v romane L'va Tolstogo 'Voyna i mir'* (Moscow, 1928).

4   J. Bayley, op. cit.

5   The Russian term is *ozornichestvo*, literally 'mischievousness'. The passage given below is from the end of Gorky's *Reminiscences of Tolstoy*, trans. S. S. Koteliansky and Leonard Woolf (New York, 1920) pp. 85–6.

5 Gorky

In January 1900 Gorky wrote to Chekhov:

> . . . the time has come for the heroic: everybody needs something
> stimulating, something striking, something, you know, that shouldn't
> be like life but should be higher than life, better, more beautiful. It is
> absolutely necessary that contemporary literature should start to
> embellish life somewhat, and as soon as it will start doing so, life
> itself will be embellished, that is people will start living more ener-
> getically, more buoyantly. And now – have a look at their wretched
> eyes, how bored, dull, frozen they are . . .

This letter epitomises Gorky's literary attitude throughout his life.

Gorky's work is inextricably bound with the kind of man he was and
the age he lived in. The peculiarities of his biography explain to a large
extent his spirit of rebellion, his contempt for philistinism, his admiration for strength and inner freedom, his deep humanity and love of man,
and his faith in the future. He not only projected these attitudes into his
work, but they actually motivated it. Though he envied Chekhov for con-
sidering literature the foremost interest in life, he admitted being unable
to do so himself. Writing for him was not primarily a creative necessity
born out of need for self-expression and self-exploration. Convinced
that the Russian people needed their writers to look up to, when he
discovered within himself a literary talent, he felt he had to use it as a
means for 'the education of man's mind and emotions, and ennoble-
ment of life' in the name of a great future. Chekhov's and Gorky's
ideals were not dissimilar. But whereas Chekhov believed that a writer
should be a witness and not a judge and that man's consciousness would
be aroused when he saw himself as he was, Gorky maintained that man
would respond better to an ideal, be it a quest for truth and justice or a
longing to believe in an illusion. Chekhov, with his restraint and understatement, was deeply suspicious of all tendencies in literature; Gorky –
exuberantly and conspicuously – never hesitated to use literature as 'a
well-aimed shaft'.

Aleksey Maksimovich Peshkov (1868–1936), better known under his pen-name of Maxim Gorky, Maxim the Bitter, was born into a provincial lower-middle-class family which was to break up during his early childhood as a result of deaths, quarrels, and financial ruin. The boy's lasting impressions of these years which crystallised later in his work were the simple optimistic faith of his maternal grandmother to whom one can also trace Gorky's love of folklore and his gift as an oral story-teller; and the tyrannical authority of his grandfather against which the boy rebelled violently and which no doubt was at the root of his later hatred of philistinism. The senseless cruelty and brutality of the background of these years filtered through to Gorky's later descriptions of 'Asiatic' Russia.

At the age of ten, Aleksey's meagre formal schooling ended and he was soon forced to earn his living 'among people'. Errand-boy in a shoe shop, apprentice to a draughtsman, kitchen hand on a Volga steamer, painter in an icon shop, he spent all his free time reading avidly and indiscriminately: 'What happiness to be literate!' He discovered eventually good literature, and later spoke of those books which reveal 'great feelings and desires that lead people to exploits'. Gorky's thirst for learning and respect for culture originated in these formative days. He also discovered his ability to tell stories and to hold an audience spellbound. Finally, at the age of sixteen, he decided 'to do something with himself', and left Nizhny Novgorod for Kazan to enter the university. Instead, he had to make the best of his extra-mural education, living in slums where he met some of the prototypes of the 'ghosts of men who had outlived themselves', and working in a bakery later described in *Twenty-Six Men and a Girl* (1899), the story about which Chekhov said: 'one feels in it strongly the locale, it smells of dough.' He was interested in everything: 'I was pulled in all directions – to women and books, to workers and carefree students . . .', but did not know where he belonged and experienced a short period of bewilderment and loneliness which culminated in attempted suicide in 1887. The experience was retold in *An Incident in the Life of Makar* (1912).

During the next four years he was constantly on the move, gaining an increased awareness of the sociopolitical scene, joining some Populists and witnessing peasant violence – an experience which impressed him for life. In 1889 he approached Korolenko to ask his opinion about *The Song of the Old Oak*, a poem a single line of which is extant: 'I came into this world to disagree.' Discouraged by the initial reaction of the writer who none the less was later to become Gorky's first literary mentor, he burned his poem and set out for two years of wandering through Russia on foot. The wealth of impressions gathered during this tramping period was to find its way into Gorky's short stories. His vagabonds and gipsies were based on life. Asked by the police why he was walking, he replied that he wanted to get to know Russia. His first story, *Makar Chudra*

(1892), was published in a local Tiflis newspaper, and from then on he never looked back.

The next ten years witnessed Gorky's meteoric literary career. After publishing several stories in the provincial press, he reached the major national journals, while earning his living as a journalist first in Samara, then back in Nizhny. In 1898 two volumes of his collected stories and sketches were sold out within a few days, and a year later a third volume was published. Gorky started corresponding with the leading writers of the time: Tolstoy, Chekhov, Andreyev, Bunin; on a visit to St Petersburg he met publishers, intellectuals, writers. Even the intelligentsia circles who were suspicious of his work were impressed by this tramp who became a writer. There was an integrity, a freshness and, surprisingly, an inner elegance about the man which commanded respect despite his frequent rudeness to the bourgeois, who was to become the greatest target of his later work. In Moscow Gorky met Tolstoy, who subsequently wrote: 'I was very happy to meet you and am happy that I liked you. Aksakov used to say that there are people better than their books, and there are worse. I liked your writings, but found you better than your writings . . .' Gorky answered characteristically: 'I don't know whether I am better than my books, but I know that every writer has to be higher and better than what he writes . . .'

Meanwhile, Gorky was constantly watched by the police for suspected participation in the world of revolutionary student circles and especially after the publication of his *Song of the Stormy Petrel* (1901), a clear allegory of the impending political storm. Arrested, he was freed through the intercession of Tolstoy. When someone suggested that it might be safer for him to go abroad, he answered that 'if a certain Gorky was killed in a street fight, this would do more good than if Gorky started playing at being Herzen.' In 1902 Gorky was elected Honorary Academician, but the election was cancelled by the Tsar. Korolenko and Chekhov resigned from the Academy in protest. In April his first play was staged, followed a few months later by *Lower Depths*, which met with tremendous success and won Gorky international fame.

A spiritual and social rebel, by 1905 Gorky became a real threat to the authorities. His popularity as a writer was incendiary enough; his police record was getting increasingly longer; and his sympathy for the revolutionaries manifested itself not only in his moral support generously given to individuals and causes, but also in his financial support given to all revolutionary factions. Besides, he had become a major fund-raiser, mainly through his friendship with Savva Morozov, later known as the 'Bolshevik millionaire' and a prototype of many of Gorky's strong merchant characters. After the events of 'Bloody Sunday' Gorky was imprisoned in the Peter and Paul fortress, but following demonstrations in his favour in Western Europe and America was released a few weeks later.

By 1906 Gorky was forced to flee abroad, and went to the United States to raise funds for the Bolshevik movement. He wrote to Andreyev: 'You lucky Russians are making a revolution at home, in your native language, and I have to do it through interpreters. Inconvenient, but just the same, it works.'

Finally Gorky settled in Capri where he stayed until 1914. These eight years of exile were mainly a period of political and journalistic work, marked by Lunacharsky's and Lenin's visits to Capri, the opening of Gorky's school for revolutionary propagandists and its subsequent closing because of Lenin's criticism of its 'fractional' orientation. One of the main areas of disagreement between Lenin and Gorky was the latter's idea of 'God-building', which he embodied in his novel *Confession* (1908), and according to which socialism was to be the new religious creed.

Following a political amnesty in 1914, Gorky returned to Russia and devoted himself to various publishing activities. Throughout the war, he published a journal, opening its pages to all political factions, angering most of them. He was to write later: 'In every group and party I regarded myself as a heretic.' The Revolution brought no miracle. In December 1917, Gorky wrote: 'There's nothing for me to rejoice at . . . The prisons are full of people . . . The "new authorities" are as crude and brutal as the old, only even less well educated . . .'

Above all, Gorky feared the destruction of Russia's culture. In the words of Trotsky, he 'welcomed the Revolution with the misgivings of a Museum director'. In April 1917 he started a daily *New Life* [*Novaya zhizn'*] which became the only independent voice in Russia at the time. In it Gorky engaged in polemic against the new régime until the paper was suppressed in July 1918. At this stage Lenin struck a bargain with him: Gorky was to stop meddling in politics, and in exchange he would be allowed to devote himself to saving Russia's intelligentsia and Russia's culture. Gorky proceeded now to use all his energy, power and influence to help scholars, artists and writers, and to preserve the cultural values of old Russia. One of his most important schemes was a grandiose project to make the world's classics available in translation to the great Russian public, providing thus a living for innumerable writers. He personally saw to it that they received food, clothing and shelter. The writer Zamyatin subsequently recalled: 'In a capital where there was no more bread, light, or street-cars, in an atmosphere of catastrophe and ruin, these enterprises seemed at best fantasies of utopia. But Gorky believed in them ("one must believe") – and with his faith was able to infect the sceptical citizens of Petersburg . . .' Gorky's generosity knew no limits; he interceded for everybody, even for men under sentence of death. When someone mentioned those he had saved, he said: 'It's nothing. For every one or two I get off, they manage to kill two or three hundred.'

By 1921 his uneasy friendship with Lenin, his strained relations with

Zinoviev, the execution of Gumilyov, the death of Blok, and the worsening state of his health made him leave Russia. He continued to write letters from abroad to raise money for the Russians faced with famine. His main concern was for the Russian intelligentsia, 'the best brains of the country' without whom he felt 'it is impossible to live as it is impossible to live without a soul.' In 1924 he settled in Sorrento where he spent some years in torment and ambiguous voluntary exile. The story of Gorky's final return to the Soviet Union has not yet been told in all its details. To decide on permanent exile meant betraying the revolutionary ideal of his youth. In the words of the *émigré* poet Khodasevich, Gorky 'finally sold out – not for money, but to preserve the principal illusion of his life, both for his own and for others' sake'. In 1928 he went to the Soviet Union for a few months. The next five years were spent between Russia and Italy. After 1933 he never left the Soviet Union again.

One of his last contributions to Russian literature had far-reaching repercussions. After organising the new Union of Soviet Writers, he helped to expound the notion of Socialist Realism – a method of writing which would reflect socialist realities and socialist mentality in a positive way, revolutionary romanticism being an essential ingredient of it. He did not foresee the consequences of this well-intentioned prescription. Nor did he foresee, or want to believe in, the impending Stalin purges. Determined to glorify every aspect of contemporary Russia, he convinced some *émigré* intellectuals to return to the Soviet Union to serve the further development of Russian literature, among them Prince Mirsky. Though he is said to have adopted a more orthodox Soviet line on political matters, he still tried to protect writers and literature, but arrests and deportations gradually assumed gigantic proportions, and there was probably little he could have done despite his considerable prestige.

Gorky died, in obscure circumstances, on 18 June 1936.

Thus ended the life of a man who had dedicated both himself and his work to the task of inspiring the new generations. A committed writer persuaded that literature can influence life, he wrote in 1895 (*The Reader*): 'The purpose of literature is to help people to understand themselves, to inspire them with a yearning for truth and to give them greater confidence in themselves . . . to waken in their souls anger and courage, so that they may become noble and strong.' Some twenty years later, he was still writing (to H. G. Wells): 'Our aim is to imbue young people with a sense of social romanticism, a love and faith in life and people. We are trying to teach them heroism.'

The theme is a constant in Gorky's work; it is repeated and reiterated far too often, drummed in, almost shouted through a loudspeaker. Yet the initial impact of the message was tremendous. The assertion of man, life, freedom and independence was met with unparalleled enthusiasm by a society which was just beginning to emerge from a period of impotent disillusionment.

Gorky began writing as a romantic. Not surprisingly he turned first to allegory, parables and legends; he always thought that folklore was the natural literature of working people. He found these forms suitable for projecting his attitudes in a simplistic but striking and symbolic manner. There is no disparity of theme and genre in *The Siskin who Lied* (1893), which expresses a striving towards freedom and happiness, or in the *Song of the Falcon* (1895), a poetical contrast between the heroic falcon and the philistine grass-snake, which extols 'the madness of the brave' against merging sea and skies, or in the later *Song of the Stormy Petrel* (1901), which released a potent feeling of revolutionary expectation. Likewise, the early heroic fables presented by their narrators in *Makar Chudra* (1892) and *Old Woman Izergil* (1895) are also romantic in their admiration of courage, pride and freedom. The gypsy Loiko Zobar who prefers to murder his beloved rather than submit to her, in the first story, and Larra, the son of an eagle and a woman condemned to eternal life, in the second story, are entirely abstract creations but have a certain haunting splendour enhanced by Gorky's picturesque impressionistic language and his rhythmic prose. The old woman Izergil is much more interesting herself than the second legend she recounts – quoted sometimes as an ideological and emotional bridge between Gorky's early and later works – in which Danko tears out his heart and holds it up aflame to light the way of his people to the land of freedom. A female variety of the tramp, set against a background of steppe and sea, she has got her own tale to tell of a life unrestricted by conventional morals, illuminated by a thirst for personal freedom, and an admiration for strength and vitality.

Korolenko, who had commented on Gorky's stubborn predilection for allegories, said about *Old Woman Izergil*: 'It's a strange thing. This is romanticism – and it is long now dead. I very much doubt whether this Lazarus is worthy of resurrection. It seems to me that you sing with a voice that doesn't belong to you. You are a realist, not a romantic, a realist!' He approved of *Chelkash* (1895), one of the best of Gorky's early stories, free of fantasy and ornamentation, but still romantic in spirit if not in form. The dramatic clash between the two protagonists who enact rather than propound the author's attitudes is not all black and white, though the moral independence of the tramp is powerfully contrasted to the servility of the peasant. A thief and an outlaw, Chelkash is almost heroically glorified, but his moment of weakness and envy for the peasant makes him an artistically credible character, while the several changes of mood add intensity to the story, and nature once again reflects the spirit of freedom. The scene in which Chelkash throws all his money into the face of Gavrila shows clearly Gorky's sympathies. Peasants never fare well with him: in *Malva* (1897), Seryozha says: 'The Zemstvo does everything for them, but they want us to believe that they are orphans'; in *Varenka Olesova* (1898), the heroine, who is temperamentally if not socially akin to some of Gorky's early self-reliant, vigorous vagabonds, knows her peasants: 'They are described everywhere as deserving pity, yet they are simply despicable.' Characteristically, she prefers to read French novels which are full of interest and excitement, and in which the hero is heroic.

Some of the best of Gorky's early short stories glorify instinctivism. 'No man should fight against his own self. If a person opposes his own self he is a lost man,' says Kuzma in *Heart-Ache* (1896). *On the Raft* (1895), a vaguely Chekhovian story, superbly illustrates the mood without elaborating the writer's point of view: the father's affair with his son's wife is not judged in terms of right or wrong. There is also no message in *Malva*, which most evocatively renders the harmony between nature and the heroine's dissatisfaction with reality. In its time, its framing sentence, 'The sea was laughing,' provoked many a comment as well as the displeasure of Tolstoy.

Most of Gorky's characters express a yearning for some sort of an ideal, whether they are gipsies, tramps, or – after 1896 when there is more truth of situation in Gorky's stories – workers and the urban poor. In *The Orlov Couple* (1897), the setting is no longer nature but a small miserable provincial town; the cobbler Orlov drinks and beats his wife. During an outbreak of cholera the Orlovs are brought to the local hospital to help as they can. In her new surroundings, among kind and considerate people, the wife flourishes, gains confidence in herself, and finds independence. The husband, who for a short while saw himself as a hero who would save Russia from cholera, soon takes up drinking again. At the end, he says: 'And so, after all, I never accomplished any heroic deeds. Yet I still long to distinguish myself . . . I was born with unrest in my soul, and my fate is to be a tramp . . .' Notwithstanding the cobbler's somewhat improbable self-awareness, the story is an important pointer to the development of Gorky's attitude to his early characters. The note of glorification is gone: the tramp by temperament is no longer heroic. And yet even Orlov was transformed when he believed himself capable of great deeds. Every man needs an ideal. In *Twenty-Six Men and a Girl* (1899), the workers in the underground bakery need to believe in the purity of the young girl who comes daily to collect bread: she is literally their only ray of light. Their disappointment when their object of worship is sullied gives rise to an ugly and cruel scene. Despite the sombre description of the bakery in which the men work from early morning to late at night, there is no direct indictment of social conditions here, nor is there in *The Orlov Couple*. Orlov was given the same chance as his wife, but did not take it. Unlike his nineteenth-century predecessors who held society responsible for its superfluous men, Gorky repeatedly makes the point that man is the creator of his own fate. The old woman Izergil spoke with contempt about those weak natures who blame faith instead of blaming themselves. Konovalov, in the story of this name (1897), asks 'Where were you when your life was made?' Kuvalda in *Creatures who Once were Men* (1897) is more specific: 'Women, shopkeepers and philosophy have been the three causes of my ruin.' The story is explicit in showing Gorky's disappointment with the tramp as a champion of freedom and independence.

Man has to rise above his environment; the future depends on the consciousness of individuals and not on circumstances. What matters to Gorky is to awaken in man that consciousness, to make him rebel and thereby make him strong, 'to inspire him with a yearning for truth'. Yet from the beginning, the theme is given added depth by an underlying doubt which mitigates the inherent crudeness of the message. The ensuing complexity is far from being sophisticated, but it provides a conflict that is basic to many of Gorky's works. The early parables – like later his theatre – lend themselves naturally to expressing the conflict, the ambivalence that was inherent in Gorky despite his protestations to the contrary. Already in *The Siskin who Lied*, the little bird bids his companions to fly with him beyond the dark woods into a brighter future. But the sceptical woodpecker accuses him of lying, for no bird, he says, can fly higher than itself. Tearfully, the Siskin admits: 'Yes, I told lies, because I do not know what there is beyond the woodland, but it is so good to believe and to hope . . . Maybe the woodpecker is right, but what do we need of his truth when it weighs our wings with stone, preventing us from flying into the sky?' There is no doubt that the Siskin voices Gorky's feelings. Did not he write to Chekhov after reading *Uncle Vanya*: 'You have a great talent, but, listen – what do you think you will achieve by such blows?' Truth can weigh man's hopes with stone. Man needs an ideal at any cost. The yearning for truth is all-important, but what is truth? Embellished truth may be more helpful to man than cruel, unadorned truth. The note is sounded many a time with varying emphasis. In *The Reader* (written in 1895, published in 1898), a poor effort but an important *profession de foi* for Gorky ('I have put into it much of *my truth* . . .'), there is the potentially dangerous question: what is it good for men to know? In Gorky's first play, *Smug Citizens* (1902), one of the characters says: 'So that man's life should not be boring and hard, he has to be somewhat of a dreamer, a castle-builder.' Once again, life echoes literature when Gorky writes to Andreyev from Capri: 'Castles in the air are always appropriate!' In *Summer Folk* (1904) Ryumin incurs the displeasures of the author's main spokesman, a 'strong' female character, for claiming every man's right to wish for an illusion. He becomes an almost tragic figure when he shouts out: 'I want to be deceived. I have learned the truth – and I have nothing to live for!'

The conflict between illusion and reality is dramatised best, however, in Gorky's earlier play *Lower Depths* (1902), which in many ways sums up the writer's early work. The setting is a sordid doss house populated with alcoholics, tramps and criminals. Luka, a somewhat enigmatic old wanderer, offers a series of comforting lies to these creatures who have now sunk to their lowest level. 'Man can do everything . . . if he only wants to,' he says. And he himself is always ready to sacrifice truth for the sake of man: truth does not always save the soul. Satin – a former convict – does not believe in the comforting lie: untruth is the religion of slaves, truth is the god of free man, he maintains. He has understood Luka, but he cannot sympathise: 'The old man is not a charlatan. What is truth? Man – that is the truth! . . . He lied out of pity for you . . . There are weak people who need this . . .' In the end Satin breaks into an unbearably rhetorical paean to the human spirit which burst on Russian audiences of 1902 with a voice of thunder: 'Man is free – man is above the lie . . .'

There is no doubt that Satin was intended to be the real hero of the play – the strong proud rebel, the fighter. And yet Luka emerged as a complex and more attractive character than Satin. Gorky was non-plussed. He admitted that truth came out rather pale in Satin's speech, but he complained that neither critics nor public had understood the play despite its success. Was this due to the outstanding talent of the actor who played Luka (Moskvin), he asked, or was it due to the short-comings of the author?

Gorky's shortcomings as a dramatist were of a different nature, however. He transposed his heroes and his attitudes on to the stage without giving much thought of how to exploit the dramatic genre best. And yet the stage appealed to him as a tribune. His first attempt at writing a play goes back to 1897 when, characteristically, he chose as his theme a legendary Russian hero, Vasily Buslayev; he abandoned it mid-way. In 1900 his contact with Chekhov and the Moscow Art Theatre encour-aged him to turn again to drama. 'Not to love the Moscow Art Theatre is impossible,' he wrote, 'not to work for it is criminal.' And though he appreciated Chekhov's plays enormously, it is interesting to note how carried away he was by a production of *Cyrano de Bergerac*: 'This is how one ought to live – like Cyrano. Not like uncle Vanya . . .' To instruct how to live heroically was more important for him than the form in which to express his aspirations and his hates.

His first completed play, *Smug Citizens* (1902), gave him consider-able trouble. He disliked it: 'It's bad. It is shrill, vain, and empty,' he wrote both to Andreyev and to Chekhov. His basic dramatic principles are already evident here. The play owes a great deal to Chekhov. The drama and the conflict between his characters take place in the everyday flow of life; the plot is weak and there is no real central protagonist. But the Chekhovian 'sub-text'[1] and fine psychological characterisation are sorely missing. Chekhov immediately diagnosed the weaknesses: 'You force new, original people to sing new songs from a score that looks second-hand; you have four acts, the characters deliver moral lectures, the long drawn-out passages cause dismay . . .' Gorky differs from Chekhov, and this is characteristic of him as dramatist, in sharply differentiating his characters according to their ideology; their personal relationships only emphasise their ideological clashes. Thus the domestic two-generations conflict in *Smug Citizens*, vaguely reminiscent of Ostrovsky's plays, is projected onto a social canvas, and the play acquires a political dimension especially topical in pre-1905 Russia. *Smug Citizens* contained a new character, the worker Nil, hailed as the first proletarian type in the Russian theatre. Though rude and callous, he is an attempt at a positive character who, like Gorky himself, hates the small bourgeoisie and their philistinism. Gorky explained to Stanislavsky that Nil was 'a man calmly confident in his strength and in his right to change life', the shortcomings of which aroused in his soul 'only one feeling – a passionate desire to do away with them'. In the play, however, the calm confidence of Nil is not as apparent as his violent hatred. He is too loud and too ruthless in his denunciation, and unrelieved by doubts or weaknesses. Chekhov rightly considered *Smug Citizens* an immature work, but he pointed out that Gorky's merit was to have been the first writer in Russia and in the world to speak with contempt about philistinism at the very time when society was ready to protest.

Lower Depths proved a better play. More complex, it had a certain 'philosophical' interest, was permeated by a feeling of compassion for humanity – more effective than the crude hatred of *Smug Citizens* – and, above all, had a striking background, so much more colourful than the drabness in the preceding work. Once again, in form it looked back to Chekhov: in its plotless structure (though the loose scenes have more nodal points of dramatic interest than in Gorky's first play), in its absence of one central hero and its concentration on a collective group (here made socially and symbolically significant by the confines of the doss-house) and, above all, in its polyphonic dialogue (parallel speeches directed at no one in particular and punctured by expressive songs), though without the finesse of Chekhov's suggestion of the inner current of individual drama. Unlike the Chekhovian delicately understated and psychologically motivated characters, Gorky's thieves, murderers and prostitutes are sharply delineated and romantically exaggerated especially in their tedious speeches on the meaning of life and truth. They are individualised not so much by their individual drama as by their response to the kind of truth they believe in. Luka's arrival has activated for a while the stagnation of his dethroned social outcasts. His departure leads to both an optimistic assertion of human dignity and an act of despair, leaving enough room for varying interpretations of his role. The play's unprecedented success at the time no doubt was due to a combination of Gorky, Stanislavsky, and its contemporaneous relevance. Its initial impact on Western audiences can be easily explained, but by now the novelty of the naturalistic setting, of the sociopolitical undertones, and of the reflections on Man, Freedom, illusion and reality should have paled, yet the play is still periodically revived in the West. One of the great theatrical prototypes, *Lower Depths* remains a challenge to both producers and actors.

After 1902, Gorky wrote a series of plays attacking the new intelligentsia. *Summer Folk* (1904) which, incidentally, saw its British *première* seventy years later, seems to take up where Chekhov's *Cherry Orchard* leaves off. It is a sprawling picture of the inheritors of the cherry orchard who, instead of creating a better world, have settled for the complacency and futility of their predecessors' lives. 'We do nothing except talk an awful lot,' says one character, while another ends a long diatribe on the intelligentsia's alienation from the masses with self-castigation: 'We have created our alienation ourselves . . . we deserve our torments.' *Summer Folk* is one of Gorky's most static plays, theatrically if not always thematically heavily indebted to Chekhov. Its characters are hardly ever more than two-dimensional. But Gorky was not interested: '*Summer Folk* is not art,' he wrote in a revealing letter to Andreyev, 'but is clearly a well-aimed shaft and I am glad, like a devil who has tempted the righteous to get shamefully drunk.'[2] The topicality of the play excited the audiences of the day.

This kind of topicality proved to be the main redeeming feature of Gorky's subsequent plays which lacked the human interest of *Lower Depths*. *Children of the Sun* (1905), *The Barbarians* (1906) and *The Eccentrics* (1910) were all directed against the intellectuals, while *The Enemies* (1906) portrayed a clash between factory owners and workers. There were also several plays on provincial merchants which were hardly ever staged. Gorky stopped writing for the theatre in 1917, but returned to it in the thirties to create his finest dramatic work, *Egor Bulychov and Others* (1932).

The three acts of the play, which Gorky called 'scenes', depict the last days in the life of Egor Bulychov, a rich provincial merchant who knows he is dying of cancer and yet has still tremendous inner strength and zest for life. The time is the eve of the 1917 Revolution. Terrified of death, surrounded by scheming relatives who are waiting to divide the inheritance, incapable of believing in God, Bulychov refuses to submit.

D

To lie down means to give up. Unrepentant of his past misdeeds ('I am a sinner, I've wronged people and I've sinned in every way. Well, all people wrong each other and it can't be helped, such is life.'), he rejects the priest's counsel to accept humbly his lot: 'Did you submit, when the bailiff offended you? You took him to court . . . In which court can I lodge a complaint against my illness, against my premature death?' He knows quacks cannot help him, and yet he would desperately like to believe them and be deceived by their 'comforting lie', but he refuses to be taken in. There is an extraordinarily effective scene in the play when Bulychov teases the trumpeter Gavrila who claims healing properties for his instrument: 'Are you a fool or a crook?' he asks. The man doesn't admit to being a fool. 'You must be a crook then,' concludes Bulychov. 'I am not a crook . . . But you know yourself – without deceit it is difficult to live.' Bulychov agrees and, amused by the man who still, without success, tries to sell him the cure, gives him money and tells him to leave. He stops him on the way, however, and asks him to blow the trumpet. The sound is deafening, but Bulychov persists: 'Go on blowing, Gabriel! It's Judgment-day! The end of the world . . . Blo-o-ow! . . .' The irony and poignancy of the scene are superb.

The end of Bulychov's world is near in more than one sense. Events from the outside world filter through to him and he responds to them through the prism of his personal problem. He is aware of the corruption of the class that is toppling just as he is aware of the corruption of his family. He feels a stranger in their midst and realises that for thirty years he has been living 'in the wrong street'. The 'right street' seems to belong to the people – the class into which he was born but which he had deserted to make money, and which was now promoting the Revolution. And the people also include the only human beings for whom this warm, full-blooded man cares – his godson, his illegitimate daughter, and his old servant and mistress.

As Bulychov is dying, he can hear the singing of marching Bolsheviks; it seems to him that they are singing his requiem.

At last Gorky the dramatist achieved what had eluded him all his life: a brilliant psychological drama with sociopolitical undertones and symbolic generalisation, closely knit together by the tragic figure of the protagonist, and illuminated by irony and humour. The political background is motivated and controlled by the psychological portraiture, and the dialogue is at once terse and suggestive. Never before has Gorky so well avoided overstatement and ideological abstraction. Despite the obvious connection of Egor Bulychov with Tolstoy's Ivan Ilyich, the play contains the whole of Gorky – his strong merchant type, his colourful rogues, the 'free' people who follow their instincts, the revolting philistines, the theme of truth and illusion – but this time handled with a sureness of touch and a restraint which reveal a truly great artist.

Only once more has Gorky achieved a successful dramatic character-isation – in *Vassa Zheleznova* (1935), a revised version of a play written twenty-five years earlier. However, it did not match *Egor Bulychov*. Nor did the sequel to the latter, *Dostigayev and Others* (1933), approach the dramatic force of its predecessor.

Gorky the playwright merits more attention than he has been given. As all his work, his plays are uneven. But in the final count, his contri-bution to drama is probably more noteworthy than his contribution to the Russian novel.

Gorky's novels illustrate well his major weaknesses and his strength as a writer. Used to the short story form which by its very nature disciplined his propensity for rambling and limited the number of characters involved, throwing into relief the frequent contrasts of mood and types, Gorky experienced difficulties with all his longer works. While the psycho-logical make-up of his characters revealed itself mainly by reaction to their opposites, the complex interrelationships of a group of characters – so memorable in Tolstoy – was outside his artistic range. Besides, the novel demanded a development of character, while the dramatic conflict which so often evaluated Gorky's protagonists in the short story was usually limited to the moment shown and did not need the light of the past on the present. Whereas structually the short stories – at their best – equalled those of Chekhov, Gorky's novels suffer considerably from an inability to bring them to a convincing end. It is notable that all his novels start brilliantly but they do not fulfill the promise inherent in the initial pages. However strange it may seem, this man who bequeathed to Russian literature new themes and a whole range of new types, had little *artistic* imagination. The striking vividness of his work is entirely due to the vividness of his experience and to that extrovert power of observation which seals the colours, words, sounds and even fragrance of every de-tail in the richness of its setting. These qualities will lead naturally to Gorky's strength – his genius as a memoirist.

Meanwhile, Gorky tried to solve his problems as a novelist by resorting to biographical narrative. He succeeded especially well if the characters he presented in a straight narrative against a background he knew were close to his heart. For, like in the sketches, and indeed in his life, Gorky gravitated towards the strong, self-reliant, dynamic men and women.

Gorky's first full-length novel, *Foma Gordeyev* (1899), was to be the story of 'a healthy, energetic man seeking scope for his energy'. In fact, the hero – though endowed with a spirit of rebellion – is a 'negative' type in the sense that he lacks driving power and a recognisable aim. Foma's conflict with his environment erupts merely in a long-winded speech which reveals his impotence as well as Gorky's own weakness. Foma's childhood and youth are interesting because his background of

Volga merchants is picturesque: the success of the novel was mainly due to the vivid painting of this unfamiliar setting and to the outstanding portraiture of the two rich merchants who dominate the scene, Ignat Gordeyev and Yakov Mayakin. The story of Ignat Gordeyev, Foma's father, a self-made man who, propelled by an immense energy and driving force rather than love of money, has created his barge-owning empire on the Volga, belongs to the best pages ever written by Gorky. His tremendous vitality finds an outlet both in business and debauchery: a man of 'broad nature', he does everything on a large scale. Mayakin, Foma's godfather, a more traditional type of merchant, is an authoritarian and ruthless man who can be benevolent provided this coincides with his interests. Gorky hates his calculating approach to life and disregard for human personality, but is fascinated by his strength of will and his 'positiveness'. The relationship between the two old merchants is excellently drawn, their differing natures being emphasised as well as the community of their class interests. Both Ignat Gordeyev and Mayakin are drawn from life, despite Tolstoy's assertion that everything in the novel was invented. Even the pathetic figure of Foma, who revolts against his father's wish to make of him a merchant and against Mayakin's eulogy of a future built on organised business lines in which every human being is merely a brick, is not invented: Foma draws too much on Gorky himself. His cry of protest is that of his begetter: 'Oh, you swine, what have you created? Not a new life and order, but a prison where you shackle human beings in chains . . . You destroy the very souls of men . . .' Like young Gorky, Foma has a critical mind and vague ideals, and like Gorky again, he talks too much. The novel suffers from verbosity, especially in its second part, and Foma disintegrates as a character because his creator is incapable of developing his potential psychological complexity. He is vitiated by an obvious, if confused, social purpose and by Gorky's inability to analyse a character from within.

The novels that follow *Foma Gordeyev* do not add much credit to Gorky the novelist despite some excellent passages. About *Three of Them* (1901), Gorky wrote himself to Bryusov: 'You have probably understood already that I simply cannot write.' A story about a young man who dreams of middle-class respectability only to be disappointed when he achieves it, it is complicated by a murder, a confession which is to be taken as an act of defiance, and a final suicide. Certainly the most disastrous of all Gorky's novels is *Mother* (1906–7). It was also his most influential work: considered in the Soviet Union as the prototype of the socialist–realist novel, its hero – a superhuman abstract industrial worker – served as a model for much Soviet fiction. The only partly acceptable figure in this black and white propagandist picture of pre-1905 revolutionaries inciting peasants and workers to rebellion, is the mother herself who comes to the revolutionary cause by way of maternal love and not through ideology. Her attitude to religion heralds the quest for God's kingdom on earth which is the theme of *Confession* (1908), the novel Gorky wrote in Capri while he was obsessed by the idea of 'God-building'. *Okurov Town* (1909) and its sequel *The Life of Matvey Kozhemyakin* (1910) are considered by some critics as Gorky's best novels. Mirsky says that of the two, the first one is better because it is shorter. An exceedingly gloomy picture of stagnant provincial life, it represents that side of Russia which Gorky called 'Asiatic' and which he knew so well.

After a break, Gorky turned again to novel-writing in the twenties. *The Artamonov Business* (1925), a story of three generations of a Russian merchant family, looks back in many respects to his first novel. More compact, it is also better structurally: it has a centre, the linen factory; and dealing with three generations over a period extending from the early 1860s to the Revolution, it pictures a changing society within a controlled framework. But the ending, like all Gorky's endings, is unsuccessful. Once again, the first part of the book is the best.

Gorky made one further attempt to portray a whole era of Russia – from the mid-1870s to 1917 – this time through the life of a liberal intellectual and his family. But the long four volumes of *The Life of Klim Samgin*, written between 1825 and 1936, are a dismal failure, unrelieved by either vivid description or successful secondary characters to offset the deliberate non-entity of his central character.

Gorky's fiction has clearly shown that his real talent consisted in describing and dramatically relating what he knew from experience. He had an uncanny gift for taking in almost simultaneously movement, speech and visual shape; and this coupled with a retentive and artistically selective memory made him achieve his greatest triumph in the recollections of his childhood and youth.

Gorky's autobiographical trilogy – *Childhood* (1913), *Among People* (1918) and *My Universities* (1923) – is notable as a record of the rich and colourful, if squalid life that happened to be the lot of young Aleksey, rather than as a work of self-revelation. For Gorky's theme is not really himself but the Russia that surrounded him. We are told of his experiences, we get some reaction to them, but there is no introspection, no attempt at explaining his innermost thoughts and feelings. This peculiarity was already evident in the portraiture of his early work: his characterisation always lacked the intensity of an inward struggle, the psychological interest of a Tolstoy or Proust. Besides, Gorky never liked to talk about himself. 'To speak of oneself is a subtle art – I do not possess it', he said once to Blok. His correspondence with Andreyev is even more significant in this respect. He never permitted anyone to touch on his personal life.

Thus it is not surprising that Gorky did not place himself in the centre of his autobiography. The selection of detail and events in *Childhood* is not related to their import on Gorky, the individual child; it is related to what any Russian child of the time and background sees around him and to what the visual memory of Gorky the writer recalls as significant. The stress is not on the first person narrator, but on the people around him coming and going in an ever-changing stream of impressions, on 'the stifling, pent-in atmosphere' of their 'savage Russian life'. This organisation of material is deliberate: Gorky recalls the 'abominations' he witnessed, for the truth 'must become known in its very roots, so as to be eradicated from man's memory, from his soul, from this whole dismal, shameful life of ours'. The subjectivity of the memoirs is in the reason why they were written. But Gorky is concerned with truth (a truth limited by what the child sees and hears), and the overall impression is remarkably objective, more so than in many of his early stories where the third person narrator often spoils the effect by philosophising.

Despite the squalor and evil depicted, the work as a whole is not oppressive. It is illuminated by Gorky's faith in humanity and in man's fortitude, by his conviction that the Russian man is sound and young in spirit and that he will surmount these abominations. After all, by the time Gorky was writing his memoirs, he knew that he himself had surmounted them.

Childhood is by far the best part of the trilogy. It contains a whole gallery of unforgettable characters connected with the Kashirin family, and especially the portrait of his grandmother which belongs to the great literary portraits of all time.

In the twenties, Gorky published his *Reminiscences* (1923), written at various stages of his life, and *Notes from a Diary* (1924), which contained portraits of some of his literary contemporaries, notably Tolstoy, Chekhov, Andreyev, Blok, and others. Together with the portraits of his autobiography, they are Gorky's highest achievement.

The fragmentary non-consecutive form of *Reminiscences of Tolstoy* (published in full in 1923) is brilliantly impressionistic, shifting from one perspective to another, the whole producing a finished, multi-faceted portrait of the great writer. Gorky's powers of observation make Tolstoy alive: 'He would come out looking rather small, and immediately everyone round him would become smaller than he'; inwardly, after his illness, the old man 'seemed to become lighter, more transparent'; 'at times he gives one the impression of having just arrived from some distant country . . . He sits in a corner tired and grey, as though the dust of another earth were on him'. Under 'his shaggy werewolf eyebrows' his sharp little eyes screwed up; he had 'a glance which at once took in anything new and instantly absorbed the meaning of everything'; his keen eyes saw everything through and through: 'in his two eyes Leo Nikolayevich possessed a thousand eyes.'

The detail is not only realistically life-like, but also extremely reveal-ing. Gorky not only observed, but also saw through Tolstoy. Unperturbed by the living legend of 'the saintly life of our blessed father, boyar Leo', he saw the man as he was, with all his weaknesses and his poses. He sensed his 'suspicious relations' with God, his 'violent resistance to some-thing . . . above him', his conceit and intolerance of 'a Volga preacher'; he remarked that Tolstoy 'always greatly exalted immortality on the other side of life, but . . . preferred it on this side'; he sensed his fox-like nature and didn't want to see Tolstoy as a saint: 'let him remain a sinner close to the heart of the all-sinful world'; through the façade of Tolstoy's peasant beard and 'democratic crumpled blouse' he saw 'the old Russian barin, the grand aristocrat', and admired 'this creature of the purest body . . . the noble grace of his gestures . . . the exquisite pointed-ness of his murderous words'.[3]

There is a certain resentment coming through the *Reminiscences* which contributes a certain tension – Gorky's resentment at being treated by Tolstoy as an object of ethnographic interest. In that sense, the *Reminiscences* also explore the relationship between the two writers.

A much greater sympathy with his subject can be felt in Gorky's *Reminiscences of Chekhov* written soon after Chekhov's death and published together with the Tolstoy memoir. But after the brilliant sketch of Tolstoy, Chekhov's portrait is disappointing and uneven. It may be that the very tenderness Gorky felt for Chekhov, and the sense of self-identification with his attitude towards philistinism prevented him from casting a more penetrating glance at his subject. Gorky's relation-ship with Chekhov comes out much more vividly in their corres-pondence.

Reminiscences of Andreyev (written in 1919, published in full in 1922), on the other hand, are superb. Despite Gorky's claim to have written them 'with no care for sequence or chronology', the long fragments are linked by a narrative which traces the love–hate relationship between the two writers from the day Gorky discovered the young Andreyev in 1898 and took him under his wing, until 1916 when, to avoid arguments, they could only speak of the past and recall their former close friendship. There is a surprising amount of self-revelation by Gorky – either direct ('I knew that I owed my success not so much to my inborn talent as to my capacity for work, my love of work') or indirect through the words of Andreyev ('A book to you is like a fetish to a savage,' or 'You speak like an atheist, but you think as a believer'). We get glimpses of Gorky's at-titudes to Andreyev's works, to Russian literature; we get a characteristic reaction to the Symbolists: 'Was it the time for "Symphony" when the whole of Russia was gloomily making ready to dance the *trepak*?' (the Symbolist poet Andrey Bely wrote two 'Symphonies' on the eve of the 1905 events). None the less, the revelation of Gorky is not overpowering, and his ideological differences with Andreyev don't distort his genuine sympathy for the man ('I never gave theories and opinions a decisive role in my relations to people').

If the portrait of Andreyev seems somewhat less perceptive than that of Tolstoy, the reason for it is probably the difference between the two subjects rather than any weakness of Gorky. The portrayal of Andreyev is remarkable in its mobility. 'He spoke hurriedly, with a dullish, booming voice, with a little crisp cough, his words slightly choking him, while he waved his hands monotonously as though he were conducting'. He was a wonderfully interesting talker: a word was enough to start him off, 'as though touched by an inner fire' he 'would instantly develop it into a scene, anecdote, character, story'. He leapt from one thought to another 'with a flexible movement of his soul, with the agility of an acrobat'. Andreyev seems alive: his quick repartee, his ability to catch a meaning in flight, the crisp dialogue – all these contribute to the sense of movement and excitement.

Gorky's narrative gift is superbly illustrated when he recounts the drunken night spent with Andreyev in St Petersburg. They met three girls in a cafe, one of them was a graceful Estonian: 'Her face was stony; she looked at Andreyev out of large, grey, lustreless eyes with eerie gravity while she drank a greenish venomous liqueur out of a coffee cup. It smelt of burnt leather'.[4] The scene in the girls' flat is told with beautiful restraint and yet with a feeling for drama and the grotesqueness of the situation. There is not a word of comment from Gorky, not a single reaction: as in the best pages of *Childhood*, he is merely a witness, 'the eyes that see it all', but he is there with Andreyev whom he feels he cannot leave alone.

The historian of Russian literature finds it hard to dissociate Gorky's writings from his personality, or at least from the person he chose to be. Seldom can art and life have been interpenetrated to such an extent.

Chronologically and symbolically, in his life and in his work, Maxim Gorky bridges two worlds. If his writings and his literary attitudes are firmly rooted in pre-revolutionary Russia, one cannot ignore his part in shaping certain aspects of Soviet culture.

Gorky's best work is retrospective. His romanticism as well as his realism, his awarenes of the spiritual stagnation of provincial life, his criticism of contemporary society, his compassion for the 'little man', his very understanding of literature as a moral and educational influence – all these can easily be traced to the nineteenth century. The difference is that his writings were a search for a means of transforming man into a hero of life, that beside compassion, he also felt anger and hate: 'We must hate suffering – that is the only way to destroy it.' His background and experience were different, and the needs of his time were different.

The timeliness of Gorky's appearance in literature can never be over-emphasised. Bunin resented his fame which, he felt, bore no relation to his talent. But one must remember the shock value of Gorky's buoyant mood on the grey and apathetic Russian literary scene of the 1890s when frustration and futility were beginning to lose their charm; the novelty of his types and settings for a literature based on a predominantly rural tradition; and the spirit of unrest and rebellion in Gorky's early work which coincided with the discontent and the mutinous temper of the uneasy pre-1905 Russian society. Gorky not only reflected the atmosphere of the moment: Chekhov maintained that he was instrumental in creating it.

His later popularity in the period of militant Communism has to be linked primarily with his belief in the potentialities of man, and his faith in work and education. It is easy to see why the new Soviet readers responded to Gorky's didacticism and optimism. Above all, by the late 1920s they regarded him as one of 'their own', although neither by birth nor by political allegiance was he really 'one of them'. He seemed to them a champion of their interests, a teacher to look up to. They did not appreciate then, perhaps, that the greatest service this so-called 'proletarian writer', who both in his person and in his art strayed from official doctrine, performed for their future benefit was to save the Russian Classics and preserve Russian culture. The image of Gorky as 'the founder of socialist literature' is based on myth, but his influence on the development of that literature has been real, both in positive and negative directions.

Gorky could not have foreseen the consequences of his social and civic commitment. He would not have approved of our view that the quality of his work was in inverse proportion to the degree and obviousness of its didacticism. We may prefer him for his retrospective pictures of a Russia he knew, for his portraits drawn from life, for his dramatic stories cut off from romanticism. We have seen that when he departed from actual observation, he more often than not failed. As he said himself, he felt things 'freshly', but did not know how to think. Permanently propelled by purpose and will, he was only too often obvious, repetitive and unrestrained. Sincerity and convictions cannot make up for artistic integrity.

And yet, ironically, to remember only the peaks of Gorky's work is to do him an injustice. He was more than a writer. A courageous and generous man, deeply devoted to the public good, he played a part in shaping the destiny of Russian literature, and thus linked the old with the new. Chekhov thought the time would come when Gorky's work would be forgotten, but not Gorky himself. For once, he was probably wrong. The essence of Gorky the writer was to combine the qualities of a witness with 'tendentiousness'. But had he been only a witness and not a judge, he would have been a greater writer.

NOTES

1 Undertones, indirect evocation of mood.
2 Excerpts from Gorky's letters to Andreyev are based on Miss Lydia Weston's translation (ed. Peter Yershov), (London, 1958).
3 The excerpts quoted are from the translation by S. S. Koteliansky and Leonard Woolf (London, 1920).
4 Translated by S. S. Koteliansky and Katherine Mansfield (London, 1922).

6 Pasternak

The Western intellectual tradition, particularly that of the post-Renaissance period, has constructed over the years and learned, at times uneasily, to live with an image of itself which it finds reflected in the life and work of countless figures of poets, artists, writers, philosophers and scientists. The alienated intellectual in this view is pictured as an individual who stands, in the final analysis, outside time and society, embodying specific values – moral and ethical absolutes which, by implication or design, pass judgement on contemporary society, politics and religion. That this view has always been open to debate and criticism, especially in the present century, does not in any way diminish the potency of this mythic image. Indeed, it could even be said to be one of its strong points.

A weighty case can be made for including the Russian intelligentsia within this general tradition. Though interpretation of the meaning of the term intelligentsia may vary, the very fact that the Russian word itself has gained such widespread currency elsewhere in Europe tends to support this case. Within the European intellectual tradition the Russian intelligentsia, by virtue of its unique historical circumstances, illustrates and symbolises the most extreme form of polarisation between the rights, duties and responsibilities of the citizen and the freedom of the speculative, imaginative or creative individual when confronted by the apparatus and values of the absolute state.

Against such a background the literary attitudes of Russian writers are far from being a ploy or a casually adopted stance. They derive from a structured, organic sense of mission. The writer is held to be the vessel of moral, spiritual and ethical values that may be frustrated but cannot be denied by an absolute secular power, whether Tsarist or Soviet. Such a stance inevitably has its tragic, heroic and prophetic aspects, in that it makes statements about human life which can only be judged outside strictly historical time. Taking past and present culture as its birthright, this stance points clear directions for future generations.

Robert Conquest, in one of the better short studies of the life and writing of the Russian writer Boris Pasternak (1890–1960), sums up the issue very well: '. . . in the great Russian writers and thinkers we find seriousness without portentousness, high aims without egotism, an un-selfconscious, un-selfregarding effort to attain complete candour and complete charity about the human being.'[1] In 1934 the Soviet cartoon team known under the acronymic title 'Kukryniksy' drew what was called, in conventional Soviet parlance, 'a friendly caricature' of Pasternak. They portrayed him as a sphinx. Many of Pasternak's readers may still share this view of a writer well known for the syntactical and imaginative complexity of his prose and poetry. Yet the Kukryniksy were less concerned with the enigmatic qualities of Pasternak's writing. They were poking fun at what, in the political circumstances of the time, they clearly felt was an outmoded and quaint literary pose, and they were drawing on one of Pasternak's own poems to do so.

The allusion is to the cycle of poems entitled 'Themes and Variations' in the collection of the same name – Pasternak's fourth in ten years – which had appeared in 1923. It is a commonplace in writing about Pasternak's poetry to point out the musical parallels in the content and form of his poetry, but in 'Themes and Variations', a cycle consisting of a 'Theme' followed by three 'Variations', this formal aspect cannot be ignored, particularly since it launches an image which was central to Pasternak's writing throughout the course of his life. Here are the opening lines of 'Theme':

> Cliff and storm. A cliff, a cloak, a hat.
> A cliff and Pushkin. That selfsame man who to this day
> Stands, eyes closed, and contemplates the sphinx as
> Something greater than the empty notions we propose
> Within our times: here, no blind surmises
> Of a cornered Greek, no riddle,
> But an ancestor . . .

In the Soviet Union of those years, with their self-proclaimed versions of 'the new man', of art as no more than a response to social demand, of collective responsibility and individual utility, or the sense of a break with the traditional pre-revolutionary culture and the founding of a new one, it was an easy matter for the Kukryniksy to raise a laugh at Pasternak's expense. Yet Pasternak was highly serious when he linked Pushkin and the sphinx – and, by implication, himself. This is one of his most telling symbols for the survival of art, poetry and truth against all the ravages of time. Traditionally, and conveniently for Pasternak's purposes, the sphinx stands in a desert. Seared by the sun, blasted and pockmarked by sandstorms down the ages, it dominates the wastes around it, an eternal and enigmatic memorial to the culture which produced it, yet so much the more imposing because that culture has long since passed away. The parallel can clearly be extended to Pushkin, arguably the outstanding Russian poet of the nineteenth century.

For Pasternak reading Pushkin was to confront not the riddle of the sphinx, not Oedipus, nor even Pushkin himself, still less the details of a life transformed into poetry. It was to be faced with the continuity of a tradition, with truths and values which are interwoven into the fabric of human history. These are Pasternak's poetic realm, and yet his own life has about it a fascination which tempts a reader to enquire further into why and how such a man came to adopt the stance he did.

Pursuing the reason inevitably leads in the first instance to biography, but the bare outline of the writer's life is merely contributory to an examination of Pasternak's literary attitude. As much as this was rooted in biography, it was also a product of the way he *experienced* life. His stance changed subtly with that experience and in accordance with his own evolution as a writer. If there could ever be a 'key' to Pasternak and his work it must lie in a subtle combination of these factors, weighed against the most careful literary and personal evidence. Both Pasternak's frankly autobiographical works, *Safe Conduct* and *An Autobiographical Essay*,[2] discuss such matters, but selectively, rather than discursively. What follows is an attempt to put both these books and the rest of Pasternak's writing into the kind of perspective which will explain the paradox of the sphinx, and if, initially, familiar factual matters predominate, it is because, as Pasternak himself said in an early poem:

> Life, like the silence of autumn,
> Is rich in detail.

Pasternak's life not only spans two centuries, but two epochs. Born into an intellectual Jewish family, he remained at all times a product of Moscow, deeply sensitive, spiritually receptive and close to nature. Not for him the estranged elegance of St Petersburg or the austere brittleness of its post-revolutionary offspring, Leningrad. Pasternak came to writing after music had taken prior claims. As a student at Moscow University between 1908 and 1913 he also had a brief brush with formal philosophy. The details of his friendship with the composer Skryabin, the agonising break with a promising musical career – 'straightforward amputation', as he later called it – as well as his brief interest in Neo-Kantian philosophy, are all discussed in Pasternak's autobiographies and need not be dwelt on at length here.

Pasternak's earliest writing attempts, poems, prose, translations and critical essays, date back to 1911. He published his first few poems in a small anthology in 1913, briefly engaging in the post-Symbolist Futurist controversies raging at the time by virtue of his membership in a Moscow literary group called 'The Centrifuge'. His first collection of poetry, *A Twin in the Clouds*, came out under the Centrifuge imprint in 1914, to a generally quiet, if not unfavourable reception. He wrote reviews and a couple of theoretical articles for Centrifuge and during the same period translated a play by the nineteenth-century German Romantic Heinrich von Kleist. He also completed a story entitled 'The History of a Contra-octave', which remained unpublished until recently. He took on work as a private tutor and then, exempted from military service at the outbreak of the First World War, he spent a considerable part of the period from 1915 to February 1917 in the Urals, working in a munitions factory. During these years he abandoned interest in the Centrifuge group and wrote poetry which eventually materialised as his second collection, *Above the Barriers*, in early 1917. He returned to Moscow after the February revolution, which he welcomed as a great emotional event. He spent the summer of 1917 writing most of the poems which were to establish his name, though they were not published immediately.

After the Bolshevik Revolution he was for a time associated with 'the Scythians', a loose-knit group of writers who welcomed the new order, but whose loyalties lay more with the Socialist Revolutionary Party. This gave Pasternak some opportunities to publish one or two short prose fragments, as well as the longer stories 'The Mark of Apelles' and 'Letters from Tula'. Work became more difficult to find during the civil war years and, though Pasternak refused to leave Russia, as his parents and sisters eventually did in 1921, he saw sufficient reason to grumble to Lunacharsky, head of *Narkompros*, the Bolshevik Commissariat of Education, in a letter in 1920:

> If the rations at the Literary Section's disposal have already been distributed, then perhaps new ones are envisaged. Perhaps there will be rations . . . which go unclaimed. Perhaps work of a literary or scientific nature can be allotted which will give me the right to this gift of life. Whatever the case, I petition for this right to be granted. I know that two grounds are stipulated. The existence of real need, let us say rather, want. I have demonstrated this as best I can . . . The other ground for receiving the academic ration is the artistic significance of the applicant and his talent . . .

Pasternak's situation as one of the old pre-revolutionary intelligentsia was, of course, precarious during these years, but he did manage to survive by translating for Maxim Gorky's ambitious World Literature series, which was a prestigious *Narkompros* scheme. When the New Economic Policy of 1921 brought better opportunities for publication, as well as an end to the paper shortages caused by the turmoil of revolution and civil war, Pasternak's third collection of poetry, *My Sister Life*, appeared in 1922. It contained basically those poems written in the summer of 1917 with some added material completed more recently, some of which had been recited in the 'poets' cafés' that were still a feature of Moscow life, even in the hardest times. Though Pasternak was to claim that the years 1919–24 were generally a lean time in terms of literary output, he wrote one long poem, another short story, 'Aerial Routes', his fourth volume of poetry, *Themes and Variations* (1923), and some fragments of prose which were clearly part of a larger design. He also married in 1923 and a son was born the following year.

In fact he was making enough of a reputation on his last two collections to be considered of interest by as perceptive a critic as Zamyatin, doyen of the literary world of what Trotsky termed the fellow-travellers. In 1925 a collection of his stories appeared, to general praise. He attempted a brief collaboration with his long-standing friend Vladimir Mayakovsky and the Left Front of Art (LEF) group of experimenting talents. The outcome of this was a final painful break with Mayakovsky, but his brief flirtation with LEF may have encouraged Pasternak to try his hand at what he called 'epic' poetry: 'Lieutenant Schmidt' and 'The Year 1905' were products of these years.

Towards the end of the 1920s two fairly comprehensive volumes of Pasternak's collected poetry were published and in 1929 there were plans for a full collection of his poetry and prose. The end of NEP, the beginning of the First Five-Year Plan and the ugly hectoring dominance of the Russian Association of Proletarian Writers (RAPP) that established itself over the Soviet literary world in that same year curtailed such a plan. Nevertheless, Pasternak managed to get *Safe Conduct*, his long prose introduction to the cancelled completed works, published in 1931. Its title is the best evidence of Pasternak's claim to individual treatment in an increasingly conformist environment.

Both *Safe Conduct* and a piece of fiction entitled *The Story* (a continuation of his 'novel in verse', called 'Spektorsky', which he had begun in 1924) now came in for some blistering criticism from RAPP writers and their supporters. So too did Pasternak's fifth volume of poetry, *Second Birth*, which appeared in 1932. His first marriage broke up in 1930. In the aftermath he decided to visit friends in Soviet Georgia during the summer of 1931, and his experiences there, coming as an exhilarating antidote to the nagging official criticism and personal tensions of previous months, led to a sweeping, affirmative collection of poetry that marked a considerable advance on even those well-thought-of previous collections. In a spirit of optimistic re-evaluation, Pasternak faced growing ostracism and difficulty in getting published by turning to translation more and more throughout the 1930s. He was drawn reluctantly into the business of the recently founded Union of Soviet Writers and spoke at its first Congress in Moscow in the summer of 1934. Amazingly, Pasternak survived the purges of 1936-8, perhaps by the great good fortune of having a recent collection of translated Georgian poetry to his credit, or for other reasons which have never been fully substantiated, though there is no question of any kind of compromise on Pasternak's part. He merely retired to the village of Peredelkino near Moscow, where he was to spend much of the rest of his life, and worked there on translations of European and Georgian poets, as well as on the first few chapters of a long novel which was taking shape. Even so, his health began to suffer from the strain of events.

When the war with Nazi Germany began in 1941 he was evacuated as a non-combatant to the Urals for a while, visited the front line briefly, then returned to Moscow in 1942. The war years saw the publication of two small collections of poetry, *Terrestrial Expanse* (1943) and *On Early Trains* (1945). His translation of Shakespeare's plays continued apace, and he even began his own play about the war years, *In This World*, which was never completed or published. His poetry came under renewed heavy criticism after the war during the phase of 'Zhdanovism', which gripped the Soviet Union at the beginning of the Cold War period and was a central phenomenon of Stalin's last, increasingly paranoid years. The criticism of Fadeyev, general secretary of the Writers' Union, may not have been as damaging to Pasternak as that of Zhdanov was to his great friend and colleague, the poetess Anna Akhmatova, but the mood of the time was crucial to Pasternak's artistic development and may also have contributed to the difficulties with his second marriage which began at the end of the war.

The trouble centred on his affair with Olga Ivinskaya, a translator, and it almost proved fatal to Pasternak, for in 1948, at the height of the 'anti-cosmopolitan' campaign, with its anti-semitic overtones, Ivinskaya was arrested and tortured to make her confess that Pasternak was implicated in a 'Zionist plot'. To her great credit, and to Pasternak's eternal gratitude, she refused to break and was eventually released in 1952. Their affair continued sporadically until Pasternak's death, though he never left his second wife Zinaida. His translation work continued during this period and he now settled to finish his long novel. Between 1946 and 1954 *Doctor Zhivago* was completed. After Stalin's death in 1953 the relaxation of tight controls and the period of relative uncertainty until the leadership question was resolved allowed some hope of publishing the novel, but all Pasternak's ambitions came to nothing in 1956 when, despite an officially approved project to bring out his complete works, *Doctor Zhivago* was rejected by the most likely publisher, the literary journal *Novy mir*. In quiet desperation Pasternak sent the manuscript abroad, where, in spite of pressure from the Writers' Union, it was published to widespread acclaim in 1957. In 1958 Pasternak was awarded the Nobel Prize for literature, which he felt constrained to refuse. He came under a storm of official criticism at home and was expelled from the Writers' Union. Meanwhile, the projected collected works had been cancelled, but the long introduction to it that Pasternak had prepared found its way abroad and was published in 1958 as *An Autobiographical Essay*.

Now ill and bitterly disappointed at the turn of events at home, Pasternak looked to the outside world for support. Another collection of poems, entitled *When the Sky Clears* and containing poems written after the completion of *Doctor Zhivago* was published abroad in 1959. Pasternak engaged in considerable correspondence with foreign admirers, scholars and writers, but still found a little time to work at a play which was to be called *The Blind Beauty*. Only one act of this play was complete[3] when Pasternak's final illness struck in the spring of 1960, and at the end of May he died, officially unmourned, but his funeral at Peredelkino was attended by thousands, the influential and the commonplace alike.

Such a bald outline of Pasternak's life loses its impact unless the bare facts are set against the broader historical realities of the period. Pasternak was in every sense a product of Moscow's pre-revolutionary intelligentsia, but his experience of two epochs makes him in equal measure a product of those same environmental forces which were at work on himself and all his contemporaries. His spiritual heritage was constantly being honed down against the history of his age. What is required here is what one writer has called a 'psycho-historic' view[4] of Pasternak.

Pasternak arrived early at the conviction that the significance of art was ultimately outside history. The reasons for this are by no means certain and cannot be examined in detail here. Speculation would suggest that Pasternak came to this conviction through his reading of Pushkin, Tolstoy, Blok and the Symbolists, the Scandinavian writers of the turn of the century and possibly the religious philosopher Fyodorov. Undoubtedly he was aware at an early age that the whole issue hinged on an understanding of immortality. It was a question which had exercised some of the neo-Kantian German philosophers to whom he had felt so attracted in his university days. He had spent the summer semester of 1912 at Marburg University in Germany, studying under Professor Cohen. Not long after his return to Russia, one of Cohen's younger colleagues, Lantz, published an article on 'Questions and Problems of Immortality', which appeared in the journal *Logos*, a publication issued by the Musaget group in Moscow under the aegis of the Symbolist Andrey Bely. In February 1913, at the height of the early Futurist controversies, Pasternak gave a lecture on 'Symbolism and Immortality', in which he contended, amongst other things, that all people when they die bequeath the sum total of their experience in symbolic form to what C. G. Jung would probably have termed 'the collective unconscious'. In sharp distinction to his famous contemporary Mayakovsky, Pasternak, product of a Jewish household and deeply receptive to Moscow's Orthodox religious traditions, felt no need to attack the cornerstones of religion. Indeed, he ended his life more quintessentially Orthodox than many a professed believer, even if there is no truth in the story of his baptism by a nurse at an early age. Pasternak was always at home in nature and comfortable within the intellectual sphere of Moscow life. Not that the blandishments of Petersburg passed him by. The turn of the century in both cities was a period marked by an upsurge of creative energy in literature, the theatre, the arts, architecture and politics, and Pasternak was very receptive to the infectious atmosphere of the time.

The intellectual climate of 1905, the year of abortive revolution, left its mark on the fifteen-year-old adolescent, and much of his writing would subsequently centre on the significance of that year. In particular he would focus on the ideas and writing of one of the intelligentsia's leading spokesmen, the Symbolist poet Alexander Blok. If Blok's version of the revolution in 1905 was discredited in some eyes by subsequent events, Pasternak preserved a lifelong fascination for the man and his work, nowhere better expressed than in his 'Two poems on Blok', written towards the end of his life .

Thus Pasternak grew to maturity in the Russia of pre-1914, the heyday of artistic experiment, a period of shattered political hopes for many, but an Indian summer for an apolitical, strongly independent scion of Moscow's intellectual *élite* like Pasternak. In *The Story*, he described the summer of 1914 as '. . . that last in a series of summers when life still impinged on individuals and when to love anything in the world was easier and more characteristic than to hate.' As a non-combatant during the 1914–18 war – he had a damaged leg following a childhood injury – he may have felt a certain guilt, which expressed itself in some of his later writing, but he never shared the jingoistic enthusiasm of some of his contemporaries, nor the outrage into which that enthusiasm quickly changed. In one piece of prose, 'Three Chapters from a Story' (1922),[5] he approaches the apocalyptic vision of Akhmatova's poem 'July 1914', but essentially his prose of the period is concerned with definition of self, the nature of poetry and inspiration, the duties of the poet, and, of course, love. His poetry experiments, and soon establishes, an idiom of minute observation of nature and the town in transition and movement, conveyed in richly sonorous metaphorical verse which largely bypasses the linguistic experimentations of his Futurist friends. Indeed, between 1909 and 1917 his experiences of three different literary groups – 'Serdarda', 'Lirika' and 'The Centrifuge' – established in him a lifelong aversion to any kind of close-knit association, an aversion which led him to quarrel with Mayakovsky and LEF in the 1920s and to avoid the Union of Soviet Writers as much as was humanly possible after 1932.

The poems of *My Sister Life* attempt to convey Pasternak's spontaneous joy about the February revolution – an essentially romantic feeling, to judge by Pasternak's subsequent description:

I dedicated *My Sister Life* not to the memory of Lermontov but to the poet himself as though he were living in our midst – to his spirit still effectual in our literature. What was he to me, you ask, in the summer of 1917? – the personification of creative adventure and discovery, the principle of everyday poetic statement.[6]

Since he was to speak of the Bolshevik Revolution in very different tones, both in his immediate response (in the incomplete 'Dramatic Fragments' and 'Dialogue') and subsequently in *Doctor Zhivago*, it is vital to examine Pasternak's view of 1917 more closely:

> In that famous summer of 1917, in the interval between two periods of revolution, it seemed as though roads, trees and stars held meetings along with the people. From one horizon to the other the air was in the grip of burning inspiration that stretched out for thousands of miles. It seemed like a personality with a name, it seemed to possess vision and a soul . . .

Somehow the Bolsheviks never revealed the spiritual exuberance Pasternak found in the work of Lermontov, and long before Stalin assumed control he had decided that the new age lacked 'vision and a soul'.

Some sense of his disappointment and dislocation is conveyed by the fragmentary nature of his work during the immediate post-revolutionary period. In spite of the formal coherence of *My Sister Life* and *Themes and Variations* it is clear that Pasternak was still feeling his way towards a definition of his position as a poet in the new age. If the figure of the sphinx goes a long way to resolving this inner tension, Pasternak's feelings were nowhere more aptly described than in his long poem 'The Lofty Malady' (1924).

Drawn for a brief period into collaboration with Mayakovsky, he soon tired of the internal wrangles within LEF. Pasternak's attempts to come to terms with the new age in the long 'epic' poems left him disappointed, and he fell back on what for him was always the vital material of inspiration – retrospective evaluation of personal experience. 'Spektorsky', *The Story* and *Safe Conduct* testify to this insistence of individual validity in an increasingly intrusive collective age. His occasional theoretical pieces began to develop the theme that the poet was both observer and judge of his era – in sharp distinction to the growing insistence by partisans of the new order that writing was merely a trade like any other and responded only to social demand. In one such short piece, in 1925, Pasternak wrote:

> The most important thing, I am convinced, is that art should stand at the extremity of its era, and not as its equal participant, that art's own stature and steadfastness should link it to its era, and only in that case will it be fit to recall its era to mind, giving the historian an opportunity to assume that such art reflected its age.

Safe Conduct, coming as a personal *profession de foi* at the height of RAPP's domineering intolerance, and with its powerful metaphorical plea for special treatment, sums up Pasternak's position with an irony made more telling by the fact that his own exemplar of the Poet is none other than Mayakovsky, who committed suicide in 1930, as much a victim of RAPP's hostility as of his own fatally divisive drives. Pasternak's revulsion against the increased organisation of literary affairs after 1932 was based in the first instance on reaction against the predominance within the Writers' Union organisation of what he considered untalented hacks. The purges only increased this revulsion when he saw careers made and lives destroyed in the name of an apparently mindless state terror. The feelings of isolation that had taken root in him during the 1920s now bore in on him as friends and colleagues disappeared and died. From the beginning of the revolution he had been depressed by the early deaths of men like Blok and Khlebnikov. The suicides of Esenin and Mayakovsky had come as a profound shock to him; now men like Mandelshtam were arrested and vanished. The same happened with the Georgian poet Tabidze. Soon another close friend, the Georgian Yashvili, committed suicide. He began to see himself as one of the few survivors of a former age and mentality; he was defending the values of that culture in an era of barbarity which was making an indelible mark on the country and the people he loved so intensely.

The inner conviction that Russia was being despoiled came to a head during the war against Hitler's Germany, though now at least he could feel that he shared Russia's common experience of those dreadful years, instead of standing outside, the appalled onlooker, as he felt he had done so much during the previous two decades. With the return to Stalinist rigidity after the war and the excesses of the Zhdanov years in 1946–8 he began to construe his own position as close to that of Hamlet – he had begun translating Shakespeare's play in the late 1930s. In official disgrace himself after the war, the times must have seemed 'out of joint' to Pasternak, for he still believed in the pre-revolutionary intelligentsia's values of humanity, individual freedom, religious humility, honesty, conscience and commitment to all-encompassing rather than expedient truths. It is this spirit which informs the whole of his novel *Doctor Zhivago.*

After the death of Stalin, and despite the scandal over *Doctor Zhivago* and the Nobel Prize affair, he managed, regardless of occasional ill-health, to come to terms in his own time with old age and international fame. His belief in the eternal value of truth in art remained unbending. For him beauty was a product of a suffering that led to resurrection and immortality of the individual through art and poetry, the ultimate synthesis of experience. This profoundly religious conception is, of course, exemplified in *Doctor Zhivago,* but it informed most of Pasternak's late poetry and brought out in him a combination of pagan awe and mystic humility in the face of life and nature that is characteristic of *When the Sky Clears*, with its metaphorical allusion to the light of new hope returning to the storm-battered post-Stalin world. This was the Pasternak who confronted fame in the late 1950s. It was also the Pasternak whom many Russians revered and respected as the sage of Peredelkino.

Though it has been stressed that Pasternak's literary attitude was essentially the product of his confrontation with an increasingly hostile environment, his evolution as a writer has its own internal coherence which justifies a more intimate perspective. Even such an acknowledged authority as Vladimir Markov makes only a tentative claim to place Pasternak in any specified literary context in terms of the influences discernible in his work: 'The sources of Pasternak's early poetry are complex and not entirely clear. Further investigations are needed, and these may disclose Annensky, Tyutchev and Blok in Pasternak's genealogy.'[7] Whatever influences are discoverable – and certainly the name of Rilke at least should be appended to the three Markov mentions – it is clear that Pasternak was essentially a post-Symbolist by inclination and philosophy. Close contact with the Futurists may have stimulated his desire for verbal play, but in the event he owes them little. His first collection, *A Twin in the Clouds*, is largely a blend of total, musical effects with glimpses into the world of nature inspired by love and passion. These latter motivating forces were to remain the basis of much of Pasternak's poetry up to 1930, and he developed his ideas on the nature of poetry, passion and 'power' [*sila*] into a complex, though coherent poetics in *Safe Conduct*.

As a prose writer his first influences must include the Austrian Rainer-Maria Rilke, whose *Die Aufzeichnungen des Malte Laurids Brigge* figured amongst Pasternak's earliest favourites, and Marcel Proust, whose *A la Recherche du Temps Perdu* evoked a sympathetic response in Pasternak in both its conception and style. In his prose, after brief ventures into a mode which owed much to the German Romantics Kleist and Hoffmann, Pasternak tended to favour specifically lyrical selective insights incorporated into a texture of past events as seen from a personal, developmental standpoint. The best example of this style is his story 'The Childhood of Lyuvers' (1918), which originated in the first chapters of a completed novel that Pasternak eventually rejected and destroyed. Pasternak also acknowledges in *An Autobiographical Essay* that the prose of Andrey Bely was a formative stylistic influence, perhaps not so much in specific emulation, but rather in that Pasternak profited from his example in experiments to try and cross the boundaries between poetry, prose and music.

In *Above the Barriers* Pasternak claimed to be consciously avoiding what he termed 'the romantic manner' – rather than impose on the world his own individual voice, as he saw Mayakovsky do, he was trying to transform himself into a passive agent through whom nature, with its wealth of spontaneous metaphor, would speak directly. If any distortion occurred – the word Pasternak used was 'displacement' [*smeshcheniye*] – then it was as a result of the poet's passionate emotional response. The cardinal principle in *Above the Barriers*, to use Pasternak's own phrase, was 'dithyrambic'. His songs of praise try to catch reality in its most vivid aspect – in motion or moments of transition, all couched in a language which attempts to capture the sensual joy of confronting the natural world and making a record of that confrontation. That Pasternak was more successful at first as a poet only serves to emphasise the gradual, initially less spectacular evolution of his prose: even *My Sister Life* is constructed as a 'novel' with 'chapters', and 'Spektorsky' is a long 'novel in verse' that finally spilled over into a prose format in *The Story*.

The triumphant mood of *My Sister Life* is tempered by its cautionary ending and gives way to the self-searching of *Themes and Variations* or 'The Lofty Malady'. Throughout the 1920s Pasternak felt an intense need to define himself as a poet in an essentially non-poetic age: perhaps the sense that he was playing a role is the source of his interest in the actor figure who appears so frequently in his prose and poetry. The turning-points in this inner struggle for identity are realised in 'Spektorsky', *The Story* and the confidently assertive *Safe Conduct*. They are resolved by 1934, when Pasternak could address the First All-Union Congress of the new Union of Soviet Writers in these terms: 'Do not sacrifice face for the sake of position . . . In the great warmth with which our people and government have surrounded us there is too great a danger of becoming a literary dignitary.'

'Spektorsky' and *The Story* are also illustrative of another of Pasternak's major concerns – the merging of prose and poetry. He understood both terms in a very individual, sometimes idiosyncratic manner:

> Poetry is prose, prose not in the sense of the collective impact of someone or other's prose writings, but prose itself, the voice of prose, prose in action and not in paraphrase. Poetry is the language of the organic fact, that is, the fact with vital consequences . . . it is precisely this, that is, pure prose in its natural tension, which gives us poetry.

In an essay published in 1922 Pasternak had called prose and poetry two inextricably linked 'indivisible poles' of artistic expression. In *Safe Conduct* he was even more explicit: 'Poetry, as I understand it, takes place in the last resort within history, in co-operation with real life.' In an earlier chapter in the same book he states categorically, 'We drag the everyday into prose for the sake of its poetry. We draw prose into poetry for the music of it.' Whatever Pasternak's concerns with prose and poetry at this time, there is little doubt that *Second Birth* was a more dramatic watershed in his poetic evolution. If 'Spektorsky', *The Story* and *Safe Conduct* resolved the question of poetic identity in Pasternak's mind, they still did not point the way to any future development. In the poem 'Waves' in *Second Birth*, scrutinising his own past at a vital stage in his emotional life and expressing some of the guilt he was feeling at the breakdown of his first marriage to Yevgeniya Lur'ye, Pasternak advanced the argument that the complexity of his previous style was a mistake and stated that from now on he would seek a simpler expression for his thoughts:

> In kinship with everything existing, assured of
> And acquainted with the future in our daily round
> It's impossible, in the end, not to plunge
> Into unprecedented simplicity, as if into heresy
>
> And we shall not be spared
> If we do not conceal it
> People need it more than anything else
> Yet the complex is more comprehensible to them.

This change in emphasis was not without internal suffering, as a reading of the poem 'Oh, had I but known that this is how it is'[8] from the same collection will demonstrate, yet Pasternak now disavowed much of his previous writing and began work on a novel about 1905 and the years preceding 1917. Though this was never finished or published in full it was the first attempt at what was eventually to grow into *Doctor Zhivago*.

The theme of prose in poetry and poetry in prose which had occupied Pasternak's attention in previous years now led him to examine the whole concept of realism, perhaps in reaction to the interminable debates of the 1930s about Socialist Realism. He had acknowledged in *Second Birth* that stylistic density did not constitute successful realism and yet he still believed fervently in the openness to life and nature which had found their best expression in *My Sister Life*. What he sought now was a combination of 'unprecedented simplicity' and this sense of almost vulnerable receptivity which could only be experienced and monitored by the sensitive, gifted individual, and yet could, by a technical sleight of hand involving no malicious deception, be conveyed to others in richly simple prose. He found what he sought in the writing of models as diverse as Shakespeare, Verlaine, Pushkin, Chekhov, Dickens and Blok. He also found it in the music of Chopin (a reflection, no doubt, of his own previous attachment to the composer Skryabin). For Pasternak, such 'realism' was a combination of total openness to inspiration, closeness to nature and other men, a recognition of predestination and the actor's role in art, and an uncluttered lucidity of style.

From the time of *Second Birth* his experiences began to make more sense in the light of these views and, with the stories of Christ and Hamlet firmly embedded in his creative consciousness, he began to see his own destiny in clearer terms. In a life of joy tempered by suffering and guilt he turned to a firm belief in resurrection through fulfilment in an art which faithfully recorded the writer's constant awe of nature and its recurring cycles. In his eyes the artist was bound by duty and fate to play a fore-ordained and foredoomed role as naturally as the best actor, to recreate in his own person the eternal virtues of the great figures of the past and to distill his experiences into prosaically simple poetry and poetically simple prose. Out of these convictions the novel *Doctor Zhivago* grew naturally as the crowning work of Pasternak's life.

The unstated inner promptings which led Pasternak to write in his characteristic manner and to take the direction he did in his development as a writer have not been examined in depth by many commentators. The work of Freud and Jung has drawn attention to the enormously varied subconscious drives which can express themselves in the output of writers and artists and it would be misleading to suppose that Pasternak's subconscious processes were not discernible in his work. A brief consideration of some of the undercurrents running through his writing seems appropriate at this point, though this is only a perfunctory attempt to bring out the most significant ones.

Pasternak was an eldest son who had held his father, Leonid Osipovich Pasternak, an artist, in great respect. As late as 1934 Pasternak wrote to him. 'It is enough for me to remember you . . . to shrink back from the comparison. You were a real man . . . a Colossus, and before this image I am a complete nonentity and in every respect still a boy.'[9] There is no question that Pasternak grew up in a loving and affectionate family environment, but it is quite apparent that his mother was a fundamental influence on his development during his early years. She herself gave up a promising career as a concert pianist to devote herself to her children, and much of her thwarted ambition and talent seems to have been projected onto her eldest, musically gifted son. This may help to explain Rosa and Leonid Pasternak's consternation and disappointment when Boris abandoned the idea of a musical career in 1909. For a time they entertained hopes that he might become a doctor. When it emerged that this was not to be Pasternak's new choice either, the study of philosophy at Moscow University was nevertheless warmly supported, especially by his mother, whose savings enabled Pasternak to travel to Marburg in 1912 and spend the summer there and in Italy. The family was far from satisfied that Pasternak then went on to try and make his living as a writer and private tutor after he graduated from university in 1913. Even if there was no outright conflict over his plans for a career as a writer, Pasternak still demonstrated from an early age a desire to be independent that was to manifest itself time and again in his later life in his dealings with literary groups, the Writers' Union and the Soviet State.

In *An Autobiographical Essay* there is a particularly revealing passage concerning Pasternak's attitude to his parents:

> I was filled too early, and for my whole life, with a compassion for women so terrible it was hardly to be borne, and with a still more anguished pity for my parents, who would die before me and whom it was my duty to deliver from the pains of hell by some shining deed, unheard-of and unique . . .

Here Pasternak's drive to be genuinely original can be seen – the same reason which led him to abandon music and philosophy, the motive behind his reaction against the influence of Mayakovsky in his own early verse and which soon led to the desire to be totally independent and self-sufficient in his art. It may also be the origin of his strong sense of mission in life, which expressed itself so clearly in the St George-like figure of Yury Zhivago.

The sources of Pasternak's 'terrible compassion' for women are less clear, but generate speculation about his psychological make-up. Jung defined the growth of the individual's personality as a process of 'individuation', in which the male and female aspects of the psyche (the *animus* and the *anima* – most closely identified with the person's parents) are gradually recognised, conflicts between them are resolved and they are then assimilated into a personality in balance. Those personal aspects of the *animus* and *anima* can be further reinforced at a deeper level by material drawn from archetypes contained in the subconscious mind and relating to the so-called 'collective unconscious' – the supra-personal residuum of all significant cultural experience. In *An Autobiographical Essay* Pasternak makes another noteworthy admission in this context:

> At moments, at the dawn of life, the only time when such folly is conceivable, I imagined that in some former period I had been a girl and that I could regain this earlier, more gracious, more fascinating personality by pulling in my belt so tight that I almost fainted. At other times I thought I was not my parents' son but a foundling whom they had adopted . . .

Here Pasternak is alluding in retrospect to just such an individuation process. Identifying most strongly with the feminine side of his make-up, he seems to seek an explanation in a form of reincarnation. The figure of Zhenya Lyuvers in his story 'The Childhood of Lyuvers' displays exactly this 'more gracious, more fascinating personality' which he unconsciously sought. The story is a study of 'an excess of sensitivity' and the manner in which a person endowed with it comes to terms with the world around. Pasternak's early conviction that he was a foundling surfaces later in his unfinished novel of the 1930s, where the central figure, Patrikii, is an orphan, and Yury Zhivago is likewise orphaned at an early age and is brought up by kindly relatives and friends.

However, it is Pasternak's attitudes to women which are most revealing. A profound compassion for two different kinds of women expresses itself most forcefully in the figures of Sashka the prostitute and Anna Tornskjøld in *The Story*, and several of his other stories deal with a love relationship and the consequences this can have for a poet or an artist. Woman as a love-object becomes a Muse-like figure in 'The Mark of Apelles', 'Letters from Tula', *The Story* and 'Spektorsky'. Yet Pasternak's experience with the women in his life was ambivalent and this very ambivalence led to considerable guilt on his own part, especially over the upsets his personal conduct produced in both his marriages. This guilt spilled over into the character of Yury Zhivago, in one of whose poems it is clearly stated that 'The urge to part is uppermost . . .'[10]

Love and passion were two interrelated concepts for Pasternak in his attitude to women, but they were also present in his work in a wider sense, in that he drew much of his inspiration from his profound love of life and nature. Here there is no question of sublimated carnal desire, rather a strong sense of kinship which led him to call life his sister, instead of a lover. It is probably no coincidence that many of the elements to which Pasternak was most strongly drawn in his life and writing have the feminine gender in Russian: life, poetry, love, passion, nature, the soul, water, earth, storm, the church and Russia herself — so often referred to as 'mother' by Russians past and present. So for Pasternak Russia seemed to embrace all those elements in an archetypally maternal or sisterly sense and they were expressed by him on one level as intimate songs of praise, in much the same way that Blok in his time had written of the Unknown Lady, Divine Wisdom. On another level these same elements are expressed in depth in the figure of Lara in *Doctor Zhivago* and Yury's lifelong love for her.

Doctor Zhivago, the book which could justifiably be called Pasternak's major work, was once referred to by him as 'my flesh and blood',[11] a term which carries overtones of the communion sacrament. On the most basic level it is clearly the product of a lifetime, in the sense that Pasternak could hardly have attempted another project of such scope, imaginative depth and insight while still drawing on a lifetime's personal experience ranging over a broad historical period. It is perhaps indicative that *The Blind Beauty*, the play on which Pasternak was engaged at the end of his life, is not only a departure in historical period, but also a change of genre. Statements Pasternak made about *Doctor Zhivago* in his last years suggest that it was intended as an ambitious synthesis of confession, testimony and bequest. He told Olga Carlisle, for instance, when she visited him in early 1960:

When I wrote *Doctor Zhivago* I had a feeling of immense debt towards my contemporaries. It was an attempt to repay it. This feeling of debt was overpowering as I progressed with the novel. After so many years of just writing lyric poetry or translating, it seemed to me that it was my duty to make a statement about our epoch – about those years, remote and yet looming so closely over us. Time was pressing. I wanted to record the past and to honor in *Doctor Zhivago* the beautiful and sensitive aspects of the Russia of those years. There will be no return of those days . . .[12]

Thus the question of form is of paramount importance in passing any overall judgement on *Doctor Zhivago*. To consider it simply as a realistic historical novel incorporating a tragic love story is ingenuous. Pasternak occasionally referred to *Doctor Zhivago* as *roman v proze*, which could be translated equally well as 'novel' or 'romance in prose'. The term is reminiscent of some nineteenth-century writers' concern to break the boundaries of mere genre by giving their work a specific, but paradoxical label: Pushkin's *Eugene Onegin* ('a novel in verse') and Gogol's *Dead Souls* ('a poem') are the two best-known examples of this. By calling *Doctor Zhivago* a prose romance Pasternak was implying that it should also be read as a poetic rhapsody. His mature style of 'unprecedented simpicity' was calculated to make such an interpretation possible. Yury Zhivago even records a similar desire himself: 'It had been the dream of his life to write with an originality so covert, so discreet as to be outwardly unrecognisable in its disguise of current, customary forms of speech . . .'[13] Pasternak was, of course, only too aware of the debt which any Russian writer owes to Tolstoy. He was anxious that there should be no confusion between *Doctor Zhivago* and the Tolstoyan novel, with its elegant procession of time and omniscient author. In 1959 he explained in a letter that in *Doctor Zhivago* he had tried to move away from the limitations imposed by Tolstoyan realism. He had wanted to get away from what he called 'the iron chain of causes and effects . . . the incontestable doctrine of causality',[14] where logical process dictates action. Pasternak therefore tries to construct a framework that sidesteps some of the conventional elements of the novel: time, historical event, accurate chronology and strictly orchestrated story development are played down. Instead, he highlights character and philosophical content, building a lattice of poetic descriptive passages, short scenes and significant encounters which he links together not as chapters, but as 'units' or 'parts'. Many of the apparent structural weaknesses of the book are a result of Pasternak's desire to show that destiny and chance still play a fateful role in the affairs of men, just as they did in classical tragedy. The book has an internal impetus which relies on the spiritual force of personalities, events and relationships. It moves, as he said in a letter to a friend, 'in the world of Malte Laurids Brigge', once more paying a debt to the influence of Rilke.

In both structure and style Pasternak has also followed the pattern of two men whom he much admired: Dickens and Shakespeare. Schematically, *Doctor Zhivago* has something in common with *A Tale of Two Cities*, while its characters cover a wide range of social type in the manner of Shakespeare's major historical plays. The tragic story of Yury Zhivago is presented against a setting of a revolutionary era, in two separate locations, Moscow and the fictitious town of Yuryatin. Much of Shakespeare's realism, to say nothing of his popular appeal, derives from the personalities and language of his comic and demotic characters. Pasternak saw that it was possible for high tragedy to be tempered and intensified by a grave-digger, a gatekeeper, a court jester or a Falstaff and he was encouraged to incorporate similar characters in *Doctor Zhivago* to give it greater social and linguistic depth.

However, Pasternak's real innovation is the novel's symbolic plane which underpins the more conventional novelistic apparatus of story, plot and character. Here, philosophy takes second place. The symbolism of *Doctor Zhivago* has been discussed at length by numerous commentators, though not all have been able to agree what part the various symbols play. Pasternak himself was more reticent about the symbology of *Doctor Zhivago*, perhaps because the matter was so close to his own private life, but on the symbolic level his book is clearly designed as a latterday hagiography, like one of the 'Saints' Lives' which were such a vital part of the Russian Orthodox Church's literary traditions in earlier centuries. In Yury Zhivago's case the great spiritual 'feat' (the *podvig* of Russia's saints) is his poetry, and Pasternak wanted to demonstrate how the life of a man with a profound spiritual outlook can be shaped by his experience and beliefs until he can produce an artistic record which transcends the limitation of historical time and human mortality. Instead of returning to the monolithic, but aloof, image of the sphinx which he had used in the 1920s, Pasternak employs a symbolism which is closer to the spiritual patrimony of Russia and Europe – that of Christianity. Yury Zhivago's personal life is described in its essentials and given an impressionistic coloration which brings it close to the ikonic styles of Orthodoxy. Starting out in the conviction that Yury was an exemplary man – and giving proof of it in his poems, which form an integral part of the book, a chapter, rather than an appendix – Pasternak traces the key experiences of Yury's life, the main influences on the development of his personal philosophy, and sets them all in a historical period whose dominant tone only serves to offset what Pasternak considered to be the vital elements in that life. Proceeding from the view that Yury Zhivago becomes progressively more estranged from the purely historical side of Russian life, particularly after the Bolshevik Revolution and the civil war, he shows that such a man can be seen first as a tortured Hamlet figure, a development of the superfluous man of nineteenth-century Russian literature, but that the course of his life takes on a new significance if his trials are seen to parallel the life of Christ. The power which sustains Yury throughout is a belief in the life-force which moulds all human life, emanating from God and omnipresent in nature. This life-force is immeasurably greater than anything materialistic man can devise or understand and it mocks his efforts at control, but for the individual who recognises its existence, accepts and respects it, it brings the reward of insight, joy and fulfilment. This is why Yury's name is based on the Russian word *zhivoy* – 'alive, vital'. It gives the hagiography a further dimension by emphasising that life will always overcome death. Yury himself believes this and considers himself predestined to affirm that this is the case in his writing: '. . . art has two constant, two unending preoccupations: it is always meditating upon death and it is always thereby creating life.'[15] The regenerative power of nature and the life-force are recorded by Yury in his poetry, which draws its spiritual potential from his recognition that man can emulate Christ by living according to his destiny, no matter how this sets him in contention with historical processes. In this sense he also represents the saintly figure of St George – Yury is the Slavonic form of the name – who fights the dragon of evil forces and triumphs.

Clearly, *Doctor Zhivago* is a deeply Christian document in the Orthodox tradition and it is this that led to its rejection in the Soviet Union. However, it is only anti-Soviet or anti-revolutionary to the extent that it rejects any system devised by man which claims to answer all questions of life or death. *Doctor Zhivago* draws on religious traditions which go back to old Muscovy and by this token it is a profoundly Russian, rather than a Soviet book. It is Pasternak's record of his understanding of a period of Russian history and it could be said to be an answer to Tolstoy and his theory of history, as well as a sequel to his novel *Resurrection*. It is Pasternak's testament to a generation whose culture and values were rejected and destroyed by the revolution, but it is at the same time an affirmation of his belief in the power of resurrection in the life of man, art and Russia.

The paradox is that the poems of Yury Zhivago were written by Pasternak and derive as much from his own experience as from that of his fictional character. Many of the Zhivago poems were comments by Pasternak on his relationship with Olga Ivinskaya, and it is possible that the 'Hamlet' poem which opens the Zhivago cycle was already written in 1946 before the book was planned in its final form. This suggests that Pasternak was writing a parable of his own experience in the figure of Yury Zhivago – the views that Yury expounds certainly coincide with Pasternak's, even if the events of his life are dissimilar.

Yury Zhivago could be criticised as a self-centred, amoral man who at one time or another betrays all the women he loves, abandons his children and his career, sets his face against the most significant historical developments of his time and produces a mere handful of poems to justify his actions and his faith in his artistic gift. His great love for Lara is sustained by the way he identifies her with Russia and it is she alone who recognises in him the Christ-like qualities which he knows he possesses. Yury loses everything, voluntarily or involuntarily, including at the last, his life – he dies young, in 1929, at the beginning of Stalin's undisputed rule. Pasternak would have us judge Yury by the poems attributed to his pen. He believes that, like the sphinx, they will withstand the ravages of time and survive with their message intact into another era, since, as Yury says: '. . . every work of art, including tragedy, witnesses to the joy of existence.'[16] In the light of both Pasternak's and Yury's convictions about poetry – 'I was born to make life simple . . .'[17] – the Zhivago poems provide the key to the book: poetry and prose complementing each other.

The cycle opens with a poem in which an actor playing the role of Hamlet uses the words of Christ at Gethsemane: 'If it be possible, Father, let this cup pass from me,' and ends with a descriptive poem about Christ in Gethsemane. If the link is still not clear, there are two poems about Mary Magdalene to make the point. That the poems are intended as a cycle is emphasised by the inclusion of several poems on the seasons and natural phenomena, with the great Orthodox feast of Easter celebrating the triumph of the resurrection over death especially prominent. There is also a poem entitled 'Fairy-tale', in which St George kills the dragon and rescues the maid, thus drawing a parallel with Yury's redemption of both Lara and Russia from evil by his sacrifices in the name of art. The Zhivago poems are an abundant proof of Pasternak's convictions, voiced through his protagonist. Life for them both is a priceless gift, to be received in gratitude, not grabbed, controlled and squandered. The cycles of nature set the rhythm of human life and prove that death is followed by renewal – spring succeeds winter and autumn and Easter is therefore man's most significant festival, since it recognises the resurrection of life in nature in the symbolic form of Christ's triumph over death. Man is privileged to witness the life-force in action within himself and in the natural world around him. The life-force expresses itself in its most tangible and miraculous form in the love and passion between man and woman. Both Yury and Pasternak felt themselves predestined to make a record of these truths for their fellow men. While they witnessed the history of their time and its tragedies they still represent qualities and insights into the human condition more lasting than those of politics, rationality and materialism.

Like Yury Zhivago, the literary creation who best represents the full spectrum of Pasternak's views on art and history, Pasternak remained something of a paradox all his life: a man outside his time but deeply integrated in it, alienated from Soviet Russia yet unable to leave it, frowned on by the state but revered by many of his ablest contemporaries, the grand old man of Peredelkino who in his time seems even to have puzzled Stalin, the representative of the pre-revolutionary intelligentsia who survived into the Khrushchev era, the Moscow Jew who became an Orthodox Christian believer. It seems that with all his talk of passion and love, nature, life and its poetry, predestination and sacrifice, he may simply have been just a twentieth-century version of nineteenth-century Russia's superfluous man – to use Ezra Pound's description of himself, 'born in a half savage country out of date'. On the other hand, his writing remains, open to the test of time. Perhaps it would be fitting for his great friend and admirer Anna Akhmatova to have the last word, in a poem dedicated to Pasternak:

> And the whole world was his inheritance,
> Yet he could share it with us all.

NOTES

1 R. Conquest *The Courage of Genius* (London, 1961) pp. 16–17.
2 The Russian text of both these autobiographies can be found in Boris Pasternak, *Sochineniya* (Ann Arbor, Michigan, 1961) vol. II.
3 A translation of the surviving draft of the play was published in Italy in 1969. A Russian text was printed in London in 1969, and in 1972 the Soviet periodical *Prostor* also published Pasternak's play.
4 The term is used by Walter Abell in his *The Collective Dream in Art* (New York, 1957).
5 'Tri glavy iz povesti' was not included in the Michigan *Sochineniya*. It first appeared in *Moskovskiy ponedel'nik*, 12 June 1922, pp. 2–3. (For further details and a translation see the present author's 'One and the same life', *Teoria e Critica*, no. 1 (1972, pp. 71–109).
6 Letter to Eugene Kayden, 22 August 1958. See *Boris Pasternak, Poems* (Ann Arbor, Michigan, 1959) pp. vii–ix.
7 V. Markov, *Russian Futurism* (London, 1969) p. 238
8 'O znal by ya, chto tak byvayet', *Bib. poeta* (1965) p. 371.
9 See Lydia Pasternak-Slater's Introduction to *Boris Pasternak, Fifty Poems* (London, 1963).
10 ['*Sil'ney na svete tyga proch'*], 'Ob'yasneniye', *Doctor Zhivago*, Russian edition, (Rome: Feltrinelli, 1957) p. 539.
11 Card to R. Schweitzer, 12 August 1958, in *Freundschaft mit Pasternak* (Vienna–Basel, 1965) p. 31.
12 Carlisle, O.; 'Three Visits With Pasternak', *Paris Review*, No. 24, 1961, p. 55.
13 *Doctor Zhivago* (London, 1958) p. 430.
14 Letter of 22 May 1959. *Encounter*, Vol XV, No. 2, August 1960, p. 4.
15 *Doctor Zhivago* (London, 1958) p. 95.
16 Ibid., p. 444.
17 Ibid., p. 408.

7 Solzhenitsyn

In examining the writing of Boris Pasternak an attempt was made to demonstrate in what relationship his artistic stance stood to the Western intellectual tradition, and in particular, how it had grown organically out of the ninteenth-century traditions and values of the old Russian intelligentsia. Pasternak's literary attitudes, his artistic *raison d'être*, were a logical extension of this view of himself as a poet with an individual vision of the world, a duty and a responsibility to bear witness to history in a style and manner which would assert eternal values in as fresh and meaningful a way as possible.

Solzhenitsyn has become more of a *cause célèbre* even than Pasternak was in his time, and there are several reasons for this. In Pasternak's case, wide international fame came only in his last years, after the publication of *Doctor Zhivago*. If before he was only known abroad amongst a small circle of dedicated experts, then after 1958 his reputation was assured by the controversy which raged over this, his most profound and lengthy book. Yet, as has already been pointed out, Pasternak was essentially a witness to, rather than a participant in, the events of Russian history to which he alludes and which form the backdrop to the personal story of Yury Zhivago. It is in the nature of our intellectual and artistic heritage – to say nothing of our mass media – that in the West the champion of individual freedom is picked on much more readily than a retiring, reticent and religious poet–novelist. One could perhaps compare the Western response to a writer like Pasternak with the treatment in recent years of men like Beckett, Hesse or Borges. Their reputations are hard won. Solzhenitsyn, on the other hand, has been 'news' from the outset. His writing has aroused continuous interest, and since he has been extremely productive, that interest has rarely flagged. His name has constantly cropped up in the literary press or on the tongues of literary commentators, both in the West and the Soviet Union – at least, until he became *persona non grata* there. Latterly, as his views have become more and more outspokenly critical of the Soviet system, his political significance has begun to overshadow his immense literary gifts and achievements.

Pasternak lived through the whole Stalin period as an established writer and poet, and certainly political circumstance helped to stifle his fame until the end of his life. Solzhenitsyn, on the other hand, achieved an international reputation with the first story he published, *A Day in the Life of Ivan Denisovich*, in 1962. His fame was earned in terms of the bitter experience which went into his writing and which came to form the core of his artistic attitude, but it was in some ways fortuitous in terms of the political circumstances which permitted such a remarkably potent critical voice to reach such a wide audience so immediately.

Comparisons may be odious, and literary ones perhaps especially so, but the differences between Pasternak and Solzhenitsyn are so instructive that they provide a convenient starting-point for a fuller consideration of Solzhenitsyn's writing and literary significance. Pasternak was and remained all his life a product of Moscow's pre-revolutionary intelligentsia. He was a published poet before 1917 and he, like many of his generation, came to terms with the new age from the standpoint of the old, though he was one of the few to write about it in this way, and one of the very few of those who did to survive the Stalin period. Alexander Isayevich Solzhenitsyn is, by contrast, a product of the Soviet era who bases his literary philosophy firmly on the right and duty of the writer to criticise, record and establish truths, and then point morals. As he is reported to have told an interviewer in 1967:

> By intuition, and by his singular vision of the world, a writer is able to discover far earlier than other people various aspects of social life and can often see them from an unexpected angle . . . It is incumbent upon a writer to inform society of all that he is able to perceive and especially all that is unhealthy and a cause for anxiety . . .[1]

It is this critical side of Solzhenitsyn's attitude which sets him apart from so many of Soviet Russia's accepted writers. Though he is a product of the Soviet period chronologically, his view of the writer is substantially the same as that of the Russian nineteenth century. Where the writer in the Soviet Union has been expected to affirm and encourage, Solzhenitsyn has preferred to analyse, evaluate, and where necessary, condemn.

Unlike Pasternak, he is not temperamentally inclined, nor so obliged by political pressure, to be reticent or elliptical in his writing. This difference is as much one of background as it is of personality and literary preference. Pasternak was a trained musician and dreamy philosopher who grew up in a privileged household. Solzhenitsyn's personal background is considerably harsher, and his down-to-earth, no-nonsense approach is backed up by a scientific training which tends to the analytic, empirical and deductive side of man's intellectual nature. When Solzhenitsyn turned to literature it was as a means of recording his

E

evaluative judgements, not, as in Pasternak's case, his poetic insights. Where Pasternak vacillated, Hamlet-like, over his duty to bear witness and write the truth, Solzhenitsyn openly confronts situations of which he disapproves, citing the moral duty of a writer, about which he clearly has no doubt. His letter to the Secretariat of the Soviet Writers' Union is as good a case in point as any to illustrate this, since it confronted the whole question of censorship and the consequences of censorship for Soviet literature:

> Literature cannot develop in between the categories of 'permitted' and 'not permitted', 'about this you may write' and 'about this you may not'. Literature that is not the breath of contemporary society, that dares not transmit the pains and fears of that society, that does not warn in time against threatening moral and social dangers – such literature does not deserve the name of literature; it is only a façade. Such literature loses the confidence of its own people, and its published works are used as wastepaper instead of being read.'[2]

Pasternak, a poet by temperament, turned to the wider horizons of the prose genre to paint a picture of his personal view of poetry in life. He may have extended the limits of the novel in *Doctor Zhivago*, but in doing so he remained a poet. Solzhenitsyn has rarely turned his hand to verse. He seeks the truth amongst men and their activities in a social environment and a political context. Yet paradoxically, because Pasternak grew out of and in time evolved away from the milieu of the nineteenth-century Russian pre-revolutionary intelligentsia, Solzhenitsyn now stands closer in many ways to the traditional values of Tolstoy, Dostoevsky, Chekhov, Pushkin and Leskov. He has turned back to rediscover these traditions for his own, Soviet generation. Pasternak nurtured and developed them without the need for discovery.

Solzhenitsyn comes closer to these traditions on several counts. First, he is firmly rooted in the Russian experience. He is not a capital city intellectual for whom the Russian landscape is a constant source of awe. He admires it and understands it, but does not, like the later Pasternak, worship it. Nor does Solzhenitsyn see art as some hermetic category beyond the ken of men or society, for him literature and art are tied firmly to the community and its everyday life. Like several of the great figures of the past century in Russia, Solzhenitsyn is essentially 'prosaic', where Pasternak was 'poetic', despite his attempts to bridge the gap between prose in poetry and poetry in prose. Solzhenitsyn is primarily a realist in the Tolstoyan tradition, whereas Pasternak tried to push the limits of the novel beyond the traditional. Perhaps the only point at which Solzhenitsyn and Pasternak meet is on the question of religion, and even here there are differences in both men's beliefs which belie any deep similarity. Solzhenitsyn appears to value the Orthodox religion for its spiritual strength and its affirmation of the living virtues of Russia. While Pasternak would probably not have disagreed with this view, his religion was less canonical than mystical. He drew on Orthodoxy for its profound symbolism, but he found God in nature to be another word for life itself. Solzhenitsyn's view of religion has developed over the course of his work and he now seems to believe in a traditional God, austere and aloof, guiding the lives of men, but rarely an inspiration to their creative desires.

Unlike Pasternak, Solzhenitsyn has not turned to autobiography as a specific genre, although he is now more inclined to make biographical information available than he was at the outset of his career. Since political events, not least amongst which is the fact of his enforced exile from the Soviet Union in 1974, have played a formative role in moulding Solzhenitsyn's life and his philosophy as it is expressed in the major part of his fictional and semi-fictional writing, it is inevitable that a study of Solzhenitsyn's literary attitudes should begin with an examination of why he is so much a product of Soviet society and its history. As Solzhenitsyn himself said in his Nobel Prize Speech, 'Man is built in such a way that his experience of life, both as an individual and a member of a group, determines his world outlook, his motivations and his scale of values, his actions and his intentions.'[3]

Solzhenitsyn's life covers all but a year of the Soviet period. An only child, he was born in 1918 in the town of Kislovodsk, in the northern part of the Caucasus. Not only was he a product of the Russian provinces, but his family background reflects some of the dislocation which Russia suffered at the very beginning of the Soviet period as a result of the First World War and the civil war. His father, himself an army officer, was killed in action while his mother was only recently pregnant, so Solzhenitsyn never knew him, a factor which may have a lot of bearing on the author's attitudes to the officer class in the Tsarist army as expressed in his novel *August 1914*. Solzhenitsyn's mother was thus faced with a problem all too familiar in those days, that of bringing up a child in straitened economic circumstances. This she seems to have succeeded in doing most admirably, and certainly Solzhenitsyn's education does not appear to have suffered, for, after a move to the larger town of Rostov-on-Don in 1924, Solzhenitsyn attended school and eventually became a student at the university of Rostov in 1936. Although his education was basically in the sciences, he was ambitious enough to pursue his literary studies even while taking university courses in mathematics and physics. Eventually he was to take a correspondence course in literature while still a postgraduate in Rostov. Thus Solzhenitsyn went through the newly established Soviet education system during the uncertain days of the New Economic Policy, moved to his senior school against the background of greater social regimentation associated with the First Five-

Year Plan and collectivisation, was in his early 'teens as Stalin tightened his grip on both the party and the country, and had just entered university when the full horror of the purge period burst upon Soviet society. It is one of the ironies of his life that the postgraduate scholarship he received in 1939 was named after Stalin, the same man who was to blight his adult life and whom Solzhenitsyn was to blame for so much that he found wrong with Soviet society.

His education hardly completed, the young Solzhenitsyn married and took a teaching job, still in the town of Rostov, but his first year as a working husband was brought to an abrupt close by the Nazi invasion in June 1941. He volunteered for the Red Army and served as a private for some time before it was discovered that his education would make him more suited to be an officer. His scientific training took him into the artillery, where he served until his arrest near the end of the war. There are echoes of his experience during these years in the figure of Nerzhin in *The First Circle*, perhaps the most nearly autobiographical of all Solzhenitsyn's great range of fictional characters. There is also a story, 'Incident at Krechetovka Station', which, although published much later, in 1963, dates back to his journey to officer training school in 1942.

Once he was made an officer Solzhenitsyn was sent to the front and served with distinction there until the spring of 1945 when the machinery of Stalinist Russia finally sucked him into its apparently insatiable maw. He was arrested on the strength of certain critical remarks about Stalin's prosecution of the war which he had included, unwisely, in letters to a friend from the front. He was charged under the notorious Article 58 of the Criminal Code and given the comparatively light sentence of eight years in camp for 'anti-Soviet propaganda and agitation'. Thus it came about that Solzhenitsyn was to experience the last, most paranoiac years of Stalin's rule as a mere number in the vast network of labour camps set up all over Russia since the twenties. It is the experience of these terrible years, when he worked first on Moscow construction gangs, then in a prison research institute, then in a special 'political' camp, that was to provide him with the drive and impetus, not only to succeed as a writer but to tell the stories and convey the dreadful suffering of the inmates. He also found in the camps the resolve to survive so that he might apportion some of the blame for what he and millions of his contemporaries had to endure. This is the experience which gave the world *A Day in the Life of Ivan Denisovich*, *The First Circle*, the play *The Love-Girl and the Innocent*, and eventually led to the controversial *Gulag Archipelago*.

As though this blow was not enough to break most men, Solzhenitsyn was put to the test in another more terrible manner. Amidst the squalor and deprivation of the labour camps he developed a cancerous tumour of the stomach in 1952, not long before his sentence was due to end.

An exploratory operation in a camp sick-bay under primitive conditions gave Solzhenitsyn some respite until his sentence came to an end. In early 1953, shortly before Stalin died, Solzhenitsyn was a 'free' man again, though only in name. In fact, he was sent into what was coyly referred to as 'administrative exile' in the harsh Kok Terek region of Kazakhstan. Soon he became ill again and was allowed to make his way to the city of Tashkent, where he was given radiotherapy and chemo-therapy, which cured his cancer. His account of these experiences, couched in fictional terms, is contained in his novel *The Cancer Ward*, which he was to complete over a decade later. Thus in 1955 Solzhenitsyn the ex-political convict staged a remarkable recovery and fought his way back to health in a manner that is all the more astonishing when one considers how low his reserves of physical strength must have been after years on a low-calorie camp diet and a work day that drained already depleted resources to the last drop. Some of the man's great determina-tion of later years can be seen in the way that he managed to survive with his intellectual and most of his physical faculties intact. It is from the same source that Solzhenitsyn finds the courage to fight round after round of patient skirmishes with those people in the Soviet Union who, in his eyes, bear most of the responsibility for what happened to him in the years between 1945 and 1955 and for the kind of political system which made such apparently pointless suffering routine.

When Solzhenitsyn eventually came to write about both the camps and his illness, his first-hand accounts had a vividness and conviction which immediately gave him immense moral stature in the Soviet Union and then abroad. They also threw into relief the work of so many other Soviet writers who had somehow got by during the same years. Small wonder that, even at the peak of his short-lived official fame in the Soviet Union, established writers like Fedin and Simonov were prepared to go to great lengths to block publication of novels like *The First Circle* and *The Cancer Ward*.

Solzhenitsyn's case, like so many others during Khrushchev's early attempts at 'de-Stalinisation', came up for review in 1956 and he was released from exile. Rehabilitated as a citizen, he returned to the Russia for which he longed. He settled in the town of Ryazan, not far from Moscow, remarried the wife whom he had divorced while in camp – a move to make her life outside less difficult – and took up a teaching post in a school. His two stories 'Matryona's Place' and 'For the Good of the Cause' are based on his experiences during this period of his life. For several years he took his maths and physics classes in the school and wrote in his free time. One of the stories he worked on in those years was to make him famous virtually overnight: *A Day in the Life of Ivan Denisovich*, his tribute to a 'lowest common denominator' prisoner in a labour camp.

To state that Solzhenitsyn's fame was a result of remarkable coincidence and a series of unpredictable chance factors does not in the slightest sense detract from his enormous literary gifts. However, it seems safe to say that, but for the actions and support of three men, Nikita Khrushchev, Alexander Tvardovsky and Lev Kopelev, Solzhenitsyn might well have died in obscurity, his artistic genius unrecognised. Between 1956 and 1964, when Khrushchev was ousted from power, a steady process of de-Stalinisation took place in the Soviet Union, beginning with Khrushchev's 'secret speech' to the Twentieth Party Congress in 1956 and culminating, symbolically, in the removal of Stalin's body from the mausoleum in Red Square following the Twenty-Second Congress in 1961. In this kind of atmosphere it was possible for a piece of seemingly unpolitical prose, as *A Day* may have appeared on a quick reading, to be considered valuable anti-Stalin propaganda by a man like Khrushchev. He had already given permission before this for Yevtushenko's poem 'The Heirs of Stalin' to be published in the official press, and here was a story, couched in seemingly optimistic tones, which attacked the camps and the years of the 'cult of personality' which produced them. For Tvardovsky, the liberal editor of the most influential Soviet literary periodical *Novy mir*, the choice was both a personal and an artistic one. Solzhenitsyn's manuscript had come his way through Kopelev, a scientist and literary critic who had become close friends with Solzhenitsyn in the Marfino prison research institute between 1946 and 1949. Tvardovsky, anxious to publish, sought influential backing and got it from Khrushchev himself. The importance which Solzhenitsyn attached to Tvardovsky's support is clear from the speech he made at Tvardovsky's funeral in 1971: 'When the voices of the young resound, keen-edged, how you will miss this patient critic, whose gentle admonitory voice was heeded by all. Then you will be set to tear the earth with your hands for the sake of returning Trifonych. But then it will be too late . . .'⁴ Tvardovsky's own feelings can be read between the lines of his wry preface to *One Day* when it appeared in the November 1962 issue of *Novy mir*: 'The subject matter of Solzhenitsyn's novel is unusual in Soviet literature. It echoes the unhealthy phenomena of our life associated with the cult of personality . . .'⁵ Thus Solzhenitsyn's first story – and the first he had submitted to any editor for publication except for some very early efforts in the late 1930s – reached Soviet readers with the full backing of the state publicity apparatus behind it. Critics wrote glowing reviews in the Soviet Union, and Solzhenitsyn's name soon became known abroad. Not only was the subject matter of the story sensational, but it was also clear the man could write exceptionally well. Both these factors might have tended to count against an aspiring writer, even in Khrushchev's time, especially after the scandal over Pasternak's Nobel Prize in 1958. However, Khrushchev also made it a habit to cultivate the more liberal members of the Soviet literary and artistic world, and at the time that *A Day* was published relations between the liberal intelligentsia and the party's First Secretary were at a high point. Yet only the next month the artistic community came in for some scathing criticism from Khrushchev at its exhibition of abstract art organised in the Manège in Moscow. A few more weeks and Khrushchev might not have viewed the publication of *One Day* so favourably.

Clearly, Solzhenitsyn produced an outstanding story at a time when the chances of it being published were higher than at any time during the period from the death of Stalin to the present day. It is quite possible that neither the politicians, nor even Tvardovsky himself, knew what kind of literary talent they had on their hands. By the time they did, it was too late for the politicians to interfere with the further progress of his career in such a way as to render him harmless. The events of Solzhenitsyn's life from 1962 to the present are a chronicle of minor and major frustrations overcome, in which it is possible to watch the writer's attitudes harden and his literary approach become more and more challenging, gradually assuming greater authority and political dimension. That this may have led him into areas of speculation and argument which appear wasteful and mistaken to some people only serves as an index of the controversial nature of his thinking.

The popularity of *A Day* caused Tvardovsky to include three more of Solzhenitsyn's stories in *Novy mir* the following year, but by now it was too late for Solzhenitsyn to ride the crest of his earlier favour with the authorities. Articles appeared in the official press criticising the stories, he was refused a Lenin Prize, and his novel *The First Circle* was rejected by publishing houses; a play in rehearsal was taken off at the last moment in Moscow. Even before Khrushchev was removed Solzhenitsyn began to run into difficulties, but after 1964 matters became gradually worse. His last published short story 'Zakhar the Pouch' appeared in early 1966, and the following year Solzhenitsyn went over to the offensive, attacking the censorship in his open letter to the leaders of the Writers' Union. As a result of this action not only was Solzhenitsyn's next novel *The Cancer Ward* refused publication, but the KGB stepped up its campaign of harrassment against him. This prompted two responses. First, Solzhenitsyn permitted the manuscripts of his two rejected novels to circulate in *samizdat* form. Secondly, he associated himself with the Soviet Campaign for Civil Rights, one of whose leading figures was the scientist Sakharov. As a consequence of their appearance in *samizdat* both *The Cancer Ward* and *The First Circle* were obtained by foreign publishing firms and in 1968 and 1969 translations of both appeared, selling immensely successfully throughout the world. Solzhenitsyn's stature was assured; not so his status in his own country. Under a storm of official abuse he was expelled from the Writers' Union in late 1969.

Undaunted by his situation he continued to write, his next task being the first of a number of connected novels. Entitled *August 1914*, this was to appear in 1971, but before it did Solzhenitsyn was awarded the Nobel Prize for Literature in 1970, although it proved impossible for him to go to Stockholm immediately to collect it. Eventually *August 1914*, after being rejected by every major Soviet publishing house, was deliberately sent abroad for publication by its author, who added a short afterword explaining his reasons for taking this step – an illegal one under Soviet law. Harassment of Solzhenitsyn and his family, their friends and political associates, gradually increased after this in the wake of the general KGB campaign to break up the activities of dissident groups of all kinds in the Soviet Union. *August 1914* was not the literary bombshell many people in the West had been expecting, but Solzhenitsyn's next work, also published abroad only, with the author's explicit permission, proved to be the last straw for the Soviet authorities.

The Gulag Archipelago appeared early in 1974. It is a downright attack, not just on Stalinism, but on the basic premises underlying the Soviet state, not just on the camps, but on the whole system of terror inaugurated by Lenin in 1918. The Soviet authorities lost patience and decided to rid themselves of Solzhenitsyn by the simple expedient of arresting him and immediately deporting him to Europe. Here he has stayed, showing some signs of irritation with Western ways, but still writing and still active in political controversy. He is not averse to initiating such controversy himself, as his Letter to the Soviet government shows. Continuing to work on the sequel volumes to *August 1914*, he has also found time to complete a study of Lenin's activities as a revolutionary exile in Zürich, a further volume of *The Gulag Archipelago*, and an account of his arrest before he was thrown out of the Soviet Union. It is still too early to estimate the eventual scope of Solzhenitsyn's output and obviously only tentative suggestions can be made about his evolution as a writer in the future.

However, Solzenitsyn's development as a writer since the publication of *A Day* does appear to fall into a distinct pattern. Between 1962 and 1967 he was a new writer seeking a reputation; from 1967 to the present he has embarked on a programme of moral and political criticism which tends to place his work into rather a different category. In the light of this, greater attention will be paid to the earlier fiction, if only because it is there, more than anywhere else, that Solzhenitsyn's literary attitudes really emerge.

A Day, like the story 'Matryona's Place', dealt with a very specific theme – that of the righteous person, or *pravednik*, in the general social context. The theme is not new, in fact it derives precisely from that literary tradition which Solzhenitsyn has been rediscovering and restating for his contemporaries: the tradition of Tolstoy and Leskov. In this early writing Solzhenitsyn seems to set himself two goals – formal polish and depth of insight. It is as if he were proving to himself and his audience that he has technical flair and is at the same time demonstrating the profundity of his insight into what he considers the 'real' Russian character. Both stories may be based on personal experience, but the point of view is shifted to two older characters, Ivan Denisovich and Matryona, who appear to stand for Solzhenitsyn's exemplary character-in-life. They may both be illiterate peasants, but by their actions, the acting out of their firmest convictions, in real-life situations, they testify to the great good which can be hidden inside the human frame, no matter how unpromising. On the level of formal polish, *A Day* stands out for its tight construction, its experimentation with genre and point of view, its linguistic accuracy, tone, modulation of register and voice, innovation — in fact all those elements which can be conveniently summed up by the Russian word *skaz*. Matryona's tragic story lacks the unity of *A Day* but reveals many of the latter's more successful traits.

There are several other stories with strong ironic overtones. Indeed, Solzhenitsyn's humour, not surprisingly, is essentially ironic, often black in its conception, and the endings of *A Day* and 'Matryona's Place' are typical of this. The irony in stories such as 'For the Good of the Cause', 'Incident at Krechetovka Station', 'The Easter Procession', 'The Right Hand' and 'Zakhar the Pouch' is meant to point a moral, not to entertain. All these stories are drawn from first-hand experience, as are the two most powerful of Solzhenitsyn's novels, but where the latter go into a detailed analysis of issues, the stories, by reason of length and scope, tend towards greater compression and linguistic polish. Such experimentation continues in the 'prose poems' — where irony, poetic glimpses and formal tension are explored almost for their own sake. The long novels, *The First Circle* in particular, are evidence of Solzhenitsyn's masterful handling of structure, building on a central metaphor and expanding on that to include character, incident, philosophical and political insight.

After the frustration of the mid-sixties, Solzhenitsyn turned to confrontation with the Soviet authorities and their supporters, beginning with the open letter of 1967 and continuing with a number of individual documents or letters which are reminiscent of the old Russian custom of the petition or *zhaloba*. At about the same time as Solzhenitsyn began to be more politically active within the intellectual community — and at the same time, to win its admiration and loyalty — he seems to have exhausted much of the artistic potential of his specifically personal experience. This had two consequences. First, he began to cast around for wider contemporary themes on which to hang his social criticisms, and second, he started to consider himself more as a chronicler and historian than a novelist. This changed emphasis is noticeable in both *August 1914* and *The Gulag Archipelago*. In the former, Solzhenitsyn takes a key event

F

in the history of modern Russia, the defeat of Samsonov at the battle of Tannenberg at the beginning of the First World War, and proceeds to build a documentary-historical novel on and around that key event. In the latter, he takes up an image which had occurred two or three times before in his writing, or in remarks attributed to him, and goes on to document the genesis and history of Soviet labour camps, using his own experience as a starting-point to a much wider factual account. Inevitably, the scope of both these separate viewpoints is enormous and the potential for further development is almost infinite. The historical series begun with *August 1914* will certainly continue with *October 1916* and *March 1917*; after the fundamental criticism of Lenin and his policies expressed in *The Gulag Archipelago* it seems possible that a full-scale critique of Marxism-Leninism might even emerge. Certainly Solzhenitsyn is not short of ambition: thus far his targets have included the Soviet government, censorship, the KGB, the established Orthodox Church, Western politicians, American foreign policy, China, and a whole host of other interrelated topics. His open letter to the Soviet government, as well as some of his recent speeches, have shown that there are limitations to his world-view that were not immediately obvious in his fiction. The pressures of practical criticism seem to tax even a man of Solzhenitsyn's discipline and powers, particularly now that he is living in an alien cultural environment whose roots he can never feel as deeply as those of his native Russia.

A *Day in the Life of Ivan Denisovich* is rightly considered by many commentators to be Solzhenitsyn's masterpiece. In it the most judicious and economical use of all the author's literary gifts are concentrated. The essence of *A Day* is its understatement. This springs from a number of formal considerations which throw light on Solzhenitsyn's literary concerns during his early period.

First amongst these was a desire to render the experience of a whole generation through the story of one man: 'Of all the drama that Russia lived through, the fate of Ivan Denisovich was the greatest tragedy . . .'[6] To do this in the most immediate fashion, Solzhenitsyn chose not to use his own, essentially intellectual, conceptualising viewpoint. Dostoevsky had already pre-empted this genre in his *Notes from the House of the Dead*, even though he was describing a different kind of prison system in a different era. For Solzhenitsyn, the intellectual viewpoint was something apart from the shared experience of the labour camps, and he was preparing to write a different kind of novel about intellectuals in the camp environment. Ivan Denisovich, as many commentators have noted, is a kind of Soviet Everyman, and because his experience is a distillate of that of an entire generation without him being aware that this is so, his story is all the more poignant, the waste of a potentially good life – and that much the more desperate.

To emphasise the limitations he has set himself – and to leave it incumbent on the reader to fill out the picture – Solzhenitsyn not only limits the setting of the story to one day in a labour camp; he limits the genre by referring to *A Day* not as a novel, but simply 'a story' [*povest'*]. For the Russian, this is somewhere half-way between a short story and a full-length novel, and the story will be limited to an examination of one character. By using the *skaz* convention mentioned above, Solzhenitsyn gets as far away as possible from the conventions of the novel. Ivan's story is told almost through his own eyes and mouth, in the kind of language he would use, including camp slang, obscenities, proverbs and aphorisms of the kind that Russians know instinctively by ear, but have rarely, if ever, seen on the printed page, at least since the experimental prose writers of the 1920s were at the height of their popularity. After the stultifying influence of Stalinism, this language alone was a breath of fresh air to most Russians. There is also in it a sense of immediacy created by the number of second-person singular verbs that appear – it is as if the whole story were being told on an intimate conversational level.

It was perhaps this very conversational simplicity and lack of comment, grim insight or open cross-reference which allowed *A Day* to please even the most censorious of literary arbiters before it was approved for publication. At first glance *A Day* could almost pass as a piece of folksy Socialist Realism: it has a typical hero, on a typical day, taking a broadly optimistic view of his situation – 'an almost happy day', Ivan Denisovich reflects after being refused permission to go to sick-bay and made to work in thirty degrees of frost, or strip-searched in the early morning cold outside. On a closer examination of the story a number of possible alternatives to this interpretation suggest themselves. Perhaps Ivan does gain a lot of pleasure from building his piece of wall, but is there not an irony in a prisoner building a wall, when the reader has already been told that the first thing the prisoners are expected to do in setting up a new building site is to build fences around it so that they cannot escape? Does Ivan's outlook really represent a positive Soviet man's attitude: is there no element of self-interest, no reliance on the drive for self-survival? All kinds of questions such as these can be suggested and hinted at, using Solzhenitsyn's method. The author aims to give a general view through a series of seemingly mundane facts and characters in a mundane situation. The camp becomes a microcosm, a tiny social unit from which it is possible to extrapolate certain general tendencies in human behaviour. There is a cross-section of Soviet nationalities and Russian types. There is something else which appears to fascinate Solzhenitsyn, to judge from both *The First Circle* and *Cancer Ward*, not to mention *August 1914*, and that is the question of individual responsibility in chains of command or social hierarchies. In many ways the camp hierarchy can be seen to parallel the social hierarchy on the outside – the bullies, the trusties, the guards, the commandant, each one in turn scared stiff of the man above him, all of them jumping in turn on those at the bottom, the prisoners.

To highlight this power hierarchy and counterbalance it, there is also a reverse kind of hierarchy, in which the power proceeds from moral principle. On this structure Ivan stands near the pinnacle and others are placed well below: scroungers, work-shy team-mates, the informer, the guard. Here Solzhenitsyn only hints at something which he explains more clearly in *The First Circle*. First of all, this moral hierarchy is based on an almost Tolstoyan concept of the ethical imperative graven on men's hearts. Secondly, there is an awful irony about being in a camp. The prisoner loses almost everything, possessions, self-respect, warmth, security, companionship with women, and yet the more that is taken away from him, the more his external freedom is encroached upon, the more uncomfortable, hungry, deprived he is, the greater his internal freedom. He can feel himself superior to his oppressors. Once the fear of arrest has gone, it can almost seem that life in camp is better than life outside. It may not be so true of Ivan Denisovich's camp, but it is certainly true of the Mavrino institute in *The First Circle*, and the wives who live on the outside sense the irony of their own and their husbands' positions. Who keeps whom prisoner?

So, by deliberately understating the horrors, by using the 'innocent eye' *skaz* techniques within a specifically limited temporal and spatial setting, Solzhenitsyn manages to suggest whole realms of further allegory and ironic sides to the story of Ivan which need never be touched on verbally. Given the familiarity of the scene described and all its social and political overtones for the average Soviet reader, it is small wonder that the story was a sensation.

What distinguishes Solzhenitsyn's next two novels from *A Day* is their construction on an allegory or a metaphor. Where *A Day* was closer to a parable, they are huge intellectual edifices constructed according to the classic conventions of the novel. The two basic questions under discussion in *The First Circle* and *The Cancer Ward* are: how far will men go before they allow themselves to be compromised and corrupted, and how do men face up to imminent death?

There are numerous parallels between Dante's *Inferno* and *The First Circle*. The title is not chosen merely as an image, the reader is being given as thorough a tour of part of hell as Virgil gives Dante in *The Divine Comedy*. The circles of Hades and the city of Dis are replaced in Solzhenitsyn's formulation by the various kinds of labour camp under the Gulag hierarchy. Just as Dante found Rome, 'the Holy City', to be a cover for degeneracy and corruption, and Hell not far away, so Solzhenitsyn shows another Holy City, Moscow, 'the Third Rome', sunk in the desolation and moral decay of the least years of Stalin in 1949. Dante's first circle of hell, the outer ring, was reserved as a limbo for the un-baptised and virtuous pagans, as well as for intellectuals and philoso-phers. Solzhenitsyn's Mavrino is reserved for scientists, engineers, mathematicians, and the like. They are nominally prisoners, but they are the next best thing to free. They eat well, they are kept warm, they are allowed the occasional visit from their wives, and when their wives are out in the world beyond the prison walls the prisoners can occasionally make contact with a woman from outside who may be working in the in-stitute. The only price they all have to pay to live and finally achieve their freedom is the enormous guilt of having to work for a system and a man they all hate and despise. As Dante enquired of Virgil before they had gone far on their journey into the Inferno:

> 'Tell me, sir, tell me, master', I began . . .
> 'did any man
> By his self-merit, or on another leaning
> Ever fare forth from hence and come to be
> Among the blest?'

The First Circle is almost two novels in one, and one of its underlying ironies arises from its structure. The prisoners in the Mavrino research institute are given projects which benefit Stalin's system of control, sur-veillance and intimidation if they can be brought to fruition. They do not help humanity and despite all the considerable funds and facilities at their disposal – more perhaps than any normal scientific establishment would be allotted – their work cannot be viewed as part of the search for scientific truth. They are trapped in a closed system which allows them freedom only as long as they co-operate and will grant liberty only if they sell their scientific expertise to the state. One strand of the story in the novel shows how the ambitious young diplomat, Volodin, is trap-ped by a voice-print detector that has been developed by Rubin, one of the Mavrino scientists. At the beginning of the novel Volodin is a free man, at least by his own standards – one of the aims of the book is to demonstrate that under a system such as Stalin's the ones who co-operate and rely most on this system are as much prisoners as the men in Mavrino. By the end of the book Volodin has been sucked down into the hell that waits for every Soviet citizen who is rash enough or unwary enough to go counter to the rules of society. So the young, successful and ambitious product of the Soviet intellectual elite is destroyed by the in-mates of hell whom he has never met until he is arrested and taken to the Lubyanka – the Moscow equivalent of Charon's ferry across the Styx.

The other main strand of the story is based in Mavrino, which stands, like Dante's enchanted castle, beyond the bounds of the Holy City. Here, amidst the comparative privilege of a settled scientific community, a number of key characters interact, debate, argue and reach various conclusions about their situation. This is the sharpest point of contrast between *A Day* and *The First Circle* – the former avoided the intellectual view of the world, preferring the neutral, uninformed vision of the peasant Ivan to convey the horrific senselessness of Stalin's camps. Mavrino, in contrast, is a hot-house of intellectual discussion, a forcing-plant for abstract ideas. The very image of the first circle of hell presupposes a familiarity with literature which no Ivan Denisovich could be expected to have. Not only is the atmosphere here heightened and unreal when seen against the harsh realities of life outside, but Solzhenitsyn also compresses all the action of the novel into three days, to heighten the tension and drama of the two story lines: will Volodin get caught, will the main Mavrino characters compromise themselves, or will they resist and be sent down to the lower, viler circles of hell, the labour camps?

Both these questions are answered by the end of the novel, but Solzhenitsyn uses this very classical unity of time, action and setting to move outside the immediate range of the apparent limits he has set himself. Going off at tangents in time and space, he fills in the backgrounds of many of the characters, showing their own particular road to hell and the reasons why they ended up there. He shows Volodin in his social milieu and passes silent judgement on it. He examines the plight of the prisoners' wives – a subject close to his own heart, since his own first wife had been in exactly this kind of position. Through them he develops both a picture of life 'outside' in Moscow, and also poses the question of where there is greater freedom, in Mavrino or the capital. As in *A Day* the answer seems to lie in the extent to which each individual manages to delve down into his deepest inner resources and stand firm on an intuitive ethical law that is beyond the grasp of the compromiser or the Stalin 'organisation man'. Mavrino becomes a point at which a skein of events, fates and lives are unravelled. *The First Circle* is at the same time a novel of drama, ideas, moral judgement and historical realism. As Solzhenitsyn himself has explained:

> Literature can never grasp everything in life. I will take an image from mathematics and explain it: Every work can become just a bunch of surfaces. This bunch of surfaces passes through one point. You choose this point according to your own personal bias, your life history, your superior knowledge and so forth . . .[7]

Mavrino is always the point to which the action returns, even in the case of Volodin – his fate is sealed there. It is the starting point for another of Solzhenitsyn's ventures up the power hierarchy of the two police structures that administer Mavrino, the Ministry of State Security and the Ministry of Internal Affairs, both headed by Beria, who is answerable to Stalin alone. Beneath him stretches the chain of command, each link becoming more insignificant and more menaced by the deadweight of the apparatus above until the chain reaches into Mavrino itself, the social microcosm, and the minions can be seen in action, prisoners of the system, no less than the scientists they are supposed to be guarding. At every apparent digression and every leap into another setting or development in another character's story Solzhenitsyn is careful to provide convincing links in time, or in place, or in such matters as the description of the weather. So impressive is his organisation that it is difficult not to see Tolstoy standing in the wings, and indeed there are many typically Tolstoyan elements in the novel. The characters are carefully paired off to give balance to personal dramas; there is the fascination with man in microcosmic settings and with the pyramidal power structure; there is even an attempt to incorporate the historical figures of Stalin, Abakumov, Poskryobyshev and the like, and finally there is the moral choice which faces all the characters in one way or another.

The underlying philosophical debate which goes on in the book is between Marxism, Stoicism and Epicureanism: 'One can build the Empire State Building, discipline the Prussian Army, make a state hierarchy mightier than God, yet fail to overcome the unaccountable spiritual superiority of certain human beings'.[8] The author and his semi-autobiographical protagonist Nerzhin are on the side of the stoics. Like Zeno, they believe ethics to be of paramount importance in human life and therefore virtue to be the prime quality in man. Health, happiness and possessions are unimportant. Virtue is the result of will and therefore every man is responsible to himself for the good or bad which is in him. Even in the face of adversity, poverty or death, man still has the choice to be virtuous. Every man has within him a perfect freedom once he removes all worldly temptations, and since no outside force can deprive a man of virtue, other men have power only over externals. Epicurus had no answer to this philosophy, believing as he did that the greatest good of all was prudence. Volodin believes in prudence, until he decides to act according to the promptings of his conscience. At that point his assumed philosophy is shattered and he goes to take his place in hell. The other main characters, Nerzhin, Rubin and Sologdin all display a side of stoicism in their search for virtue, but the man who sums it up as neatly as any of them is the old handyman Spiridon, a character not unlike Ivan Denisovich. He tells Nerzhin his rule of thumb for understanding the world: 'Wolf-hounds are right, cannibals are wrong'.[9] This Delphic piece of folk wisdom is the key to the ethical basis of *The First Circle*, and it is significant that none of the intellectuals, for all their education and soul-searching, can come up with a better one.

Of his next longest work, *The Cancer Ward*, Solzhenitsyn has said, 'I would like it noted that I consider this work to be not a novel, but a *povest*'.[10] Completed after *The First Circle*, *The Cancer Ward* is in many ways a more personal document for Solzhenitsyn, based as it obviously is on the circumstances of his own illness, and perhaps it is for this reason that Solzhenitsyn wanted to limit its scope. Where *The First Circle* had obvious political overtones, set as it was in a prison, under Stalin's rule, near to Moscow, *The Cancer Ward* has a more unspecified, less taut construction. Its setting is a hospital in Tashkent and the action runs from February to March 1955. The novel is inevitably a comment on certain aspects of the post-Stalin years, particularly in the clash between two of the main characters, the ex-prisoner Kostoglotov and the Stalinist functionary Rusanov. In the same way as *The First Circle*, however, whether it is a novel or an extremely long 'story', *The Cancer Ward* is constructed on an interlinking system of metaphor which gives its action extra dimensions of irony and symbolic significance.

The Russian title of Solzhenitsyn's book uses the word for a 'block' [*korpus*], and so the English title loses one of the first of the author's allusions. This is not simply a story about a number of patients in a ward, although much of the action centres on them. It is also about the people who nurse them, service their essential needs, and try to cure them. Thus Solzhenitsyn has again chosen a microcosmic setting in which to examine the problems that beset Soviet man, one in which the fascination for hierarchies can be given full play. This hierarchy and its workings can point a number of interesting parallels with society outside. Within the cancer block and its wards the doctors have a monopoly over the manner in which patients are treated and the knowledge which is supposed to cure them. Yet, one of the best doctors, Dontsova, is sick with cancer herself and fails to recognise the fact. This leads Solzhenitsyn to speculate, through his protagonist Kostoglotov, whether doctors really have an unrestrained right to practice their profession on other, less knowledgeable human beings. There is a chapter of the novel entitled 'The Right to Treat' in which Kostoglotov confronts Dontsova over this issue. The parallel between the doctors within and the party members outside is too clear to be avoided.

Cancer itself carries other associations which Solzhenitsyn exploits to the full. The first is the irrational fear which surrounds the very mention of it in Western societies, for whom it seems to have replaced tuberculosis as the *maladie interdite*. The seemingly incurable nature of the disease puts those who suffer from it beyond the pale of their fellow men – a feeling which was shared by the eponymous hero of Tolstoy's story *The Death of Ivan Ilyich*. However, as Solzhenitsyn was quick to point out, 'If a man never became ill, he would never know his own limitations.' Doctors and patients alike are confronted with their own inadequacies and respond according to their character, some changing profoundly, some modifying their attitudes out of expediency and reverting to type the second they see a glimpse of a cure. It is no coincidence that the cancer ward patients are reading a copy of Tolstoy's book *By What Do Men Live?*

The allegory and allusion do not end here. As the book progresses it becomes clear that Solzhenitsyn is likening the camp system in the Soviet Union to a cancer on the body politic. Kostoglotov even asks himself at the very end of the book, 'A man dies from a tumour, so how can a country survive with growths like labour camps and exiles?'[11] Kostoglotov becomes the mouthpiece for a constantly critical evaluation of events both inside and outside the hospital, and the bitter ironies of his own imprisonment and the harshness of his exile have combined to give him a forceful sense of self which will brook no compromise and accept no excuses for failings. In his defence of the first part of *The Cancer Ward* before members of the Soviet Writers Union Solzhenitsyn commented on his use of title:

> About the title. There was a battle over this in *Novy mir*. I lost that battle. The prison camps were, of course, a tumour. But I was not afraid to use such a title because I reckoned I would overcome it. I did not want either to depress or crush the reader. I hope to triumph on the main issue – the conflict of life with death.[12]

Like *The First Circle*, *The Cancer Ward* is a novel which is written from the intellectual point of view. Its characters cover a broad spectrum of Soviet society, even though it is set in the city of Tashkent rather than more familiar Russian territory. Few of these characters are intellectuals in their own right, unlike the prisoners in *The First Circle*, and Kostoglotov has a coarseness and down-to-earth forthrightness which cuts through any pretensions in his fellow patients. Nevertheless, the main focal point of the novel is Kostoglotov and while most of the action is seen from his standpoint, the organising voice behind all the events is that of an omniscient author in the Tolstoyan tradition. Thus the novel can be seen as a powerful discussion of the moral issues of disease and evil in man and society, and of the wider problem of freedom and personal independence.

Where *The First Circle* ended on a distinctly pessimistic note, tinged with Solzhenitsyn's brand of heavy irony, *The Cancer Ward* appears to end well for both of its main characters. The old Stalinist Rusanov returns to the bosom of his family, apparently none the worse for his ordeals, but faced with the growing trend towards de-Stalinisation in Soviet politics. Kostoglotov is apparently cured and even has the possible chance of rehabilitation and a return to Russia. This is symbolically conveyed by his sudden, poignant glimpse of the *uryuk* tree in full blossom in a Tashkent courtyard on the first day after his release from hospital. His first tentative steps into the world outside bring him face-to-face with nature's first signs of full spring to come. For him this can only be an omen. After all his sufferings in camp and exile, closely followed by the debilitating onslaught of cancer, Kostoglotov at last gets a glimpse of freedom. In *The Cancer Ward* the reader is left to wonder at what faces him in his new-found freedom and to ponder the question of why Rusanov and his like will never change.

The answer to this last question is left unresolved, but there is more than a suggestion that major evil, as represented by Stalin in *The First Circle*, can be traced to the pettiness and meanness of ordinary men. Kostoglotov is as outraged by the gratuitous viciousness of the man who blinded the monkey in the zoo 'just like that, for no reason', as he is by the more far-reaching evils of a Rusanov or the spineless compromises of an 'ethical socialist' like Shulubin. Like Solzhenitsyn himself, Kostoglotov's experiences have taught him to be tough and uncompromising, to face what he believes to be evil whenever and wherever he finds it. Like Nerzhin in *The First Circle* he is a stoic, and his stoicism is tempered by a rough scepticism. He does not believe in nor desire material things, but he demands the right to dispose of his own life. For him intelligence means trusting the evidence of your own eyes. Education on its own will not make a man smarter, but life can. Trust between people can only be established on the grounds of a commonly shared experience and common goals. He sees through the pretensions of a man like Kostoglotov immediately, and contemptuously dismisses his values and goals with an incontrovertible logic derived from his camp experiences. He aims for an inner moral perfection which will be an example to others, and yet he can still learn from his fellow men. He wants to understand the theory behind practice and to defend himself from the excesses of people who act under instruction, yet at the same time he clings to the belief that it is impossible to know everything, that man still dies in ignorance. His personal convictions lead him to question logic, economics, political theory and even physiology, yet he knows in the end that all this is somehow secondary to the problem of facing up to imminent death: '. . . these arguments, counter-arguments, technical terms, bitter, angry glances suddenly seemed so much squelching in a swamp . . . None of this was to be compared with the disease that afflicted them or with death, which loomed before them'.[13] Kostoglotov does not die. He survives to continue his fight outside both hospital and labour camp, and in the breath of optimism that is detectable at the end of *The Cancer Ward* Solzhenitsyn offers some hope for the future and a justification of his protagonist's blunt willingness to confront all the odds, to criticise shortcomings and evil, to evaluate honestly and to give praise where it is due.

With the completion of *The Cancer Ward* Solzhenitsyn reached a definitive stage in his career. Still pursuing his long-term literary and moral aims, he now set out to become a chronicler and commentator on broader historical topics. If his work up to this stage had criticised Stalin and his system, the legacy it left behind, and the cost in human terms, he now turned his attention to the underlying causes, not just of Stalinism, but of the failings of the Soviet system as a whole.

He began work on the first of a series of historical novels which aimed to examine the origins of the Soviet state in a semi-fictional form. The main concern of *August 1914*, the only one of this series yet published, is to establish responsibility for the defeat of General Samsonov's Second Army by the Germans at the battle of Tannenberg shortly after the beginning of the First World War. The next two in the series, *October 1916* and *March 1917*, will no doubt bring a clearer picture of the manner in which Solzhenitsyn wants to approach his treatment of the origins of the Soviet Union, but for many readers outside Russia *August 1914* was something of a disappointing departure from the writing of the early Solzhenitsyn, if only because it dealt with matters a little less familiar than those of the camps or a cancer ward. Perhaps Solzhenitsyn's own words will help to explain some of his intentions in this series of interlinked works:

> What is the most interesting genre for me? The polyphonic novel with precise indications of time and place. The novel without a principal hero . . . How do I understand polyphony? Each character becomes the principal character on entering the field of action. The author must then be responsible for thirty-five heroes. He does not give preference to any one of them. He must understand and motivate them all.[14]

August 1914 is a polyphonic novel as defined here, founded as it is on a broad array of characters and placed accurately in time and space. What is missing is the strong metaphorism of the earlier novels, despite the fact that Solzhenitsyn is asking the reader to accept that Samsonov's story has immense relevance for his own contemporaries, if only for the fact that his fate was that of a victim of social and historical processes which were beyond his grasp and control.

This same lack of metaphorical focus is evident in the most recent of Solzhenitsyn's longer books, *The Gulag Archipelago*. Here, Solzhenitsyn is attempting to discover the truth about the whole labour camp system, the historical reasons for its establishment, its history and the fate of many of its inmates. It does not purport to be a fictional work, but like *August 1914* it follows logically from the task that Solzhenitsyn set himself years ago – to uncover and record the facts about Soviet life which were hidden and suppressed for so long, to submit these facts to a careful evaluative analysis and to draw conclusions. In these books it is Solzhenitsyn the writer–scientist who comes to the fore, and he is unafraid to state the moral and political conclusions at which he arrives, no matter how much opposition and objection this may lead to in the end. *August 1914* is part of an as yet unrealised 'grand scheme', and *The Gulag Archipelago*, with its dominant but unrealised metaphor of a chain of labour camp 'islands' dotted in a Soviet sea, is what its author calls 'an experiment in literary research'. It may therefore be a little premature to judge the later Solzhenitsyn by the literary standards of his earlier works. Certainly his publicistic activities during the last two years have been both prodigious in amount and controversial in content: an open letter to the Soviet government, an attack on the writer Sholokhov, a series of literary–political essays in *émigré* publications, speeches on a range of contemporary political issues, a book on Lenin in exile, and a descriptive account of his own recent experiences with the KGB immediately prior to his expulsion from the Soviet Union. All these activities reflect a desire to move away from the position of a novelist into that of a moral commentator on issues affecting every aspect of modern life. It may well be that in the light of posterity Solzhenitsyn's later activities will come under the same critical scrutiny as those of the later Tolstoy, but there is no denying that the driving force is constantly his conviction that, as he put it in his Nobel Prize Address, 'one word of truth outweighs the whole world.'

Significantly, for all the controversial nature of Nobel Prizes themselves, Solzhenitsyn was awarded his 'For the ethical force with which he has pursued the indispensable traditions of Russian literature'. Obviously the Nobel committee understood that Solzhenitsyn did not fit the accepted view of a 'Soviet' writer, but derived his basic attitudes from the pre-revolutionary era. In his concern for truth, his unwillingness to compromise, his need to bear witness and chronicle as much as in his experimentation with form, genre and language, Solzhenitsyn has more than justified his link with his greatest predecessors.

NOTES

1 L. Labedz, *Solzhenitsyn: A Documentary Record* (London, 1970) p. 8. Hereafter: Labedz.
2 Ibid., p. 66.
3 The translation used here is *'One Word of Truth'*, *The Nobel Speech on Literature 1970*, trans. members of the BBC Russian Service (London, 1972) p. 10.
4 L. Labedz (ed.), *Solzhenitsyn: A Documentary Record* (Bloomington, Ind., 1973) p. 268.
5 Ibid. (London, 1970) p. 9.
6 Ibid., p. 7.
7 Ibid., p. 61.
8 *The First Circle*, trans. M. Guybon (London, 1968) p. 71.
9 Ibid., p. 486.
10 Missing in Labedz translation, p. 46, but contained in M. Aucouturier and G. Nivat (eds), *Soljénitsyne* (Paris, 1971) p. 225.
11 *The Cancer Ward*, trans. N. Bethell and D. Burg (London, 1968) p. 556.
12 Labedz, pp. 60–61.
13 *The Cancer Ward*, p. 441.
14 *Soljénitsyne*, p. 118.

Bibliography

PUSHKIN

IN ENGLISH

For an account of the earliest translations from Pushkin see E. A. Osborne in the *Bookman* (London, August 1932). For a list of the principal translations before 1900, see Maurice B. Line, *A Bibliography of Russian Literature in English Translation to 1900* (London, 1963).

Among the main twentieth-century translations, one has to note:

Arndt, Walter, *Pushkin Threefold* (London, 1972) is an interesting volume which presents the original poems with linear and metric translations.

Cornford, Frances, and Polianowsky Salaman, Esther, *Poems from the Russian* (London, 1943) contains some sensitive translations.

Fennell, John, *Pushkin* (Harmondsworth, Middlesex, 1964) is an excellent selection in Russian with plain prose translations.

Morison, Walter, *Pushkin's Poems* (London, 1945).

Yarmolinsky, A. (ed.), *The Works of Alexander Pushkin* (London, [1936]). Uneven translations by various hands, but the most comprehensive selection.

Nabokov's translation of *Eugene Onegin* (1964) is a work of scholarship but does not read easily; Oliver Elton's translation (1937) occasionally renders the spirit of the original, but is superseded by Walter Arndt's and Eugene M. Kayden's renderings (1963 and 1964, respectively).

Most of Pushkin's prose works are available in Everyman and Penguin editions.

Pushkin's letters and critical articles have been published in English in well-annotated editions:

The Letters of Alexander Pushkin, trans. J. Thomas Shaw (Madison, Wisc., 1967).

Pushkin on Literature, selected, trans. and ed. Tatiana Wolff (London, 1971).

Biographies

Magarshack, David, *Pushkin* (London, 1967). Eminently readable, but unreliable in detail.

Simmons, E. J., *Pushkin* (Cambridge, Mass., 1937). Probably still the best biography in English.

Troyat, Henri, *Pushkin* (London, 1974). Somewhat popular, but extremely well written.

Critical works

Bayley, John, *Pushkin: A Comparative Commentary* (Cambridge, 1971). The most serious study in English.

Davie, Donald, *The Heyday of Sir Walter Scott* (London, 1961) contains some interesting pages on *The Captain's Daughter*.

Eng, Jan van der, Holk, A. G. F. van, and Meijer, Jan M., *The Tales of Belkin by A. S. Puškin* (The Hague, 1968).

Fennell, John (ed.), *Nineteenth-Century Russian Literature* (London, 1973) has a stimulating chapter by the editor.

Freeborn, Richard, *The Rise of the Russian Novel: Studies in the Russian Novel from 'Eugene Onegin' to 'War and Peace'* (Cambridge, 1973).

Lednicki, W., *Pushkin's Bronze Horseman* (Berkeley, Calif., 1955).

Mirsky, D. S., *Pushkin* (London, 1926). A good general introduction.

Nabokov, Vladimir, *Eugene Onegin, A Novel in Verse by Aleksandr Pushkin*, 4 vols (London, 1964). More important for its commentary than for its translation.

IN RUSSIAN

The most complete edition of Pushkin's work establishing the basic texts and providing all textual variants is the Academy sixteen-volume edition, *Polnoye sobraniye sochineniy*, 16 vols in 20 (Moscow, 1937–49) supplemented by *Spravochny tom: dopolneniya i ispravleniya, ukazateli* (Moscow, 1959) which contains an index. The six-volume 'Academia' edition, *Polnoye sobraniye sochineniy*, ed. by M. A. Tsyavlovsky (Moscow, 1936, 1938) is the best annotated of all complete editions of Pushkin's works. More readily available, and an excellent working edition with good notes, is the small Academy edition in ten volumes, *Polnoye sobraniye sochineniy v desyati tomakh* (Moscow, publ. first in 1949), several editions.

There is no comprehensive monograph on Pushkin that is really satisfactory, though there are several excellent monographs on various aspects of his work. Among the principal recent critical works are:

Blagoy, D. D., *Tvorcheskiy put' Pushkina (1813–26)* (Moscow, 1950). This most comprehensive Soviet monograph has a sequel which still does not cover the whole of Pushkin's work:

——, *Tvorcheskiy put' Pushkina (1826–30)* (Moscow, 1967).

——, *Masterstvo Pushkina* (Moscow, 1955). Useful on the structure of Pushkin's works.

Brodsky, N. L., *Evgeny Onegin, roman A. S. Pushkina*, 4th ed. (Moscow, 1957). A classic textual commentary.

Gorodetsky, B. P., *Dramaturgiya Pushkina* (Moscow, 1953). The most comprehensive study on the subject.

——, *Lirika Pushkina* (Moscow, 1962). The most scholarly and detailed study on the subject.

Gukovsky, G. A., *Pushkin i problemy realisticheskogo stilya* (Moscow, 1957). One of the best studies on *Eugene Onegin*. Covers also *Boris Godunov, Graf Nulin, Poltava*, and the post-1830 period.

Lezhnev, A. Z., *Proza Pushkina*, 2nd ed. (Moscow, 1966). Mainly an analysis of style.

Slonimsky, A. L., *Masterstvo Pushkina* (Moscow, 1959). A fairly popular but useful analysis of some aspects of Pushkin's work; stress on genres.

Stepanov, N. L., *Lirika Pushkina* (Moscow, 1959). Very selective and much inferior to Gorodetsky's work.

——, *Proza Pushkina* (Moscow, 1962). More comprehensive than Lezhnev; thematical, not chronological treatment.

Tomashevsky, B., *Pushkin*, vol. 1 (Moscow, 1956); vol. 2 (Moscow, 1961). The best Soviet 'life and work' monograph, but stops at 1825.

Vinogradov, V. V., *Stil' Pushkina* (Moscow, 1941).

——, *Yazyk Pushkina* (Moscow–Leningrad, 1935).

Despite Mirsky's dictum that 'the English enthusiasts of Russian literature are not a race likely to understand Pushkin,' it is hoped that the above select bibliography will help to prove him wrong.

DOSTOEVSKY

There are many translations of Dostoevsky's works into English, but the best of these are by Constance Garnett and David Magarshack. Recently the notebooks for his major novels have been appearing in English translation, published by the University of Chicago Press and by Ardis, Ann Arbor, Michigan.

BIOGRAPHIES

Grossman, L., *Dostoevsky*, trans. Mary Mackler (Harmondsworth, Middlesex, 1974). Very detailed biography. Orthodox Soviet treatment of Dostoevsky's works.

Magarshack, D., *Dostoevsky* (London, 1962). A straightforward biography.

Mochulsky, K. V., *Dostoevsky*, trans. M. A. Minihan (Princeton, N. J., 1967). A deeply sensitive study of Dostoevsky's life and work especially valuable for its analysis of the structural features of the major novels.

Troyat, H., *Firebrand: The Life of Dostoevsky* (London, 1946).

CRITICAL WORKS, ETC.

Bakhtin, M. M., *Problems of Dostoevsky's Poetics*, trans. R. W. Rotsel (Ann Arbor, Mich., 1973). The most important single work of Soviet criticism on Dostoevsky in a courageous but uneven English translation. Important for its brilliant examination of the polyphonic character of the major novels. Originally published Leningrad, 1929; 2nd ed. (Moscow, 1963); 3rd ed. (Moscow, 1972).

Belknap, R. L., *The Structure of the Brothers Karamazov* (The Hague, 1967). Idiosyncratic, occasionally brilliant structuralist interpretation with little concern for the ideas in Dostoevsky's novel.

Fanger, D., *Dostoevsky and Romantic Realism* (Cambridge, Mass., 1967). Valuable study of Dostoevsky in relation to Dickens and Gogol.

Hingley, R., *The Undiscovered Dostoevsky* (London, 1962). A treatment of some aspects of Dostoevsky's 'undiscovered' humour.

Jackson, R. L., *Dostoevsky's Quest for Form* (Yale U.P., 1966). A study of Dostoevsky's philosophy of art. Compare Sven Linner, *Dostoevskiy on Realism*, Stockholm, 1967.

Jonge, A. de, *Dostoevsky and the Age of Intensity* (London, 1975). Revealing, stimulating comparisons between Dostoevsky and Baudelaire; interesting readings of the major fiction, but over-emphatic in its insistence that Dostoevsky's is 'a Russia of the mind'.

Lampert, E., 'Dostoevsky', in *Nineteenth-Century Russian Literature*, ed. John Fennell (London, 1973). A short general essay on Dostoevsky with short bibliography.

Peace, R., *Dostoyevsky: An Examination of the Major Novels* (Cambridge, 1971); paperback, 1975. Valuable study, especially for its examination of the close association between homicide and the Russian religious sects in Dostoevsky's work.

Simmons, E. J., *Dostoevsky: The Making of a Novelist* (London, 1940). Interesting pioneer introduction to Dostoevsky's novels; now rather dated.

Terras, V., *The Young Dostoevsky (1846–1849)* (The Hague, 1969). An admirable and comprehensive study of Dostoevsky's early fiction.

Wasiolek, E., *Dostoevsky: The Major Fiction* (Cambridge, Mass., 1964); paperback, 1971. Short, useful guide to major novels, with excellent bibliography.

Wellek, R., (ed.), *Dostoievsky: A Collection of Critical Essays* (Englewood Cliffs, N.J., 1962). Contains excellent – in some cases famous – essays by Freud, Lukács, Chizhevsky, Howe and others.

WORKS IN RUSSIAN

A useful guide to Soviet and Russian emigre writing on Dostoevsky is V. Seduro's *Dostoevski's Image in Russia Today* (Belmont, Mass., 1975). Noteworthy contributions to the study of Dostoevsky in the Soviet Union have been made by B. I. Bursov, A. S. Dolinin, G. M. Fridlender, V. Ya. Kirpotin, V. S. Nechaeva, V. Pereverzev, V. Shklovsky, to name only some of those who have published significant monographs. Soviet scholars have undertaken vast research and editorial work on Dostoevsky, one product of which is the currently appearing thirty-volume collected edition of his works (Leningrad, 1872–).

DOSTOEVSKY AND TOLSTOY

The contribution of Dostoevsky and Tolstoy to the development of the novel are dealt with in the following works:

Bayley, J., *Tolstoy and the Novel* (London, 1966). An excellent study of Tolstoy, though inevitably it touches on the problem of the relationship between Dostoevsky and Tolstoy.

Freeborn, R., *The Rise of the Russian Novel* (Cambridge, 1973). Contains studies of *Crime and Punishment* and *War and Peace*.

Gifford, H., *The Novel in Russia* (London, 1964). Brief, stimulating chapters on Dostoevsky and Tolstoy in the context of the development of the novel in Russia.

Merezhkovsky, D., *Tolstoy and Dostoevsky* (London, 1902). Earliest comparison between the two writers; mostly on Tolstoy.

Reeve, F. D., *The Russian Novel* (London, 1966). Densely written, erudite, aphoristic forays into Dostoevsky's and Tolstoy's novels.

Steiner, G., *Tolstoy or Dostoevsky* (New York, 1959). Many editions. Much fine pertinent commentary on the principal differences between Dostoevsky and Tolstoy. Ultimately tends to strain for effect in its effort to offer a universalising treatment of the differences.

TOLSTOY

There are many translations of Tolstoy's work into English, but those by Aylmer Maude, Constance Garnett and Rosemary Edmonds are the best.

BIOGRAPHIES

Leon, D., *Tolstoy, his Life and Work* (London, 1944).

Maude, A., *The Life of Tolstoy*, 2 vols. (Oxford, 1930).

Simmons, E. J., *Leo Tolstoy* (London, 1960). Several editions. Probably the best biography in English; by a noted American scholar.

Troyat, H., *Tolstoy* (London, 1968). Translated from the French; good, but inclined to be gossipy.

CRITICAL STUDIES, ETC.

Benson, R. C., *Women in Tolstoy* (Champagne, Ill., 1973).

Berlin, I., *The Hedgehog and the Fox* (London, 1953). A famous examination of Tolstoy's view of history as expounded in *War and Peace*.

Christian, R. F., *Tolstoy's War and Peace, A Study* (London, 1962). *Tolstoy* (Cambridge, 1969). A very sound and useful general work. It is subtitled 'A Critical Introduction' and this describes it very well.

Gifford, H. (ed.), *Leo Tolstoy, A Critical Anthology* (Harmondsworth, Middlesex, 1971). An excellent collection of critical materials in translation.

Greenwood, E. B., *Tolstoy: The Comprehensive Vision* (London, 1975). Sensitive, informative, tending to become fussily heated over other (predominantly English) critical interpretations; valuable for its sober treatment of Tolstoy's ideas.

Lampert, E., 'Tolstoy', in *Nineteenth-Century Russian Literature*, ed. John Fennell (London, 1973). Many useful insights, especially into Tolstoy's philosophical attitudes and use of language.

Matlaw, R. E. (ed.), *Tolstoy: A Collection of Critical Essays* (Englewood Cliffs, N.J., 1967). Contains interesting essays by Renato Poggioli, Isaiah Berlin, Georg Lukács, R. F. Christian, R. P. Blackmur and others, but little specifically on the major novels.

Spence, G. W., *Tolstoy the Ascetic* (London, 1967). An interesting discussion of the dualism in Tolstoy's thought.

WORKS IN RUSSIAN

Tolstoy has been more fully studied in Russian critical works than Dostoevsky. The best studies are B. M. Eykhenbaum's *Molodoy Tolstoy* (Berlin, 1922), *L. Tolstoy, 50-e gody* (Leningrad–Moscow, 1928) and *L. Tolstoy, 60-e gody* (Leningrad–Moscow, 1931). Though dated, these studies, chiefly of Tolstoy's attitudes, his ideological evolution and the influences on him, rather than his writing, are excellent. Of equal interest is Eykhenbaum's *L. Tolstoy, 70-e gody* (Leningrad, 1960). Valuable pre-revolutionary studies by K. N. Leont'yev's *O romanakh grafa L. N. Tolstogo. Analiz, stil' i veyaniye*, reprinted (Providence, Rhode Island, 1965), V. V. Veresayev's *Zhivaya zhizn'*, and those by Ivanov-Razumnik and Ovsyaniko-Kulikovsky. Important in Soviet criticism are V. Shklovsky's *Material i stil' v romane L. Tolstogo 'Voyna i mir'* (Moscow, 1928) and the same author's biography, *Lev Tolstoy* (Moscow, 1963, 1967). A definitive chronicle of Tolstoy's life is offered in N. N. Gusev, *Letopis' zhizni i tvorchestva L. N. Tolstogo*, 2 vols (Moscow, 1958 and 1960). Works of value have been contributed by B. I. Bursov, N. K. Gudzy, M. B. Khrapchenko, E. N. Kupreyanova, T. Motyleva, A. A. Saburov, E. Zaydenshnur. Further bibliographical guidance can be obtained from K. D. Muratova, *Istoriya russkoy literatury xix veka, Bibliograficheskiy ukazatel'* (Moscow, 1962).

The most complete edition of Tolstoy's work is the monumental centenary edition in ninety volumes (1928–59). It contains prefatory articles and textual commentaries.

GORKY

WORKS IN ENGLISH

Many selections of Gorky's stories have been published in England and in the United States at the beginning of this century. For a bibliography of these and Gorky's other works in English, see A. Ettlinger and J. M. Gladstone's *Russian Literature, Theatre and Art: A Bibliography of Works in English published between 1900–1945* (London, 1945).

The Foreign Languages Publishing House in Moscow has also issued several selections of short stories and articles. One of the most comprehensive of these is M. Gorky's *Selected Works in two volumes* (Moscow, 1948).

Among the more recent translations available are:

Best Short Stories, ed. A. Yarmolinsky and M. Budberg (New York, 1947).
Unrequited Love and Other Stories, trans. M. Budberg (London, 1949).
Twenty-Six Men and a Girl (New York, 1957).
A Sky-Blue Life and Selected Stories, trans. G. Reavey (New York, 1964).
Foma Gordeyev, trans. Margaret Wettlin (New York, 1962).
Mother, trans. Isidor Schneider (New York, 1949).
Mother, trans. Margaret Wettlin (New York, 1961).
The Life of Matvey Kozhemyakin, trans. Margaret Wettlin (Moscow, 1960).
The Artamonov Business, trans. Alec Brown (London, 1948).

Seven Plays of M. Gorky, trans. A. Bakshy, H. Milford (Oxford, 1945; New Haven, Conn., 1947).
Autobiography: My Childhood, In the World, My Universities, trans. Isidor Schneider (London, 1953).
My Childhood, trans. Ronald Wilks (Harmondsworth, Middlesex, 1966).
Literary Portraits, trans. I. Litvinov (Moscow, n.d.).
Reminiscences of Tolstoy, Chekhov and Andreyev, new ed. trans. Katherine Mansfield, S. S. Koteliansky and Leonard Woolf (London, 1949).
Letters of Gorky and Andreev, 1899–1912, ed. Peter Yershov (London, 1958).
On Literature: Selected Articles, trans. J. Katzer and I. Litvinov (Moscow, 1960).
Untimely Thoughts: Essays on Revolution, Culture and the Bolsheviks, 1917–1918, trans. H. Ermolaev (New York, 1963).

BIOGRAPHICAL AND CRITICAL WORKS

Borras, F. M., *Maxim Gorky the Writer: An Interpretation* (Oxford, 1967). A rather pedestrian but painstaking analysis of Gorky's works, better on the novel than on other genres.
Hare, Richard, *Maxim Gorky: Romantic Realist and Conservative Revolutionary* (London, 1962). A general introduction with a stress on Gorky's political development.
Kaun, Alexander, *Maxim Gorky and his Russia* (London, 1932). Still the best biography of Gorky up to 1931; little literary criticism.
Levin, Dan, *Stormy Petrel: The Life and Work of Maxim Gorky* (London, 1967). An idiosyncratic but interesting interpretation distinguished by a most extraordinary style.
Muchnic, Helen, *From Gorky to Pasternak: Six Modern Russian Writers* (London, 1963). Contains an excellent sensitive essay on Gorky, pp. 29–103.
Weil, Irwin, *Gorky: His Literary Development and Influence on Soviet Intellectual Life* (New York, 1966). A clear and interesting work divided into two parts: the first attempts to analyse Gorky's works in some detail; the second provides new material in English on Gorky's influence upon Soviet literature.
Wolfe, Bertram D., *The Bridge and the Abyss: The Troubled Friendship of Maxim Gorky and V. I. Lenin* (London, 1967). An excellent account of Gorky's relationship with Lenin.

WORKS IN RUSSIAN

M. Gor'ky, *Sobraniye sochineniy,* 30 vols (Moscow, 1949–55) is the most complete edition of Gorky's works to date. This is being superseded currently by the first full Academy edition of Gorky's collected works:
M. Gor'ky, *Polnoye sobraniye sochineniy* (Moscow, 1968–).
    Among the most useful reference works in Russian are:
Letopis' zhizni i tvorchestva A. M. Gor'kogo, 4 vols (Moscow, 1958–60). A year-by-year selective chronicle of Gorky's life and works.
Balukhaty, S., *Kritika o M. Gor'kom: Bibliografiya statey i knig, 1893–1932*

(Leningrad, 1934). A Bibliography of criticism devoted to Gorky up to 1932. This may be supplemented by:

Muratova, K. D. (ed.), *Istoriya russkoy literatury kontsa XIX–nachala XX veka: Bibliograficheskiy ukazatel'* (Moscow–Leningrad, 1963) which lists the main editions of Gorky's works, including collections of letters, as well as critical items.

PASTERNAK

TRANSLATIONS

Most of Pasternak's prose and selections of his poetry have appeared at one time or another in English translation. Generally he has been very badly served by his translators and only a very few stand up to careful examination. For full detail about English editions of Pasternak see the bibliography attached to Volume Three of the Michigan Russian edition of Pasternak (see below). The following are the most readily available in English:

Safe Conduct. An Early Autobiography and Other Works, trans. A. Brown (London, 1959). Contains Pasternak's early stories and first autobiography, plus a few poems, in an appallingly inaccurate and mutilated translation.

Boris Pasternak. Prose and Poems, ed. S. Schimanski (London, 1959). Revised edition. Similar to the previous volume. Contains *Safe Conduct*, four stories and selected poetry in poor to indifferent translation.

The Poetry of Boris Pasternak 1917–59, trans. with a critical introduction by G. Reavey (New York, 1959). Generally the most useful collection of translated poetry with a helpful introduction.

An Autobiographical Essay, trans. Manya Harari (London, 1959). Pasternak's second autobiography. A shorter version of this text, together with the short prose fragment 'Journey to the Army', appears in *Novy mir. 1925–67,* ed. M. Glenny (London, 1973).

Doctor Zhivago, trans. M. Harari and M. Hayward (London, 1958). Readable, but an occasionally inaccurate and slipshod translation.

The Last Summer, trans. G. Reavey (London, 1959). Poor translation of *Povest'*, slightly revised in a Penguin edition, 1960.

Boris Pasternak. Poems 1955–59, trans. Michael Harari (London, 1960). Among the best translations, but covers too narrow a period to replace previous collections.

In the Interlude. Poems 1945–60, trans. H. Kamen (London, 1962). Slightly wider selection than the previous collection, but less well translated.

Pasternak. Fifty Poems, trans. L. P. Slater (London, 1963). Pasternak's younger sister attempts to render selected poetry into comparable English with some success.

Sister My Life, trans. P. C. Flayderman (New York, 1967). An ambitious attempt to present one of Pasternak's most popular collections of poetry in an English version. Rather florid style and an uninformative introduction detract slightly from its value.

The Blind Beauty, trans. M. Hayward (London, 1970). Reliable translation, with useful foreword, of Pasternak's play.

Many of Pasternak's letters have appeared in various languages in separate Russian, European and American journals and periodicals, but the only collection thus far published is *Letters to Georgian Friends*, trans. D. Magarshack (London, 1967). This is a generally poor translation.

BIOGRAPHIES

Conquest, R., *The Courage of Genius. The Pasternak Affair* (London, 1961). A valuable study of the Nobel Prize scandal with numerous relevant documents and an interesting analysis of Pasternak's life and writing.

Dyck, J. W., *Boris Pasternak* (New York, 1972). An ambitious, though occasionally faulty study of Pasternak, but it is the first attempt at a full 'life and works' treatment.

Payne, R., *The Three Worlds of Boris Pasternak* (London, 1961). A popularising account of Pasternak's life and writing which is neither thorough nor reliable.

Ruge, G., *A Pictorial Biography* (London, 1959). Contains many photographs, supported by a journalistic text. The work of an ex-Moscow correspondent who knew Pasternak personally.

CRITICAL WORKS

Davie, D., *The Poems of Doctor Zhivago* (London, 1965). Interesting analysis, but spoilt by over-reliance on the basic premise that the Zhivago poems are directly linked to the prose text.

——, and Livingstone, A., *Pasternak* (London, 1969). A rather disconnected selection of translated critical essays on Pasternak's poetry and prose, but valuable for assembling Jakobson, Tsvetaeva, Tynyanov, and Sinyavsky in the same volume.

Muchnic, H., *From Gorky to Pasternak* (London, 1963). Contains a useful chapter on *Doctor Zhivago*.

Plank, D., *Pasternak's Lyric. Sound and Imagery* (The Hague, 1966). A scholarly enquiry into the formal principles employed in Pasternak's earlier poetry along lines suggested by the eminent critic Roman Jakobson.

Rowland, M. and P., *Pasternak's Doctor Zhivago* (Carbondale, Ill., 1967). An extended examination of the symbolism of the novel which tends to develop its argument to absurd lengths.

Readers of French may find the following of interest:

Aucouturier, M., *Pasternak par lui-même* (Paris, 1963).

Proyart, J. de, *Pasternak* (Paris, 1964).

IN RUSSIAN

The fullest edition of Pasternak's writing in Russian is the generally excellent three-volume collection containing prose, poetry and essays, with *Doctor Zhivago* as an extra, fourth volume: *Boris Pasternak. Stikhotvoreniya i poemy* (Ann Arbor, Mich. 1959–61). Despite its occasional errors and omissions this collection has only partly been superseded by the definitive Soviet edition of

Pasternak's poetry, B. *Pasternak. Stikhotvoreniya i poemy* 'Poet's Library' Series (Moscow, 1965). For further information about Pasternak's writing and work on him in Russian, see *B. L. Pasternak 1890–1960. Bibliografiya*, compiled by N. A. Troitsky (Ithaca, N.Y., 1969). This is by far the fullest bibliography of writing by and about Pasternak, though it does not cover translations into English, nor critical material in English or other non-Russian languages. Troitsky is a valuable complement to the bibliography contained in Volume Three of the Michigan collection.

Interesting critical insights and personal recollections are contained in the following:

Sbornik statey, posvyashchonnykh tvorchestvu B. L. Pasternaka (Munich, 1963). This is essentially a critical collection, not a monograph, but it contains studies of Pasternak by several leading Western authorities.

Gladkov, A., *Vstrechi s Pasternakom* (Paris, 1973). A book of personal reminiscences and observations about Pasternak by a younger contemporary. An illuminating antidote to most official Soviet criticism of Pasternak.

SOLZHENITSYN

All of Solzhenitsyn's stories, plays, novels and articles have been translated at one time or another and in some cases several different versions may be available. For fuller and more detailed information about these, see *Solzhenitsyn: An International Bibliography of Writing By and About Him, 1962–73*, compiled by D. Fiene (Ann Arbor, Mich., 1973).

The following are the most readily obtainable English editions of Solzhenitsyn's writing in English:

A Day in the Life of Ivan Denisovich, trans. R. Parker (London, 1963). Also available in translation by M. Hayward and R. Hingley (New York–London, 1963); G. Aitken (London, 1971).

For the Good of the Cause, trans. D. Floyd and M. Hayward (London, 1964).

Short Stories and Prose Poems, trans. M. Glenny (London, 1971). Contains all of Solzhenitsyn's shorter prose works in a rather inaccurate, but readable translation. For other, sometimes more reliable translations of individual stories see Fiene, op. cit.

The First Circle, trans. M. Guybon (London, 1968). Also in Fontana paperback (London, 1970).

The Cancer Ward, trans. N. Bethell and D. Burg (London, 1969). Also in Penguin paperback (Harmondsworth, Middlesex, 1971).

The Love-Girl and the Innocent, trans. N. Bethell and D. Burg (London, 1969). One version of Solzhenitsyn's *Olen' i shalashovka*. There is an American version of this entitled *The Tenderfoot and the Tramp*.

August 1914, trans. M. Glenny (London, 1972). Also in Penguin paperback (Harmondsworth, Middlesex, 1971).

Candle in the Wind, trans. K. Armes (London, 1973). Solzhenitsyn's second play.

The Gulag Archipelago, trans. T. Whitney (London, 1974).

Other separately published texts include:

The Nobel Prize Lecture, available in two translations: *'One Word of Truth . . .'* The *Nobel Speech* (London, 1972) and *The Nobel Prize Lecture,* trans. N. Bethell (London, 1972).

Letter to the Soviet Leaders, trans. H. Sternberg (London, 1974).

Letter to Patriarch Pimen of All Russia, trans. K. Armes (Minneapolis, Minn., 1972).

The following should also be consulted:

Solzhenitsyn. A Documentary Record, ed. Labedz (London, 1970). (Subsequently in a number of up-dated editions, the latest being the Indiana University Press edition (Bloomington, Ind., 1973).) This contains texts of interviews with Solzhenitsyn, letters, speeches and an assortment of related documents in occasionally indifferent translation and with unspecified editorial cuts in places.

Soljénitsyne, ed. M. Aucouturier and G. Nivat (Paris, 1971). A French edition, similar to Labedz, but using fuller texts and with the addition of critical articles and full bibliography.

BIOGRAPHIES

Björkegren, H., *Aleksandr Solzhenitsyn: A Biography,* trans. K. Eneberg (New York, 1972). A spare, but well-informed combination of text and documentary evidence.

Burg, D., and Feifer, G., *Solzhenitsyn. A Biography* (London, 1972). The fullest biography in English, tends to over-use unacknowledged quotation from Solzhenitsyn's writing to bulk out its own thinness. Solzhenitsyn withdrew co-operation with its authors before the book was completed.

Grazzini, G., *Solzhenitsyn,* trans. E. Mosbacher (London, 1973). Like Björkegren, the author was a Moscow correspondent and his view of Solzhenitsyn is generally journalistic.

Medvedev, Zh., *Ten Years after Ivan Denisovich,* trans. H. Sternberg (London, 1973). Interesting for its account of the way in which *One Day in the Life of Ivan Denisovich* came to be published in the Soviet Union.

CRITICAL WORKS

Moody, C., *Solzhenitsyn* (Edinburgh, 1973). Short but reliable and useful introduction to Solzhenitsyn's life and writing.

Lukács, G., *Solzhenitsyn,* trans. W. D. Graf (London, 1970). Critical articles on *One Day, Cancer Ward* and *First Circle* by the veteran Hungarian Marxist critic. Sensitive and original; amongst the best critical writing about Solzhenitsyn.

Rothberg, A., *Aleksandr Solzhenitsyn. The Major Novels* (Ithaca, N.Y., 1971). Generally unoriginal and uninspiring study by an American literary academic.

IN RUSSIAN

There is a six-volume edition of Solzhenitsyn's writing up to 1969, *A. Solzhenitsyn. Sobraniye sochineniy v shesti tomakh* (Frankfurt-am-Main, 1970).

Aleksander Solzhenitsyn, Sochineniya, Frankfurt-am-Main, 1966, contains the text of the early short stories up to 1965.

Since 1970, when Solzhenitsyn made agreements with the Swiss lawyer to handle authorised texts and copyrights outside the Soviet Union, YMCA Press in Paris have been responsible for the Russian editions of Solzhenitsyn's separate books. Amongst these have been:

Avgust chetyrnadtsatogo (1971).
Arkhipelag Gulag 1918–56 (1974–5). Three volumes so far.
Bodalsya telyonok s dubom (1975).

Index

This index contains all names, titles and major place names in the text and notes. It does not contain fictional names and it does not include the bibliography.

DATE DUE			